T0342485

THE POWER OF BEING DIVISIVE

THE POWER

OF BEING DIVISIVE

UNDERSTANDING NEGATIVE

SOCIAL EVALUATIONS

THOMAS J. ROULET

STANFORD BUSINESS BOOKS
AN IMPRINT OF STANFORD UNIVERSITY PRESS
STANFORD, CALIFORNIA

Stanford University Press
Stanford, California

Special discounts for bulk quantities of Stanford Business Books are available to corporations, professional associations, and other organizations. For details and discount information, contact the special sales department of Stanford University Press. Tel: (650) 725-0820, Fax: (650) 725-3457

Printed in the United States of America on acid-free, archival-quality paper

Library of Congress Cataloging-in-Publication Data

Names: Roulet, Thomas (Thomas J.), author.
Title: The power of being divisive : understanding negative social evaluations / Thomas Roulet.
Description: Stanford, California : Stanford Business Books, an imprint of Stanford University Press, 2020. | Includes bibliographical references and index. |
Identifiers: LCCN 2020008446 (print) | ISBN 9781503608207 (cloth) | ISBN 9781503613904 (ebook)
Subjects: LCSH: Management. | Business enterprises—Public opinion. | Industries—Public opinion. | Occupations—Public opinion. | Evaluation—Social aspects. | Stigma (Social psychology)
Classification: LCC HD31.2 .R685 2020 (print) | LCC HD31.2 (ebook) | DDC 303.3/8—dc23
LC record available at https://lccn.loc.gov/2020008446
LC ebook record available at https://lccn.loc.gov/2020008447

Cover design: Rob Ehle
Cover sheep: Shutterstock

CONTENTS

PREFACE

The Relevance of Negative Social Evaluations

There is no better example to start this book than Donald Trump, one of the most incredibly divisive leaders we have experienced in the modern era. As these lines were being written, Donald Trump was visiting the United Kingdom for the first time since he became president of the United States of America in 2016. After fearing a chilled welcome, he had already postponed the trip once. He was welcomed in London by tens of thousands of protestors displaying "World's Number One Racist" and "Dump Trump" placards. Above the British parliament in Westminster, an inflatable "Trump Baby" in nappies was floating as a sign of defiance and an attack against the immaturity of the most influential person on the planet. This demonstration was arguably the biggest one in the U.K. since the opposition to the Iraq war in 2003. In short, Trump was exposed to "negative social evaluations"; that is, he was the target of demeaning and critical judgments.

Trump was beyond deaf to the critics, and he discarded all of it. When asked about it on the following day aboard Air Force One, he had this incredible answer: "Some of them are protesting in my favor, you know that? There are many, many protests in my favor." Needless to say, those protests in favor of Donald did not exist outside of his fertile imagination.

Whether Trump was delusional to that point, living in his little bubble, or whether he rightly saw himself as a profoundly polarizing character, is in fact hard to say. He was right on one point: despite the intense hostility, with many opponents at home and abroad, he also maintained tremendous support, with 43 percent favorable opinion among U.S. voters. Forty-three percent! One would have expected that with his multiple controversial positions, his numerous tweets "stirring the pot," and his deeply divisive political choices, he would have garnered a much stronger antipathy. In fact, he *has* garnered significant enmity, but paradoxically won the election against all odds and has been able to maintain a high rating.

This puzzle, of how a heavily criticized and in some cases vilified individual such as Donald Trump can still garner significant amounts of support, also applies to firms. One might think of Goldman Sachs or Bank of America (representing an industry that will be covered extensively in this book) as among the most hated firms. But surprisingly, the video game giant Electronic Arts is at the top of a list compiling employee reviews and customer satisfaction scores to rank the most reviled firms in the United States. Electronic Arts regularly antagonizes its hardcore gamers, who frequently accuse the firm of offering disappointing game features or misleading advertising. Hardcore gamers are passionate customers and most of the time do not hesitate to flood social media with complaints. On Reddit—the infamous online forum where a significant share of those complaints are published—a topic regarding the game dynamics of EA's *Battlefront* game has 683,000 negative votes. This topic triggered by far the most negative reaction to a Reddit post. The second worst post was one that asked to receive adverse reaction, and it piteously reached 23,000 downvotes only.

The company set up a rehabilitating plan under new leadership in the spring of 2013, but Electronic Arts remained stuck among the worst-reputed companies. Despite all the fuss, this has not prevented the firm selling more video games and doing extraordinarily well, with a stock price continually rising to new highs. How is it even possible for a firm to trigger such hatred from customers and still be incredibly successful? Hate, love, as the famous saying goes, there might only be a thin frontier between the two. What if Electronic Arts is just one of those firms customers love to hate?

Other firms are familiar with public hostility: Uber, Monsanto (Bayer since 2018), AT&T. However, despite this hostility, those organizations have managed to survive, and even sometimes to capitalize on outsiders' anger. For these firms, public disapproval has not been an obstacle for growth, and it has opened a world of new opportunities.

At an even more abstract level, entire sectors and practices can be simultaneously stigmatized and booming. Among them, pornography is a classic example of an entire field and nexus of practices shaped by stigma (Voss 2015). Despite the taboo and the ethical concerns with the way it is produced, pornography has remained an intensely consumed product (Tarrant 2016). In 2013, three hundred thousand attempts to access porn websites were traced back to . . . the British Houses of Parliament.[1] How, precisely, did the controversial and shady nature of the practice and its products make it so successful to the point that members of parliaments and peers cannot resist the urge?

A bad reputation, media bashing, and the intense lobbying of hostile social movements have for a long time been seen as a significant corporate risk, more commonly known as the "reputation risk." A negative corporate image deters customers, business partners, and potential job applicants. Equally hostile social movements can be just as damaging, by convincing vital stakeholders to withdraw their support of the targeted firms. Governments could potentially cut funding and stop supporting the attacked firms' activities. Employees become too afraid to talk about whom they work for. And for those individuals who face negative social evaluations themselves, coaching sessions are offered to improve their work relationships.

More than ever, the practices, individuals, and organizations in the fields of politics and business, but also beyond, are familiarly exposed to "negative social evaluations" when they are adversely perceived and presented by key audiences. As the examples of Trump and Electronic Arts—and the many others we will look at in this book—suggest, those "negative" social evaluations are not always that bad, and this book is aimed at uncovering the mechanisms through which they can yield benefits for their bearers.

In this Preface, justifying the modern relevance of the concept of negative social evaluations will be central. Negative social evaluations were especially interesting to me, and in the following section I will discuss my own journey as a researcher in this area and what got me hooked.

Why Study Negative Social Evaluations Today?

There has been no better time to examine and understand negative social evaluations. Why? First, the nature of audiences has experienced a profound change with the move toward digitalization. The rise of social media has created low-cost access for any individual to use his or her voice to participate in public debate (Roulet and Clemente 2018). Anybody with an internet connection and a mobile phone can express his or her rage in a tweet or more if they feel inspired. According to the Pew Research Center, nearly two-thirds of Americans are Facebook users.[2] Like David versus Goliath, scandalized, upset, or just bored individuals can take their emotions onto social media to attack public figures, companies, and organizations or entire nations. In an era when information flows at the speed of light via social media and on twenty-four-hour news channels, no organization can hope to protect itself from this onslaught of public anger. A spark can trigger a destructive fire in the blink of an eye. However, what if things were not as simple and straightforward as we may think?

Trump and other modern political phenomena remind us that we live in a "post-truth" society that relies more on appealing to emotions and rejects the use of factual evidence. When emotions matter, social evaluations are more about gut feelings than elaborate demonstrations and arguments—going back to the Reddit and other social messages against Electronic Arts' *Battlefront* game, it does not seem that outrage and hostility always go hand in hand with compelling reasoning!

Second, in a related phenomenon, this "post-truth" society is also hosting a turn toward the inflation of social evaluations. From AirBnB to Uber and other such services in the new platform economy we are almost addicted to, we are evaluated and we evaluate everything. Indeed, the role of platforms linking service or products providers with customers has exclusively relied on the idea of mutual reviewing. If we are addicted to those services, we are also addicted to the mechanism of evaluating as a way to reward or punish those with whom we engage in market interactions.

When we feel wronged by our AirBnB host because they forgot to empty the ashtray, or by our Uber driver because they cut through Trafalgar Square, sucking up thirty more minutes of our life stuck in London traffic, what better way to take it back to them than complaining online, when we cannot be exposed to the consequences of our bitter rhetoric (it's very likely that the disgruntled AirBnB host or Uber driver will want to punch in the face many of their negative evaluators). I personally have to confess that I am the first one to go immediately on TripAdvisor when, for example, I have liked or disliked the last restaurant I have experienced. In fact, I use my TripAdvisor profile to provide only five- or one-star reviews, thinking I will have no impact on the restaurant I evaluate if I offer neutral, apathetic, or lukewarm evaluations. Writing negative evaluations is arguably more fun and distracting than writing good ones—positive evaluations of a service are more likely to stick to the facts and the reality of the experience. In comparison, providing negative social evaluations will act as a catharsis, an opportunity to express bitter emotions—and it feels good to be mean sometimes!

In this new evaluation-obsessed society, we are not only judgmental producers of social evaluations, we are also avid consumers: we can hardly spend a day without thinking about what others think of us. As Vidaillet (2016, 20) puts it, we "are under the permanent gaze of the other," and from a Lacanian perspective, this is what shapes our identity and gives us a sense of existence. We exist beyond our mom's gaze! Service providers are also addicted to reading their evaluations, mostly because they seek positive gratification, though in fact they often end up being exposed to disgraceful criticism that they perceive as a critical identity threat (Wang, Wezel, and Forgues 2016). My favorite barber around the corner obsessed for more than two years over a single negative review he got on Google Maps—telling me about it pretty much every time I would go for my monthly haircut. He would never need to worry about such negative evaluations considering his steady flow of loyal customers—yet he did. He spent hours discussing which competitors might have left such a nasty review and he asked his customers, including myself, to defend him online—which I did. However, since then it looks like many other disgruntled customers' reviews have been added to the list!

As academics, we get evaluated continuously by our peers, but also by our students, mostly anonymously. How many times have we heard about colleagues losing sleep over or being intensely depressed by the one demeaning comment received from one of their disgruntled students? We tend to only see the negative evaluations. We obsess about them because they stand out, and they stick. When I taught for the first time my Theories of the Firm elective at SciencesPo in Paris, though I received a very positive assessment overall, I remember going mad about the one student who thought I was reading too much off of my slides and was atrociously dull. It was one of my first teaching experiences—maybe I was! I accumulated clues to track down the student and confront him. In retrospect, there was no rationale for such behavior: only more evidence that we are hypersensitive to negative social evaluations.

A third factor makes negative social evaluations particularly relevant. Corporate scandals seem increasingly more common, singling out misbehaving organizations, individuals, and sometimes entire industries (Daudigeos, Roulet, and Valiorgue 2020). But are controversies and scandals more common nowadays, or is it that we are simply more aware of them? It is hard to believe firms were more virtuous in the past (although we would love to believe so, so that we could repeat the standard litany, "Things are not what they used to be"). They are just more likely to be caught, more likely to be exposed, and more likely to have their tales told all over town via individual and collective media voices, in print, and on screens. However, this sometimes plays in favor of those who want to be noticed. Boris Johnson, the former mayor of London who was voted prime minister of the United Kingdom in 2019 and led his party to a parliamentary victory in the wake of it, is a good example. To make it that far he went on to say something outrageous each time he was on the verge of being forgotten. Also, even his staunchest supporters would not disagree with it, or object to him doing that!

The practical relevance of negative social evaluations as a conceptual tool is thus becoming increasingly apparent. It does not mean that researchers, public relations and communications specialists, and political and industry leaders have all the answers we need to decipher this new brave world. In fact, questions accumulate as the conditions under which we produce and consume social evaluations evolve. In this book, before I try to identify the positive aspects of negative social evaluations, those fundamental questions will be dealt with. What is the social purpose of negative social evaluations? Why do they even exist? Why are some individuals and organizations negatively evaluated? How? Why do some individuals, organizations, and fields survive, despite hostility, media bashing, and public pressures—even managing to capitalize on those forces? And empirically this book will engage with such questions as, How did Trump win the U.S. election while bashing U.S. citizens, firms, and neighboring nations indiscriminately? How do Electronic Arts and companies like them thrive amid the multiple controversies their products trigger? How can porn be at the same time one of the most controversial and the most consumed products across the globe?

While public relations and communication professionals have often focused on how to repair a damaged reputation (see, for example, Earl and Waddingon 2013; Baer 2016; Dietrich 2014), this book offers to look beyond defensive perspectives: there may be no point in repairing a lousy reputation if it is an asset to an organization and/or a driver of change. The work of organizational sociologists and management scholars can complement the existing communication research to better understand the different ways in which being negatively perceived can yield surprisingly positive outcomes for organizations and individuals.

How I Got Caught Up in Researching
Negative Social Evaluations

Negative social evaluations were not just a topical subject of enquiry. They were of specific interest to me as a researcher, and I have seen the subject as a fruitful path for my own work. Before adequately introducing and reviewing the academic and scientific work on negative social evaluations in the Introduction, it is appropriate to give credit to the fundamental works at the basis of this literature. As our dear Google Scholar reminds us every day, we only "stand on the shoulder of giants."

It all started when, as a first-year PhD student in 2010, I read a paper by Bryant Hudson on organizational stigma published in 2008 in the *Academy of Management Review* and edited by Kim Elsbach. The idea that organizations could be stigmatized was a revelation for me, who had come to my PhD from the investment bank industry as it was facing a global backlash during the financial crisis. I immediately thought I wanted to work on this. In fact, this paper did not have this effect just on me, it also accelerated the development of an emerging stream of work in organization theory on negative social evaluations in general. At the same time that I was starting my PhD, another negative social evaluation scholar was finishing his: Jean-Philippe Vergne was about to publish his dissertation on the arms industry and the ways industry members had been able to reduce the disapproval they were facing as members of a vilified line of business (Vergne 2012). I was also deeply inspired by the work of other colleagues in the field of social evaluations emerging from my PhD program at that time: Deborah Philippe and her work at the intersection of reputation, status, and legitimacy, and Julien Jourdan and his rising interest in corporate scandals and institutional logics. I did not need more signs of destiny: this is what I wanted to do with my dissertation!

From this, I went on to Goffman's original work on stigma at the individual level (1963), which is actually at the origins of it all (yes, that is where I should have started!). Building on examples and illustrations, Goffman established the foundational conceptualization of negative social evaluations by linking deviance, norms, identity, and the dynamics of discredit. While coming from the field of organization theory, I quickly discovered that sociologists shared my interest in negative social evaluation (Vaughan 1999; Link and Phelan 2001; Pescosolido and Martin 2015) and mass communication scholars (Wolfe and Blithe 2015; Noelle-Neumann 1974).

As I was developing my dissertation, I became interested in giving a positive spin to negative social evaluations. Remembering my days on the trading floor of BNP Paribas in London, during the most significant financial turmoil of the century, I was intrigued by the way investment bankers dealt with the rising hostility faced by their industry. How were they reacting? Did they mind at all? If they did not, why? I certainly struggled at dinner parties to explain I had worked in that industry, as people were losing their jobs and the public and the media were blaming it on the industry I was working for. So what made them different? How could they still experience pride to work for such companies, and how were those companies at the same time still seen as prestigious by young graduates? I started asking those questions and listening to the answers of my former investment banker colleagues, then expanded my work to stigma and negative social evaluations at the individual level.

That is how I became part of a group of scholars working on how organizations can deal with negative social evaluations but also trying to show that being disapproved of can also surprisingly yield positive outcomes (Helms and Patterson 2014; Tracey and Phillips 2016; Roulet 2017; 2019a).

Despite the fact that I had found such an exciting and growing body of work, toward the end of my PhD I started thinking about a broader perspective linking the various forms of negative social evaluations—their antecedents and consequences (especially the positive ones). Thus in 2015 I started accumulating notes for a book project to develop a comprehensive social theory explaining the benefits of negative evaluations, taking this as an excuse to dig more systematically for inspiration from a broader range of disciplinary fields. One paper would not have been enough to cope with this ambition! Giving way to some severe sense of megalomania, I felt like I needed an entire book to develop the idea but also clarify some key definitions and conceptual arguments. I only realized I should have curbed my obsessionalism when I actually had to write the book—but at last, here it is.

Purpose and Structure of the Book

This book takes a radical and provocative view by arguing that organizations and individuals facing negative social evaluations can be ultimately better off because of it. This book is primarily targeted at the advanced PhD student as well as both junior and senior management, and sociology, communication, or ethics faculty who are interested in gaining a more profound understanding of negative social evaluations to use in class or in their research. Reading this book it is hoped will aid them in developing potentially new ways of thinking about the antecedents and consequences of social evaluations and how a negative taint can result in positive outcomes.

The argument is that facing disapproval has actually *helped* the most hated companies to foster a stronger corporate culture, attract the right set of customers or employees, radically change themselves, and in turn generate growth opportunities. Stigmatized actors can also thrive on the frustration of being marginalized. The book will explore how individuals in contested occupations maintain their self-esteem and what we can learn from such mechanisms.

To make this argument compelling, the Introduction will bring together the existing literature on negative social evaluations and provide a multilevel conceptual framework to explain why, when, and how negative social evaluations can be beneficial for individuals and organizations. This conceptual framework will build on the existing empirical and theoretical work and some illustrative examples. This interdisciplinary dialogue will build bridges between concepts in different kinds of literature, but also show how various levels of analysis can inform each other (for example, how the research on dirty work can inform the identity dynamics of stigmatized organizations). Ultimately, the book is aimed at comprehensively covering the negative social evaluations literature at multiple levels, including their antecedents and consequences, in a coherent manner.

The Introduction is the cornerstone of the book, as it will first define the range of adverse social evaluations and touch upon the role of audiences and media. The Introduction presents an overarching framework connecting the different kinds of literature on negative social evaluations. It introduces a model of three steps: looking first at the antecedents of negative evaluations, then at the resistance and reaction to negative evaluations, and finally at how individuals and organizations capitalize on negative evaluations and use them strategically. Each of the following chapters will flesh out the different parts of the model. Chapter 1 covers the antecedents of negative social evaluations by identifying different forms of deviance. Chapter 2 focuses on resilience: How do organizations and individuals endure, confront, and deal with negative social evaluations? Chapter 3 will flesh out the core argument of the book by explaining how organizations and individuals can go beyond resilience and capitalize on those negative social evaluations. Chapter 4 will discuss the practical implications. What can individuals who experience stigma or hostility, leaders, stigmatized organizations, and industries learn from this extensive body of research? Finally, the Conclusion will explore the contribution of this work and pave the way for future research on the topic.

ACKNOWLEDGMENTS

I'm grateful for the continuous moral support but also the constant intellectual stimulation of my second half, Kiran Bhatti. I am thankful for the editing work of Steve Catalano at Stanford University Press, and previously Margo Beth Fleming. I recognize the key contributions of the three reviewers who evaluated my work at various points in time.

I also want to thank all of those who inspired and shaped this book: colleagues in the field of negative social evaluations (in no particular order, Bryant Hudson, Wes Helms, Karen Patterson, Alessandro Piazza, Julien Jourdan, J.-P. Vergne, Deborah Philippe, Mark de Rond, Jan Lodge, Lionel Paolella, Paul Tracey, Christian Hampel) but also beyond that field (Joel Bothello, Marco Clemente, Olivier Cristofini, Heloise Berkowitz, Olivier Germain, Claudia Gabbioneta, Daniel Muzio, Bertrand Valiorgue, Andrew Von Nordenflycht, Sabina Siebert), and colleagues in the institutions I have worked for (in particular Dirk Vom Lehn for his intellectual input and support, Howard Gospel, and my fantastic colleagues at Girton). I am grateful for the excellent and useful feedback I got in various institutions when presenting this book: at GREDEG-University of Cote D'Azur, University Paris-Dauphine, University of Clermont Ferrand, University of Toulouse 1, Concordia University, Lancaster University, Girton College.

I also sincerely thank all the negative reviews I received over the years, from the one I got when submitting my proposal at Stanford University Press to my high school teacher who told me I would never be able to use the English language. I have trumped as many of those negative evaluations as I could, and I would not be here without them.

INTRODUCTION

A Framework to Understand Negative Social Evaluations

The idea of this book emerged as I discovered myself exploring how negative social evaluations could paradoxically be beneficial. In my PhD dissertation, I started looking at how investment banks and investment bankers could resist public hostility during the financial crisis and even capitalize on it (Roulet 2015b; Roulet 2019a). Those ideas germinated as a growing body of work began to stress the identity, opinion, and impression dynamics triggered by public hostility. Being up against everybody else is an active driver of organizational identity (Tracey and Phillips 2016): in many cases, big firms facing public scrutiny build a robust company culture by making their staff feel like they are in the right and everybody else is wrong. Whether businesses create alignment between their employees' values or recruit employees who fit with the desired mold (Turban and Greening 1997), it becomes possible to create a corporate culture that is resistant to public hostility. At the individual level, I was fascinated by the way those in negatively perceived occupations such as janitors or exotic dancers could build a positive sense of self (Ashforth and Kreiner 1999; Ashforth et al. 2007), or how stigmatized individuals experienced frustration that could lead them to be better entrepreneurs (Bacq et al. 2018).

However, before exploring those examples in more detail in the following chapters, as in every social science literature, some housekeeping is necessary. The literature on negative social evaluation and in particular on stigma has boomed in the past decade and seems to promise continued growth, considering how well-attended conferences and forums are on this topic. A research query on stigma in Google Scholar yields 128,000 results from 1990 to 2000, 417,000 from 2000 to 2010, and 331,000 from 2010 to 2018. While a number of factors can explain this growth, it seems that growth there is. Negative social evaluations—as an umbrella term including all forms of adverse appraisals of a target by an audience—seem to have emerged more recently. A search on this term yields 156 results from 1990 to 2000, 628 from 2000 to 2010, and 1,640 from 2010 to 2018. We can attribute the increasing use of this term to the need of federating a literature that was being populated by a range of new concepts in the past decade. This phenomenon emerged conjointly with the burgeoning of a broader literature on social evaluations, and the need to also unite the different concepts under the same banner (see Bitektine 2011).

The literature on both social evaluations and negative social evaluations in particular has ranged across the disciplines of sociology (often seen as the birthplace of stigma because of Goffman's foundational work), psychology (where social stigma has been the subject of thousands of social experiments), management (where we apply it all!), communications (with a focus on the reaction of audiences), and ethics (with a focus on antecedents of negative social evaluations). However, those different disciplines have engaged in a limited dialogue over those concepts. For example, there is still reasonably limited agreement over what exactly are social evaluations, and also what are the boundaries and overlap of the various concepts under this umbrella. How does a bad reputation differ from stigma (Mishina and Devers 2012; Pollock et al., forthcoming)? What does celebrity bring to an organization that reputation does not (Pfarrer, Pollock, and Rindova 2010)? Are legitimacy and illegitimacy two sides of the same coin (Hudson 2008; Roulet 2015b; Helms, Patterson, and Hudson 2019)?

In a conference in the summer of 2018, I happened to sit in a room full of negative social evaluation scholars (sort of my vision of academic paradise!) whose central debate was for each case, whether they were cases of stigma or not. I heard that colleagues in a neighboring room working on the construct of legitimacy had the same sort of disputes. In fact, some make the argument that the multiplicity of existing concepts, measures, and terms in this field have considerably slowed down research on negative social evaluations (for example, Pescosolido and Martin 2015). In this context, I thought the first objective of this book would be to clarify the links between the different concepts and provide a more precise framework regarding boundaries and overlapping characteristics of the various constructs that emerged in the negative social evaluation literature.

After covering basic definitions, and clarifying the links between different concepts and streams of literature, the Introduction will provide the reader with the critical conceptual pillars to understand the framework developed in the book. This framework is aimed at explaining resilience to negative social evaluations—how actors confront and resist them—and how those negative evaluations can have beneficial outcomes—how actors capitalize on them. The role of media as intermediaries and audiences will also be discussed. Finally, the last bit of this Introduction will present the key arguments of the book and the framework that connects those arguments and give them an overarching coherence.

A Brief History of the Negative
Social Evaluations Literature

Before diving into the negative social evaluations literature, it is interesting to look at the rising interest and complexities in the broader field of social evaluations from a long-term historical perspective. A Google NGram search browsing its considerable library of digitized books from 1800 to 2008 reveals the competitive dynamics between the different terms used in the literature (see Figure 1). Although in some ways anecdotal, the evidence provided by this NGram search gives us a few pointers on the most ancient terms used to refer to social evaluations. While *reputation* happened to be the dominant social evaluation concept in the nineteenth century, it was progressively taken over by *status*, or the more generic term *approval*, in the turn of the twentieth century. In the meantime, *legitimacy* has emerged as a critical contender since the 1960s.

A similar search for negative social evaluation concepts is more puzzling (see Figure 2). *Stigma* has always been center stage despite a drop in interest between the two world wars, followed by a rise in the 1960s. The generic term *disapproval* took prominence in the twentieth century but did decline after a peak following the Second World War. *Stigma* and *disapproval* are more widely used terms than *illegitimacy* or even the notion of "bad reputation" that will be explored later on.

The first venture into the world of negative social evaluation started with the first discussion of deviance and stigmatization by French sociologist

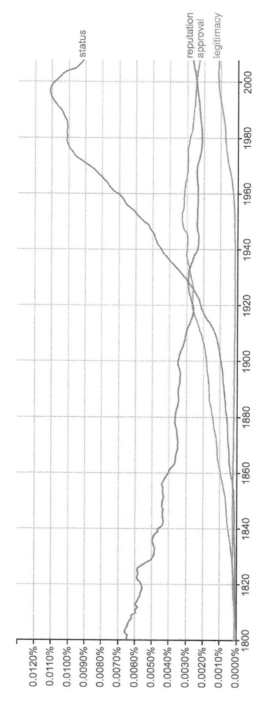

Figure 1. NGram Search for Social Evaluation Concepts. Source: Google Books Ngram Viewer, http://books.google.com/ngrams.

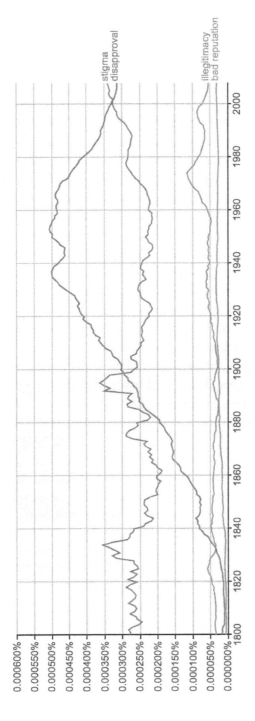

Figure 2. NGram Search for Negative Social Evaluation Concepts. Source: Google Books Ngram Viewer, http:/books.google. com/ngrams.

Emile Durkheim in *Les Règles de la Méthode Sociologique* (Rules of Sociological Method) (1865), and Erving Goffman (1963) and his foundational work *Stigma: Notes on the Management of Spoiled Identity*. Nevertheless, the term *stigma* initially comes from ancient Greece, where it referred to a physical mark, signaling ownership but also pointing out a taint or a negative label of some sort. Etymologically, *stigma* in Greek implied a puncture, or the idea that the marking itself was a painful process. In fact, *stigma* referred to the scarification used to mark criminals and slaves and expose their lower status to those who would interact with them or simply be in their presence. Such bodily signs played a social role, excluding and marginalizing individuals, while at the same time reminding them of their status by giving them an attribute they could not get rid of.

Sociology has since taken over from the Greeks. Emile Durkheim came with a broad social approach to deviance (Durkheim 1865/2017), and while often cited as a precursor of the concept of stigma, Durkheim does not mention stigmatization in the *Rules of Sociological Method*. His contribution to the topic does matter though, as he was the first to explain crowd behavior as a mode of social control to deal with crime—when groups would turn against a criminal, cut ties, and marginalize him or her. Such mechanisms can be compared to the stigmatization of the deviant. Durkheim attempted to conceptualize crime in a broad sense, and how society can collectively process deviance. In his analysis, punishment for the deviant is not a way to change the course of individuals' actions but rather is aimed at creating a collective societal conscience.

By contrast with Durkheim's top-bottom approach, Goffman's focus was on the stigmatized individuals themselves and the way they internalize negative social evaluations. He wanted to understand how individuals experience being considered deviant and abnormal, the impact on their identity, and how they manage this negative label. He also looked at the stigmatizing process by exploring how deviance and abnormality lead to adverse evaluations—when negative perceptions are voiced out by audiences. A large number of his illustrations focus on the mentally ill, but he also builds a number of his arguments on the stigma faced by homosexuals, disabled individuals, and prostitutes.

More recent research has focused on new forms of stigma such as the one caused by mental health conditions (Pescosolido and Martin 2015), or that of sexuality, a question for which there is rising awareness in the workplace (Stenger and Roulet 2018). From Goffman's original interest around the identity of the stigmatized, many researchers focused on the management of stigma—or how individuals could overcome stigma (Clair, Beatty, and MacLean 2005; Ragins 2008; Jones and King 2014). As explored later in this book, research has also followed recent changes and evolution in the stigmatization process: the nature of our social interactions has evolved, for example with the changes in the media landscape and the rise of social media (Castelló, Etter, and Nielsen 2016).

Building upon Goffman's original work on stigma at the individual level (1963), scholars have expanded on the study of stigma in a variety of fields including sociology (for a review in this field, see Link and Phelan 2001; and Pescosolido and Martin 2015) and in psychology under the broader agenda of research around intergroup bias (Hewstone, Rubin, and Willis 2002) and stereotypes (Hilton and Von Hippel 1996). As a result, the psychological perspective on negative social evaluation has had a significant focus on the mutual perceptions of groups of actors.

Extending Goffman's discussion of how prostitutes experienced their everyday lives, further research fleshed out the concept of "dirty work" and explored the ways that individuals experience despised occupations (Ashforth and Kreiner 1999). The dirty work research focuses on the stigmatization of entire occupations and the hostility their practitioners face in their everyday lives (Ashforth et al. 2007). Moving up to the organizational level, scholars have fleshed out the concept of stigmatized organizations (Hudson 2008; Devers et al. 2009), organizations that are collectively perceived as discredited. Other similar constructs such as public disapproval (the hostility from a broad audience) (Vergne 2012); negative media coverage (adverse depiction in the media) (Zavyalova et al. 2016); or a bad reputation (a judgment on the capability of an actor) (Mishina and Devers 2012) have also emerged. At a macro level, research has looked at contested industries (Galvin, Ventresca, and Hudson 2005; Roulet 2015a), or entire fields facing and resisting public hostility. This body of work is highly interdisciplinary, spanning various fields including management, organization theory, sociology (Cain 1994; Voss 2015), and mass communication (Wolfe and Blithe 2015).

This literature emerged as a response and alternative to a large body of work around "positive" social evaluations in the 1990s such as legitimacy (Suchman 1995) or organizational image (Treadwell and Harrison 1994). One of the first works of this kind was the qualitative study of Sutton and Callahan (1987) on how employees of failing computer firms would experience the "spoiled" image of their organization. At the organizational level, whether the evaluation is produced by audiences that are external or internal to the organization is crucial. One of those evaluations produced by the internal audience of the organization is organizational identity, the shared representation of an organization by its members (Albert and Whetten 1985; Wang, Wezel, and Forgues 2016).

The development of the legitimacy concept has fueled the interest in social evaluations, and ultimately negative social evaluations. Ruef and Scott (1998, 877) credited Max Weber (1968) for the concept of legitimacy and define legitimate actions as "forms of action that were guided by a belief in the existence of a legitimate order" guided by conformity to the collectively generated formal and informal laws. Ruef and Scott present legitimacy as a mechanism of social control with normative, regulative, and cognitive dimensions (see also Scott 1995). According to them, social acceptance can be given to actors who conform to norms (the normative pillar) or to explicit laws (the regulative pillar), or who are visibly prevalent to audiences (the cognitive pillar). Instead of the regulative aspect, Suchman (1995) put forward the idea of pragmatic legitimacy—social acceptance based on the self-interest of the audience.

More generally, legitimacy has been a central concept in institutional theory and the subject of inquiry for a vast literature (such as Suddaby, Bitektine, and Haack 2017). Because it is defined as a form of social acceptance and seen as conferred to actors that conform to norms (Heugens and Lander 2009), legitimacy is associated with mimicry (Deephouse 1996). The best way to acquire legitimacy is thus to yield to isomorphic pressures (ibid.). Hudson, Devers, Mishina, and colleagues turned this around by asking, What happens to those who do not conform to norms? Because Suchman (1995) presented legitimacy as a resource, the consequences of not having legitimacy became a question of strategic interest for business and management scholars. How can it be strategic to avoid illegitimacy and acquire legitimacy to operate? How does this variable constrain and enable relationships with stakeholders? As discussed later, Hudson (2008) went one step further by looking at how it was possible to be and not to be legitimate at the same time.

Because of this interest in legitimacy triggered by institutional theorists, illegitimacy took center stage and became arguably the second most crucial form of negative social evaluations after stigma. Illegitimacy as an attribute was given to a variety of objects. Bryant Hudson (2008) went on mapping out the early literature on negative social evaluations, and taking stock of work that looked at illegitimate practices (Dougherty and Heller 1994), illegitimate actions (Elsbach and Sutton 1992), illegitimate symbols (Glynn and Marquis 2004), or illegitimate products (Zuckerman 1999). He was the first in organization theory to try to create linkages between different conceptualizations of negative social evaluations, in particular by using the dichotomy of core stigma (actors that are negatively labeled because of core attributes) and event stigma or "stigma that results from discrete, anomalous, episodic events" (Hudson 2008, 253). One of the very first empirical studies expanding on the link between negative social evaluations at the individual and organizational levels (at the exception of the work by Sutton and Callahan 1987) was his study of men's bathhouses (Hudson and Okhuysen 2009). This work focused on how gay saunas used a variety of strategies to avoid passing on stigma to their users and network partners.

The most recent work in the area of negative social evaluation has focused on the processes and causes of negative social evaluation such as corporate scandals (Daudigeos, Roulet, and Valiorgue 2020; Piazza and Jourdan 2018), contested markets (Vergne 2012; Durand and Vergne 2015; Shantz et al. 2019), and misconduct (Palmer 2012; Palmer, Greenwood, and Smith-Crowe 2016). This stream of work has further theorized the links between event stigma and core stigma, that is, how punctual negative social evaluations of an actor become anchored in audiences' minds so that the negative label sticks.

This book will very much focus on a fairly recent but also most intriguing argument in this stream of work on negative social evaluations. Contemporary work focusing on the way organizations can deal with negative social evaluations has indeed revealed that being disapproved of can also surprisingly yield positive outcomes (Helms and Patterson 2014; Tracey and Phillips 2016; Roulet 2017; Roulet 2019a).

To fully understand and flesh out this argument, a broader perspective linking the various forms of negative social evaluations—their antecedents and consequences (especially the positive ones)—is still missing. Establishing a more rigorous framework linking different mechanisms and concepts is the purpose of this Introduction.

What Exactly Are Negative Social Evaluations?

As previously stressed, it is critical first to clarify the differences and convergence of the concepts that can be found under the broader umbrella of negative social evaluations. I use "negative social evaluations" as a general term to depict any assessment of an actor that has a negative valence.

DEFINING STIGMA AT DIFFERENT LEVELS

Stigma at the individual level is used "to refer to an attribute that is deeply discrediting" (Goffman 1963, 3), although Goffman noted in the same sentence that stigma was first and foremost about social relationships—the bonds with others—rather than characteristics that are limited to the self. Stigma is indeed a relational construction: Graham and Grisard (2019) look at how poverty can be stigmatizing in the eye of the beholder and because of a contrast with the self. Goffman's conceptualization of stigma relied on a typology. Character stigma is related to the conduct of the stigmatized and associates a social, moral, or behavioral characteristic with a negative stereotype. In this category, Goffman includes the mentally ill (as the mentally ill were long considered not as suffering from an affliction but rather as having played an active part in their situation), sexual minorities, and negatively labeled occupations. The second form of stigma is based on physical aspects—it negatively labels individuals because of characteristics that are visible to the eyes. Physical difference leads to marginalization when this difference triggers repugnance. Goffman tends to see disability as the primary physical stigma. Finally, the stigma of group identity is a third category, that of belonging to a group that is negatively perceived by a majority. The borders between those categories are naturally porous: the mentally ill, for example, are publicly cast out, but mental illness, which was initially seen as a given attribute, became considered a developed one (Phelan et al. 2000). Racial stigma is related to a group identity but also associated with adverse behavioral characteristics through the stereotyping process.

Goffman also made an essential distinction between the different parties involved in the stigmatization process. The "stigmatized" are those who bear the stigma—whose marks signal them as abnormal for the rest of the community. The "normal" are those outside of the stigmatized category—those who are not marked. The "wise' are those who do not bear the stigma but sympathize with the stigmatized and are accepted as allies by them. Recent research has shown that network structures also reflect this division in three groups (Smith 2012). A modern example of "wise" groups are LGBT allies in the workplace—those who are particularly aware of the stigma and engaged in supporting the stigmatized. Stonewall, the main NGO supporting LGBT rights in the United Kingdom, identifies allies as listeners of the stigmatized, challengers to the stigma, and influencers of others.[1] While the term *ally* is used mainly to designate "straight" ally, the boundaries of the LGBT categories (and the wording used by Stonewall) in fact leave room to include a variety of individuals who consider themselves belonging to the LGBT group to various degrees. In other words, the "wise" are those who experience an overlap between their identity and that of the stigmatized. From a Goffmanian perspective, though, the idea that there are "wise" individuals with regard to a stigmatized group is a sign of stigma in itself—they would not exist or be needed in any way if there was no stigma. Moreover, those wise do suffer from what Goffman calls "courtesy stigma" or stigma by association (Neuberg et al. 1994). Besides, this partition into three groups depends on the social context, and from one situation to another a normal can become stigmatized, and vice versa.

A wide range of studies shows the discrimination and other adverse consequences faced by the stigmatized (Link and Phelan 2001). Evolutionary perspectives suggest that natural selection drives stigmatization and stigmatization processes are aimed at creating a social distance for the "normal" to avoid being contaminated by the "abnormal" (Kurzban and Leary 2001). As a consequence, stigmatized individuals see their social network shrink as stigma spreads, and their number of social interactions plummets (Carter and Feld 2004). In the workplace—especially in contexts that encourage the marginalization of some individuals because of rules, culture, or norms clashing with the identity of those individuals—the stigmatized experience social discomfort that can severely hamper their careers (Stenger and Roulet 2018).

While psychological theories assumed for a while that stigma had a negative impact on the perception of self, empirical results seemed to contradict this proposition (Crocker and Major 1989). Looking at the "self-concept" and how it develops as "a reflection of those others' appraisals of oneself" (610), Crocker and Major were the first to report that there was scarce evidence of generalized low self-esteem among the stigmatized. In fact, they point out that high self-esteem was found among ethnic minorities (Hoelter 1983) or the mentally ill (Willey and McCandless 1973). Taking a step further, Hughey (2012) shaped the concept of "stigma allure" by observing how individuals used stigma as a positive signal of authenticity and moral purity. Stigma is a scar that can be used to impress and make a point to convince audiences about adherence to a specific identity. This argument will be explored in more detail in Chapter 3 in the section on how the stigmatized and disapproved of resist hostility.

At the organizational level, arguably the most established concept is the one of organizational stigma (Hudson 2008; Devers et al. 2009). An organization is stigmatized when "collectively perceived by a specific stakeholder group as having values that are expressly counter to its own" (Devers et al. 2009, 157). Stigma researchers assume that there is some homogeneity in the stakeholder group stigmatizing the organization (Helms, Patterson, and Hudson 2019)—such as when they share the same value incongruence with the stigmatized organization. For example, a broad range of stakeholders and audiences stigmatize gay saunas because they perceive them as enabling a form of sexuality they cannot tolerate (Hudson and Okhuysen 2009). However, "for a stigma to materialize, the social labeling and categorization process . . . must diffuse across a critical mass of members within a stakeholder group" (Devers et al. 2009, 162). This collective labeling process thus requires a diffusion process through the audience constituted by the stakeholder group (Roulet 2015a). The different stakeholders and intermediaries within this group display their stigmatizing perspectives, thus creating consensus around their position and diffusing the stigma (ibid.).

Stigma has also been brought to other levels of analysis, with the stigmatization of practices (Clemente and Roulet 2015). Helms and Patterson (2014), in particular, looked into the practice of mixed martial arts. Entire fields of consumption can be stigmatized: Lopes (2006), for example, discussed the stigma around popular culture, in an attempt to explain why comic books are commonly despised. In the case of porn, it is the whole organizational field from producers to consumers that is stigmatized (Voss 2015).

What makes for a stigmatized characteristic? Goffman (1963, 3) stressed early on that not all undesirable characteristics lead to stigma, but "only those which are incongruous with our stereotype of what a given type of individual should be." In other words, the cultural and social contexts play a crucial role in making an undesirable characteristic a source of stigma. Here we are talking about culture in broad national terms, but also in more localized contexts such as the workplace. Minority sexuality is more stigmatized in some countries than in others because of cultural, social, and religious influences (Whitaker 2011), but also in some specific professional contexts such as professional service firms, where the rhetoric around performance penalizes minority sexuality because it deviates from the ideal masculine, straight employee (Stenger and Roulet 2018).

The process of stigmatization has often been presented in the literature as a case of social categorization (Tajfel et al. 1971): the stigmatized are put in a category that is negatively labeled, and the question is whether they are perceived as belonging in this category. In that sense, stigmatization is a dichotomous process. Goffman (1963) explains stigma categorization as the creation of a boundary between "us" (the "normal") and "them" (the "abnormal"). In modern work on stigma (for example, Vergne 2012), this argument on categorization often relies on existing work on the stigmatization of AIDS, making the point, for example, that HIV patients cannot be "in-between," they are either sick or not (Leary and Schreindorfer 1998). From a category perspective, stigmatized actors, whether they are organizations or individuals, are "deindividuated" because they are associated with a tainted group (Devers et al. 2009, 157). They lose their specificity when being negatively stereotyped. Open-access journals, for example, are often stigmatized because of the overlap between the category of predatory outlets and open-access ones (Daudigeos and Roulet 2018). However, at the same time, a stigmatized organization becomes "emblematic of the negatively evaluated category to which it is linked and, thus, caricatured as an embodiment of values that explicitly conflict with those of the stakeholder group" (Devers et al. 2009, 157).

BEYOND STIGMA

In 1995, Cahill and Eggleston (p. 681) noted that "the concept of stigma is so inclusive as to be uninformative," thus acknowledging the burgeoning of a variety of concepts well beyond stigma. As previously stressed, illegitimacy is another crucial construct among the various conceptualizations of negative social evaluations. While illegitimacy has often been used as an attribute for objects and symbols (Glynn and Marquis 2004), it has also been used to understand the link between illegitimate actions and illegitimate organizations (Elsbach and Sutton 1992) and the way in which products become more broadly accepted (Zuckerman 1999). Illegitimacy is often considered as a state preceding stigmatization (Suddaby, Bitektine, and Haack 2017). Hampel and Tracey (2019, 6) actually argue that stigmatization is an extreme form of moral illegitimacy, "when an audience deems an organization as being morally 'undesirable' because it regards the organization's activities as being harmful to society." Building upon Kraatz and Zajac (1996), Devers et al. (2009) contend that engaging in an illegitimate practice is what triggers the stigmatization of an organization. As one would expect, there are penalties for being illegitimate, mostly because illegitimate objects and actors are more likely to be ignored or disdained (Zuckerman 1999). Because illegitimacy is seen as either a lack of legitimacy or a negative legitimacy (Hudson 2008), some have however considered stigma and illegitimacy as two distinct concepts (Helms, Patterson, and Hudson 2019).

Less developed streams of research exist on other negative evaluations at the organizational level, such as disapproval (Vergne 2012; Roulet 2017; 2019b), infamy (Zavyalova, Pfarrer, and Reger 2017), negative media coverage (Zavyalova et al. 2016), or a spoiled image (Sutton and Callahan 1987), although many of those concepts are often assimilated to stigma (Devers et al. 2009; Hudson 2008). Some of those concepts directly relate to the nature of the audience producing the negative social evaluations, for example, the media when it comes to negative media coverage (Zavyalova et al. 2016; Roulet and Clemente 2018). Many concepts imply a gradation in the negative evaluation—disapproval, like illegitimacy, is less extreme than stigma (Vergne 2012), while infamy implies a critical mass of stakeholders agreeing on having an unfavorable opinion of the targeted actor (Zavyalova, Pfarrer, and Reger 2017). A spoiled image evokes the same taint as for stigma but suggests that the image of the organization or the individual became spoiled by an exogenous event (Sutton and Callahan 1987) or what Hudson (2008) would call an event stigma.

Those constructs also need to be disentangled from positive evaluations (Mishina and Devers 2012; Devers et al. 2009; Pollock et al., forthcoming; Roulet 2019b). Devers and colleagues and Pollock and colleagues made a significant effort to consider the connections, overlap, and differences between reputation, status, legitimacy, and stigma. Reputation is a signal of quality regarding the value a social actor can add when other information is not available or is too costly to obtain (Fombrun and Shanley 1990). The concept of reputation is anchored in signaling theory (Milgrom and Roberts 1986; Spence 1974), meaning that reputation is a social clue that is visible and interpreted by audiences (Shymko and Roulet 2017). Mishina and Devers (2012) add that while a bad reputation is a visible indicator predicting poor performance in the future for a given activity, stigma is a negative label being given to exclude an actor from a community. In this sense, stigmatized actors can still have a positive reputation—for example arms producers can be stigmatized and at the same time have a top-notch reputation for providing deadly weapons (Vergne 2012; Durand and Vergne 2015). Status is the rank of a social actor in a given hierarchy (Podolny 1993), and it captures "a pecking order—in which an individual's location within that hierarchy shapes others' expectations and actions toward the individual" (Podolny 2010, 11). Status is why elite jewelers reject the idea of selling turquoise, a stone they despise, despite strong demand, because their higher status makes them see themselves as untouchable and above and beyond economic consideration (Podolny 2010). Reputation denotes an expectation regarding the value of a product or service offered, while status is "tied to the pattern of relations and affiliations in which the actor does and does not choose to engage" (ibid., 13). Low status will translate into difficulties for a social actor to establish relations (Piazza and Castellucci 2014; Devers et al. 2009), but to a lesser extent than stigmatization: social actors will avoid associating themselves with stigmatized individuals and organizations, while they will just ignore low-status ones, and prefer creating ties with higher-status partners if those are available. Status and the related concept of prestige also found roots in early anthropological work by Clyde Mitchell, who mobilized those constructs to explain the heterogeneity of African societies (Smith 2019).

The concept of celebrity comes from the sociology of media (Gamson et al. 1992; Gamson 1994) and is attributed to social actors that are considered noteworthy and of interest by crucial evaluators such as the media (Roulet and Clemente 2018). Celebrity is constructed through narratives that make the actor stand out (Ohanian 1991). Shielded by their celebrity, organizations and individuals tend to conform less to norms (Rindova, Pollock, and Hayward 2006; Devers et al. 2009). Celebrities are credited with trustworthiness (Ohanian 1991), and for this reason they would not be stigmatized by the same audience. Thus an actor seen as a celebrity for one audience can be stigmatized by another. For example, Alek Minassian, a member of the Incel community—an online group of male supremacists—killed ten pedestrians in a vehicle-ramming attack: he was a celebrity for his peers, who perceived media reports as a celebration of their subculture, but he was despised and stigmatized by a broader audience.

The concept of legitimacy is the most closely linked to stigma, to a point that the overlap between the two is the subject of a significant controversy among social evaluations scholars (see the dialogue that took place in *Journal of Management Inquiry* between Helms, Patterson, and Hudson (2019) on one side and Hampel and Tracey (2019) on the other; see also Roulet 2019b). Legitimacy is usually defined as the social acceptance of an actor (Deephouse 1996; Roulet 2015b) or as a "generalized perception or assumption that the actions of an entity are desirable, proper or appropriate within some socially constructed system of norms, values, beliefs and definitions" (Suchman 1995, 574; cited in Suddaby, Bitektine, and Haack 2017). By contrast, as pointed out by Hudson, illegitimacy is either seen as a negative form of legitimacy (building upon Elsbach and Sutton 1992) or the absence of legitimacy (following Zuckerman 1999). Hampel and Tracey (2019) argue that moral legitimacy and stigmatization are on a continuum ranging from positive to negative social evaluations. By contrast, Helms, Patterson, and Hudson (2019) clearly distinguish legitimacy, illegitimacy, and stigmatization, as they argue that legitimacy is an evaluation shared across broad audiences, while stigma is audience specific. Suchman (1995) differentiated three types of legitimacy: pragmatic, cognitive, and moral or normative. First of all, pragmatic legitimacy is an evaluation that relies on "the self-interested calculations of an organization's most immediate audience" (ibid., 578) and in this sense is comparable to reputation. By contrast, cognitive legitimacy is related to an audience taking for granted an object or an actor (Jepperson 1991) and in this sense is not an evaluation per se (Suchman 1995). The last type of legitimacy—moral or normative legitimacy— is the most relevant to the study of negative social evaluations (Hampel and Tracey 2019). Moral legitimacy is an "interest-free" judgment relying on the conformity to societal norms (DiMaggio and Powell 1991; Suchman 1995, 579). In this sense, audiences evaluate the legitimacy of actors without thinking about the benefit they can obtain as a consequence of their evaluation. While the absence of taken-for-grantedness may signal a lack of cognitive legitimacy, it does not imply illegitimacy. Similarly, a lack of pragmatic legitimacy indicates the inability to deliver value to an audience or a partner. In this sense, illegitimacy evaluations are likely to solely rely on a moral or normative judgment (Hampel and Tracey 2019; Pollock et al., forthcoming).

Since Hudson (2008) and Devers and colleagues (2009) wrote their foundational pieces on negative social evaluations, other constructs that can be useful to understand negative social evaluations have emerged in the literature, focusing on the characteristics of the evaluating audiences, in particular peer evaluation (Shymko and Roulet 2017), expert evaluation (Cattani, Ferriani, and Allison 2014), and market identity (Wang, Wezel, and Forgues 2016). The two first forms of evaluations are self-explanatory: peers are members of the same field, and engaging in the same activity as the targeted actor, while experts are key audience members that are legitimately sought out to judge the targeted actor. Wang and colleagues define market identity as the shared representation of a social actor by an audience. In their case, they study the identity of hotels as a perception shared by their customers. While peer or expert evaluation can be positive, they can also be unfavorable as peer or expert stakeholder groups formulate a common criticism and evaluative threat toward the targeted organization or individual. The concept of peer evaluation (Cattani et al. 2014; Aadland, Cattani, and Ferriani 2019) has been used to understand how audiences can negatively evaluate other social actors in their field because of relationships with adversely perceived stakeholders (Shymko and Roulet 2017). Concretely, in our work on Russian theaters (ibid.), we show that their peers despise the theaters that receive corporate money. In this sense, peers and experts are crucial audiences when it comes to both positive and negative social evaluations.

In parallel, concepts under the negative social evaluation umbrella are themselves considerably intertwined (Roulet 2019b). The label "contested industries" encompasses the tobacco or gambling industries (Galvin, Ventresca, and Hudson 2005), and organizations within those industries are usually seen as core-stigmatized companies. Stigmatization as a categorization process has also been directly linked to the concept of disapproval, as Vergne (2012), in his work on the arms industry, argues that disapproval is the variance in discredit within a same stigmatized category of actors. Media disapproval is commonly seen as an operationalization of stigmatization (Roulet 2015a; Vergne 2012; Piazza and Perretti 2015) and can be used to capture a more fine-grained understanding of the negative perception of a social actor. In my work on investment banks (Roulet 2015b; 2019a), I captured particular media depiction, focused on the adverse evaluations of investment banks' practices. One thing that negative social evaluations at the organizational level have in common is indeed the often acknowledged role of media in transmitting evaluations of all stripes (Roulet and Clemente 2018; Zavyalova, Pfarrer, and Reger 2017).

In Chapter 1, we will explore in more detail the antecedents of negative social evaluations.

How Can Social Actors Simultaneously Have a Good Reputation and a Bad Rap?

With the concept of negative social evaluations pinned down, another critical argument to introduce is that positive and negative social evaluations can be on different continua (Hudson 2008). In other words, social actors can be both illegitimate and legitimate, have a good and bad reputation, be at once stigmatized and esteemed. This idea is a particularly important point of conceptualization for the arguments explored in this book: one key mechanism through which negative social evaluations become beneficial is when they generate positive social evaluations from other audiences, thus yielding positive consequences. In fact, we have already considered some cases in which organizations or individuals have simultaneously received positive and negative evaluations: Alek Minassian, terrorist but also the hero of the male supremacists; a frowned-upon arms dealer that does a have a positive reputation for selling deadly weapons; Trump, hated by the Democrats but loved by a strong base of supporters; Electronic Arts, a company that is despised by hardcore gamers but a favored provider for casual gamers.

Social actors are rarely negatively evaluated by all audiences at the same time (Hampel and Tracey 2019). While Hampel and Tracey see stigmatization as an extreme form of moral illegitimacy, Helms, Patterson, and Hudson (2019) make the point that some organizations can be stigmatized while at the same time being legitimate. For example, the Catholic Church is deeply tainted by scandals of sex abuse, while some crucial audiences still confer legitimacy to the organization and identify themselves with it (Gutierrez, Howard-Grenville, and Scully 2010; see also Piazza and Jourdan 2018). Walmart is another big firm heavily targeted by social activists and social movements for its labor practices and unfair competition (Ingram, Yue, and Rao 2010) while at the same time maintaining sales and a loyal customer base. For Helms and colleagues, stigma requires a critical mass of stakeholders sharing the negative perspective (an argument also made by Devers et al. 2009) and is not inherent to the targeted social actor. That is, stigma is not an intrinsic attribute—unless it is internalized by the stigmatized—it is a label provided by particular audiences. Helms, Patterson, and Hudson argue that legitimacy and illegitimacy, in comparison, reflect the evaluation of broad and generalized audiences (see Suchman 1995) while stigma reflects the perspective of one homogenous group of stakeholders.

To explain this conundrum, it is crucial to explain the role of audiences— different stakeholder groups that evaluate social actors and may or may not affect their economic and social prospects by formulating those evaluations. Audiences indeed play a crucial role in determining whether there are benefits in negative social evaluations. Negative social evaluations matter as much as positive evaluations of reputation (Deephouse 2000), legitimacy (Deephouse

and Suchman, 2008), and status (Piazza and Castellucci 2014) *because* negative and positive social evaluations can coexist on different continua (Hudson 2008). Such a situation can be due to the boundaries and scope of the
audiences. A high-status individual or organization within a given field may
attract hostility outside of this field. This situation might also be explained
by the opinions of the evaluating audiences (Clemente and Roulet 2015) and
their heterogeneity (Roulet and Clemente 2018). A highly reputed individual
for one medium might be despicable for another one at the opposite end of the
political spectrum.

This consideration of audience is an opportunity to flesh out the function of media as essential intermediaries (Entman 2007; Schultz, Utz, and
Göritz 2011; Zavyalova, Pfarrer, and Reger 2017). Media play a crucial role of
intermediaries between audiences and are commonly acting as a heterogeneous ensemble (Roulet and Clemente 2018). In the era of "fake news," media
may even disagree about truth and facts (Allcott and Gentzkow 2017). In this
context, media may appeal to emotions rather than reason when depicting
social actors, criticizing or praising them on the basis of their emotional
appeal rather than on their track records (Pollock et al., forthcoming). Such
a phenomenon can generate even more polarization between supporters and
opponents.

The divergence in the perception of the behaviors of those evaluated often
explains this dual continuum of positive and negative social evaluations for
a single actor. Illegitimate or disapproved of actions or practices can lead to
positive evaluations for the organizations or individuals who engage in them.
Hudson (2008) himself built upon the study by Elsbach and Sutton (1992) in
which they explore how two activist organizations became legitimate in the
social movement arena by engaging in illegitimate actions. In my studies of
investment banks, I show that organizations that are disapproved of by the
media for engaging in typical practices of their industry are also praised by
their corporate clients (Roulet 2017) and their peers (Roulet 2015b) because it
signals their proximity to the core of their field. Politicians often try to shock
opinion with controversial statements, to make the headlines and be noticed
in the media. Being controversial and being visible are quite often correlated.

Some organizations can have a high-level reputation or status, for example
within their industry or their field, and face strong public hostility (Roulet
2015b). Goldman Sachs, in particular, is considered as a must-go or must-
work-for for investment bankers or investment banker wannabes, but the

bank was heavily attacked in the media for their responsibility in the financial crisis (Roulet 2019a). In short, social actors can be highly esteemed by their peers and condemned by outside audiences. In a similar way, popular movies that were despised by the critics and experts or other cinema professionals can be successful in terms of box office receipts—in this case, peer and expert evaluations are unfavorable, while the public is supportive. The horror teen movie *Final Destination* was one of the biggest and most successful horror franchises from 2000 to 2011. However, soon after the first release, *the New York Times* wrote, "Even by the crude standards of teenage horror, *Final Destination* is dramatically flat," and the *Washington Post* in an even nicer critique stated to the viewers that "[their] own final destination just might be the box office, to demand [their] money back."

It might even be that the support of the public is actually partly motivated by the critique formulated by the elites. Social evaluations coming from different stakeholders are deeply intertwined, and a negative evaluation for one actor may mean a positive one for another actor (Shymko and Roulet 2017). The key to assessing the consequences of those social evaluations—whether positive or negative—is to identify the key audiences that will significantly impact the social and economic prospects of the social actor under the microscope (Roulet 2019a).

The fundamental role of audiences in understanding the divergence of social evaluations for a single social actor will enable us to build boundary conditions and limitations to the arguments regarding the benefits of negative social evaluations (see Chapter 4).

A Cross-Disciplinary and Multilevel Framework to Understand Negative Social Evaluations

Now that the various concepts in this literature have been reviewed, it is time to set the foundation for the overall theoretical framework offered in this book. While a range of existing work has focused on the "reputational" risk, or the extent of damages that negative social evaluations can cause (Westphal and Deephouse 2011: Mishina and Devers 2012), the opposite argument is made here—the idea that negative evaluations can be beneficial to those who receive them.

This Introduction started by identifying clues suggesting that negative social evaluations may, after all, not be that bad. The evidence suggesting that negative evaluations can be in some ways beneficial has started accumulating, from Crocker and Major (1989) examining the link between stigma and self-esteem, Ashforth and Kreiner (1999) looking at positive self-conception in dirty work occupations, and Elsbach and Sutton's (1992) study of activists to the more recent work on mixed martial arts (Helms and Patterson 2014) or organizations providing support to migrants (Tracey and Phillips 2016). This stream of research defends the same counterintuitive argument, but more work is needed to differentiate the mechanisms that lead negative social evaluations to have positive outcomes, to identify the overlap between them and the conditions under which they materialize. In addition, there is limited research on how those different processes can be generalized and expanded to different levels. For example, there are implications of the psychology of dirty work for organizations, and inversely there are lessons we can draw from work on contested industries management to understand individual stigma. This book will look into the individual and organizational levels of analysis, but also at the field as a critical echelon experiencing negative social evaluations. Fields are composed of actors sharing the same activity and having a common belief and value system (DiMaggio and Powell 1983; Bourdieu 1977; Thomson 2014), and they play a crucial role when it comes to defining the scope and boundaries of audience evaluations (Shymko and Roulet 2017).

The model offered here is thus aimed at answering the following research question: How can negative social evaluations be beneficial? To answer this research question, I will bridge the gap between antecedents and consequences of negative social evaluations by better fleshing out existing links to relevant work on misconduct (Palmer, Greenwood, and Smith-Crowe 2016) and scandal (Kuhn and Ashcraft 2003; Entman 2012), but also bringing in complementary literature such as on crisis management (Williams et al. 2017) and organizational change (Rousseau and Tijoriwala 1999). The objective is to better connect the impact of social evaluations with their roots and starting points. Moving toward exploring how social actors resist and capitalize on negative social audiences, the key roles of audiences and media will be stressed. Media in some ways enable the coexistence of positive and negative social evaluations and explain the boundary conditions under which negative social evaluations can bring about positive consequences.

Figure 3 summarizes the architecture of the model offered in this book. Ultimately, the model will lead us to discuss the practical implications (Chapter 4), where we will be exploring what organizations and individuals can do about negative social evaluations.

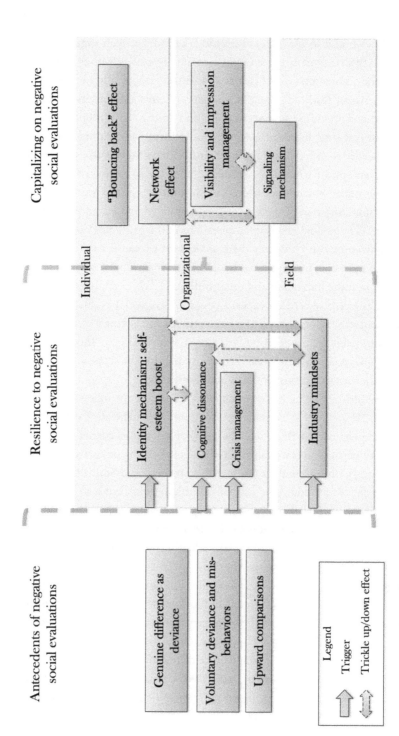

Figure 3. Theoretical Framework for Understanding Negative Social Evaluations. Source: Made by author.

An exploration of the antecedents of negative social evaluations will be the starting point of the book. Chapter 1 will form the groundwork for the left-hand side and the starting point of the model. To understand why and how negative evaluations can be beneficial, it is crucial to understand where they originate and what triggers them, but also, simply, why do they even exist in the first place? In that chapter, the *raison d'etre* of negative social evaluations will be covered: looking at their very existence and the motivations of actors producing them. The antecedents of negative social evaluations are divided into three broad categories. The first two categories fall under the general notion of deviance. Practices, individuals, and organizations can interrelatedly deviate from norms. Diverging from Falk's (2001) differentiation of societal and contextual deviance, the argument formulated here relies on the notion of agency to establish a typology of deviance. There is a distinction between "genuine" deviance and "voluntary" deviance from norms. Genuine deviance is the idea that social actors can unintendedly deviate from norms because of their very nature. They have not chosen to deviate—they do so because of who they are, where they are, or the groups they belong to in spite of themselves—but still have to suffer the consequences. In contrast, individuals and organizations may purposefully be deviating from norms: in this case, deviance is voluntary. Instrumental motives are usually behind the choice of voluntary deviance, but one can imagine more complex reasons why actors want to deviate from the norms, for example when they are pressurized by their peers. There is a less common reason why hostile audiences target individuals or organizations: being on the receiving end of upward comparisons, when the status, the reputation, or the legitimacy of an organization or individual attracts jealousy and hatred. For example, actors at the top of social hierarchies might be more often targeted with negative evaluations from envious counterparts. By contrast with deviance, this last explanation resides in the characteristics of the producers rather than of the target of the negative evaluation. Finally, this chapter will finish on the dynamic aspects of negative social evaluations: How do they stick? How and why do they spread? How can there be variance in the extent to which individuals and organizations belong to stigmatized categories? The final section of the chapter is aimed at explaining how and why negative social evaluations persist and mutate over time. What motivates the production of a social evaluation might be quickly lost as the evaluation is diffused through audiences.

Chapter 2 will investigate how individuals and organizations confront and resist negative social evaluations. The term *resilience* will be used to encompass the different mechanisms through which social actors endure negative evaluations. How can negative labels be experienced in a favorable light by their targets? Each of those reactive mechanisms will be covered, including how they overlap and how they relate to each other. In particular, genuine and voluntary deviance and upward comparisons can all have a positive impact on self-esteem at the individual level through a variety of identity mechanisms. Identity mechanisms relate to the self-image: how individuals perceive themselves, including by contrast with others. Developing this argument will take us to a discussion of how common enemies are constructed to build group cohesion, the identity mechanisms through which stigmatized groups resist hostility, and how they build a positive self-perception. The implications of this phenomenon for organizations will be discussed. At the organizational level, deviance can cause cognitive dissonance as organizational members refuse to confront the reality of outsiders' claims: they bunker themselves against outsiders' claims and arguments, and their own beliefs end up being reinforced. Taking the argument to a more macro level, the chapter will then cover the emergence of industry mindsets as a consequence of deviance and upward comparisons. Finally, the last two sections of this chapter will focus on the dynamics of resilience: how it develops over time and how reactions are deployed. One way negative social evaluations are managed is through crisis management, as misbehaviors, voluntary deviance, and subsequent scandals are put under control. In the penultimate section of that chapter, the ways in which individual relations change as a consequence of negative evaluations will be explored. Overall, we will also consider how those processes affect each other across levels, in particular through the trickling up and trickling down effects explaining cascades of reactions to negative social evaluations (Clemente and Roulet 2015; Harmon, Haack, and Roulet 2018; Roulet et al. 2020).

Chapter 3 will be more radical and will focus this time on the benefits of negative social evaluations, unveiling a number of overlapping processes. At the individual level, those who "bounce back" after a negative evaluation experience the frustration of being negatively evaluated, which has consequently pushed them to better themselves. Engaging in negatively evaluated practices and actions, and being negatively evaluated in itself, gives visibility to both organizations and individuals. Both genuine and voluntary deviance can trigger effort by deviating actors to manage the "impression" they produce—the opinion of what they are like according to their audiences. Ultimately those actors can manage impression so that they stand out. In the same way, organizations that receive an unfavorable label because of upward comparison can also capitalize on that to obtain visibility and reinforce their superior position even more. Those mechanisms will be illustrated by looking at the strategies used by divisive politicians to attract voters. As in the previous chapter, the dynamics aspects of negative evaluations will be covered. At the individual and organizational levels, we will explore, for example, the role of network effect, when hostility from some audiences and stakeholders generates positive evaluations from others. Those network effects depend on the willingness of the network members to spread and diffuse negative social evaluations, but also on the nature of those evaluations. This process is deeply intertwined with the signaling mechanism of fields and organizations through which internal and external audiences signal to each other their proximity or distance to social actors. Taking stock of those arguments, a summary of the theory of beneficial negative social evaluations will be presented before discussing its boundary conditions.

Chapter 4 will be used to reflect on the framework to appraise and list the practical implications of this model. While the arguments explored throughout the book are theoretically rich, readers can use them in their daily work lives. More broadly, there are ramifications of the literature on negative social evaluations for stigmatized individuals, contested organizations and industries, and communication and public relations practitioners. The research reviewed in this book and the conceptual model can be harnessed by those practitioners. In particular, how can individuals within organizations concretely elicit beneficial evaluations and mitigate the adverse consequences of negative ones? This work also feeds approaches to leadership and customer relationships building on the relevant theoretical mechanisms identified earlier in the book. Firms can also manage employees' self-concept when they are facing public hostility by focusing on the implications of the book for firms' internal communication. Turning toward external communication, negatively perceived actors can manage their relationships with their stakeholders to survive. Finally, this chapter will touch upon the societal implications of divisiveness—in particular looking at the negative role of fake news and conspiracy theories.

The Conclusion will take stock of the model and its implications, in particular from an ethical point of view and at a more macrosocietal level. This section will set out methodological avenues and an agenda for future research on social evaluations, across disciplines. This will lead to a debate around the "evaluative society" in which we live, and how it feeds new phenomena that may threaten democracy.

CHAPTER 1

WHERE IT ALL BEGINS

Understanding the Antecedents of Negative Social Evaluations

Before digging into the positive consequences of negative social evaluations, let's look at what causes and triggers those evaluations, what precedes them, and how they take shape. What sort of behavior or characteristics can bring a negative label to individuals and organizations? How does this behavior translate into a negative social evaluation? This chapter will look at how the literature on negative social evaluations can benefit from a closer comparison to existing work on misconduct (Palmer 2012; Palmer 2013; Palmer and Yenkey 2015), deviance (Burke 1994; Lawrence and Robinson, 2007), social comparisons (Festinger 1954), and scandals (Adut 2008; Entman 2012; Puglisi and Snyder 2011; Piazza and Jourdan 2018; Daudigeos, Roulet, and Valiorgue 2020). There are essential processes to bridge the theoretical gap between different levels of analysis, for example, by explaining how identity dynamics of dirty workers (Ashforth and Kreiner 1999; Kreiner, Ashforth, and Sluss 2006) inform the case of industry mindsets (Phillips 1994) surviving public hostility.

As this chapter begins to dive into the model, it will cover the antecedents and triggers of negative social evaluations. As a first step, it will explore why social evaluations exist and under which forms, independent from the characteristics of audiences and target. It will expose two antecedents of negative social evaluations explained by the characteristics of the evaluated parties: genuine deviance (deviance that is not sought after and is caused by the very nature of the social actor) and voluntary deviance (when actors purposefully refuse to conform with norms). Turning toward one antecedent of negative social evaluations, focus will then be on the interaction between the recipient and producers of those evaluations: upward comparisons (when the status, the reputation, or the legitimacy of an organization or individual attracts jealousy, envy, and hatred). Fleshing out the causes of negative social evaluations will help us better understand the responses and reactions of individuals, organizations, and fields in later chapters.

The following section will answer three fundamental questions to help map the antecedents of negative social evaluations fully. Why do we even need negative social evaluations in the first place? Why do audiences and stakeholders feel the need to attribute negative labels? And what use do society and communities have for negative labeling?

Raison d'etre and Motives for Producing Negative Social Evaluations

WHY DOES STIGMA EXIST?

Going back to the etymology of the word *stigma* in Ancient Greece, the idea was to hurt the targeted individual (as it involved a scar or a bodily modification) and mark him or her as different and deviant. Criminals or slaves were the main stigmatized individuals at that time. Stigma was playing a societal role by signaling either dangerous individuals or those with lower status so that they could be avoided. The stigmatized become isolated, and their peers start to avoid them for fear of being contaminated (Kurzban and Leary 2001). The fear of "being contaminated" makes full sense when the label is associated with the idea of contagion, such as in the case of the stigmatization of AIDS, in which one marginalizes the sick because of a fear of getting sick him- or herself (Leary and Schreindorfer 1998). Stigma is thus playing a crucial social role, casting out those who were thought to be harmful to others or more broadly to society's cohesion.

While one would survive a one-star review on TripAdvisor or AirBnB without a fleshly scar, the marking is still there, although in this case more digital than physical. We single out those restaurants or hotels on TripAdvisor so "others know" that they are subpar and can consequently avoid them. We go on providing a negative rating for a host or a guest on AirBnB to alert other users to stay away from those reprobate business partners. By reporting those miscreant businesses and individuals, we ensure that they are less likely to engage in fruitful partnership in the future, and others are less likely to suffer from their substandard offering. To some surprising extent, engaging in such a process makes us feel good and proud. We see ourselves as citizens, contributing to society—although hopefully not in the way the Greeks were disfiguring their criminals. In the same way, consumer boycotts are driven by individuals opposing and wanting to change the behavior of a firm by making it more prosocial (McDonnell and King 2013).

Societal Role of Negative Social Evaluations and Personal Motives

What sort of roles do the production and the consumption of negative social evaluations play in society? How can their instrumental use inform our understanding of what motivates them?

First of all, negative social evaluations can be motivated by the willingness to create alignment between what are perceived as the firm's values and as the activists' values, when the latter consider theirs as more legitimate or morally acceptable. Or in other words, social movements generate negative evaluations of a target so that this target will start following the same norms of behavior. In 2011, it became known that the American fast-food chain Chick-fil-A was funding a number of anti-lesbian-gay-bi-trans (LGBT) associations, and the firm's president and CEO appeared on radio only to confirm his business's hostility to the LGBT community. This disclosure was followed by a strong backlash, with a call for banning the chain on university campuses, because this lack of tolerance was profoundly at odds with the moral norms prevailing among students. In the meantime, the former Arkansas governor Mike Huckabee politically capitalized on the situation by federating the opponents to the opponents and creating a Chick-fil-A Appreciation Day movement. Those opponents to the boycott felt it was threatening their values and beliefs with regard to the conception of the family. The Chick-fil-A case is an excellent example of how a clash in values can lead to an attempt to realign the principles enacted by the target and the values of different audiences. The boycotters wanted Chick-fil-A to change its values, but their efforts only signaled the contrast, and helped the firm gather even stronger supporters, thus providing incentives for the firm to become even more radical in its values.

Thus negative social evaluations play a crucial role in society. However, another perspective on our motivation to provide negative social evaluations is less flattering: we also often take the time to provide a nasty comment online because we want revenge, we want to harm those that have wrong us, we want to see them suffer. Richard Smith, a professor of psychology at the University of Kentucky, spent his whole career studying the concept of *Schadenfreude* (see Smith 2013 for a thorough review), or the "malicious pleasure at an out-group's misfortune" (Leach et al. 2003, 932), from a unique German word that can be literally translated as "harm-joy." Smith, Leach, and colleagues are building upon the work of the psychologist Heider (1958) but also Nietzsche's foundational work *On the Genealogy of Morals* (1887/1967) as they explore how we can enjoy and take pleasure in seeing others suffer.

Another motivation is to be found in egoistic rather than prosocial motives. Nietzsche distinguished between the pleasure of seeing others suffer passively and the pleasure of actively triggering suffering and enjoying it. In our case, this distinction is similar to enjoying reading nasty criticisms of a neighboring restaurant on TripAdvisor, or actively writing such a criticism and taking pleasure in thinking it will be read and enjoyed by others, and will ultimately make the target suffer. If we go back to the case of my local barber, who is getting the most unpleasant Google reviews from customers on a regular basis (although the barber wants to believe those are only comments from malicious competitors), we can see how the motives for *Schadenfreude* differ from the motives to produce negative social evaluations. As I was writing on this example for this book, I went back on Google and read a few more reviews: I do confess I had a good laugh reading that my hairdresser was called a "melt" (apparently a slang word for idiot!). I could not prevent myself from thinking that he probably at least partially deserved the insult, and reading those lovely reviews did provide me with good entertainment. That would definitely be *Schadenfreude*. If, by contrast, my hairdresser had decided to cut my hair in the shape of a Mohawk without my consent, I would have enjoyed writing a noxious review myself.

Such feelings of enjoying others' demise is in "human nature," as Richard Smith stated in a *New York Times* interview in 2002.[2] Buckels and colleagues (2019), in a recent piece in the *Journal of Personality*, investigated the relationship between online trolling and a sadistic personality. They found that online trolling and sadism triggered the same pleasure among individuals exhibiting those behaviors. In addition, the authors note that online trolling as a behavioral transgression causing pain to others is judged morally acceptable because it brings enjoyment and amusement. Online trolls, like sadists, are found to minimize the pain of others when they rationalize their judgmental behaviors. In practice, if online trolls see the suffering of someone online (for example, someone whose appearance is affected by chemotherapy) and make fun of it, they negate the pain they can observe (for example, "this person seems fine, despite the chemotherapy—so this whole thing is probably not that bad") to feel less guilty.

Another key malicious motivation explaining why we enjoy reading others' poor reviews or producing ones can be found in social comparison theory, a framework that goes back to a *Human Relations* article written by Leon Festinger in 1954. Because of the difficulty in objectively assessing their abilities, individuals constantly engage in social comparisons with each other. Instead of capturing their own absolute value they evaluate their value in comparison with others. In this sense, any negative reviews of others provide reassurance in our own ability to succeed. Seeing co-workers receive negative performance feedback can potentially bring comfort and confidence. In fact, Vidaillet (2016)—elaborating on the Lacanian perspective on envy—even argues that the benefits of reassuring ourselves drive the very existence of performance systems, because "it is a means of situating oneself in relation to, of comparing oneself to, the other, to watch the other" and "to show that we can 'distinguish ourselves from the rest'" (9). Providing negative reviews can be motivated by the intersection of social comparison and fairness—by comparison, nonperforming services or product providers deserve to receive a negative evaluation. There is also significant enjoyment in providing to others the satisfaction of being rewarded for their work when they receive positive social evaluation (Vidaillet 2016). In comparison, the pleasure of providing a negative evaluation, because it can trigger suffering, can potentially "suppl[y] an intense awareness of our power" (Soll 1994, 180). Within organizations, differences in social evaluations usually closely mimic power hierarchies (Smith, Merlone, and Duffy 2016).

Online complaints can also simply be motivated by power trips. Customer experiences can leave those same customers with a sense of powerlessness, and negative social evaluations can be the only way to regain control over the relationship with a product or service provider. By posting an unpleasant evaluation, taking advantage of anonymity, we exert our power of judging, for want of any better opportunity for retaliation. Such a situation has reached the point that hotel and restaurant managers often report clients trying to extort upgrades or additional services by threatening them with negative evaluations. A *Telegraph* article reported the frustration of an English pub owner: "We get it frequently, people who sit in and say 'if you don't take this

off my bill, we will put it on TripAdvisor'."[3] Since 2013, TripAdvisor has put
in place a process through which hotel and restaurant managers can report
attempts of blackmailing by customers. However, the difficulty is to assess
the ex-ante intention of the evaluators: from a hotel or restaurant perspective, any negative social evaluation is malicious, while from the evaluator perspective it might be motivated by a genuine attempt to share a documented
point of view. Besides, the review of research on *Schadenfreude* by Smith and
colleagues (2009) reports that enjoying others' demises is strongly driven by
a quest for fairness: we enjoy even more reading the negative evaluations of
others if we think they deserve it. Going back to the case of my hairdresser, if
I had truly appreciated him, I would not have enjoyed him being treated as a
"melt" on Google reviews, and in some way, a part of my own perception of
him felt validated.

Performance and evaluation systems in organizations are potentially fueling envy and motivating individuals to appear favorably in social comparisons (Smith, Merlone, and Duffy 2016). In fact, something that scholars of
stigma agree on but have not always focused on is that stigmatization, and
negative social evaluations more broadly, are first and foremost contributing
to a process of *social control* (Goffman 1963). Those processes "produc[e] and
reproduce[e] relations of power and control" (Parker and Aggleton 2003, 16)
and rely on marking those who deviate from social norms to make them easily
identifiable and punishable. As I pointed out, negative evaluations of hotels,
restaurants, or hairdressers are aimed at socially controlling others to avoid
those service providers. Punishment is aimed at correcting future behaviors
or preventing those of individuals potentially at risk of engaging in a stigmatized practice. However, Blume (2002) mathematically modeled the impact
of stigmatization on deviance and showed that the longer the stigma lasts,
the less efficient is the process of social control, because individual actors lose
incentives to correct their behavior if there are no opportunities to minimize
the penalties received for deviating from the norms. The author mentions
the case of the United States, where in some states, businesses cannot obtain
licenses if they employ former felons, no matter when the crime was committed: such a system excludes those former criminals from finding legitimate
jobs and returning to normal social life, thus potentially forcing them into
new felonies.

To explain why some individuals and organizations are stigmatized, hostile audiences engage in what Goffman (1963) called *"stigma theorizing"* (see

also Roulet 2015b, for the use of the concept at the organizational level), an "ideology" to rationalize the inferiority of the stigmatized actors (Goffman 1963, 5). We create arguments, articulate values, and form beliefs with what we see as evidence to convince ourselves and others that the stigmatized are indeed inferior and must be avoided by other social actors. Research has, for example, shown that auditors are prone to stigmatize homosexual colleagues because of pervasive male-focused rhetoric of performance that condemns divergence from expected gender roles (Stenger and Roulet 2018). Investment banks faced public hostility during the financial crisis because media and audiences were attributing the turmoil to their typical behaviors and practices, and the values on which they relied (Roulet 2015a; Roulet 2019a).

CONSPIRACY THEORIES: WHEN NEGATIVE EVALUATIONS ARE COLLECTIVELY SHAPED BUT REMAIN ELUSIVE

Negative evaluations can take different shapes and fuel much broader movement than what we have explored so far. Their nature also depends on the vehicle that enables their diffusion. The "Yellow Vest" crisis in France, Trump in the United States, Brexit in the United Kingdom, and the new politics of populism in many Western countries have revealed the strength and acceleration of a specific source of negative social evaluations: conspiracy theories. Conspiracy theories are not a novel phenomenon (Goertzel 1994), but they are now fueling radical political movements on the basis of misleading information usually aimed at discrediting and tainting another party (Nougayrede 2019).

Examining conspiracy theories in conjunction with negative social evaluations is fruitful, because the diffusion of those theories relies on the emotional nature of the negative evaluations they produce. They generate shock and outrage because of those negative evaluations. In this case, they have a societal impact, but are harnessed by smaller groups to create a division that will benefit those smaller groups.

Conspiracy theories are a collective narrative that produce elusive negative evaluations, usually leading to more divisiveness. As noted by Nougayrede (2019), conspiracy theories do not only target groups of people, they now commonly target entire countries. In the current context, even the biggest and the most absurd claims gain traction. Nougayrede listed a range of contemporary stories used as political tools. In January 2019, the meeting in Aachen of the German chancellor and the French president was claimed to be about the sellout (or the return) of Alsace-Loraine, a region of France, to Germany, an idea that, for most people and in particular those living in Alsace Lorraine, would be impossible to believe. Yet this theory had a range of believers. In the same vein and in the same period, members of the Italian government claimed that African countries were still factually (and not metaphorically!) under colonization by French forces. Those conspiracy theories also linked up with the belief that emerged at the same time according to which the UN migration pact was designed to accept millions of migrants in Europe. There was thus a system of theories, connected to each other, mostly used to feed a fear of migrants, which would ultimately benefit extremist parties.

The best-known conspiracy theories in history are the ones claiming that the assassination of John F. Kennedy was part of a full plot or that men never landed on the moon. They rely on the stigmatization of elusive enemies, in this case enemies "from the inside," such as members of the government. In this sense, the targets of the conspiracy theories are unclear, which helps the theory followers believe in a common enemy.

As I have previously noted, social media play a crucial role in spreading negative evaluations and in particular broader systems of evaluations such as conspiracy theories. Allcot and Gensklow (2017) specifically examined the role of social media in the 2016 U.S. election. In a post-election survey they present in their paper, 13.8 percent of Americans reported that their primary sources of news related to the presidential election were on social media and 14.8 percent on websites. Those who said social media was their primary source of news were significantly more likely to believe in fake news (mostly targeted at discrediting Hillary Clinton). Some specific media have made conspiracy theories their primary business, activity, and *raison d'etre*. One example is Alex Jones's Infowars—a website and associated radio show that has built its audience on the basis of fake news, harassment, and conspiracy theories. Infowars famously sparked controversy by repeatedly claiming 9/11 was an inside job.

Conspiracy theories give an unusual form to negative evaluations: like stigma, they are collectively shaped. As previously stressed, they remain elusive in who and what they target, and they articulate together sets of incorrect facts that give each other coherence. In fact, they are like religion or logics, and they are erected in systems of beliefs, especially including negative evaluations of outside parties. Conspiracy theorists "spin . . . alternative universes" (Nougareyde 2019). By contrast with sole "fake news," erroneous facts that are widely shared without necessarily any intent, conspiracy theories are spread by individuals and groups that have an instrumental motive—they want to serve a political objective or gather support in favor of or against a group, and usually serve their interest in the meantime. The conspiracy theories around France at the end of 2018 and the start of 2019 were mainly aimed at destabilizing the French government and serving the extreme right before the European elections. They relied on the negative evaluation of the president and the ministers in power, erected as a common enemy. The conspiracy theories regarding JFK or 9/11 have been used to blame a whole range of actors depending on the originating party, but usually the government (as elusive as it can be!) and people in power. Populist politicians from Donald Trump in the United States to Jarosław Kaczyński in Poland to Viktor Orban in Hungary have made use of such theories to serve their political destiny. In the case of Hungary, Orban forged conspiracy theories to blame national issues on the billionaire George Soros, whose Open Society Foundations was forced to flee Budapest.

Early research on conspiracy theories showed that believing in one conspiracy theory makes one believe in other conspiracy theories (Goertzel 1994). Hannah Arendt, in the *Origins of Totalitarianism* (1973), looks at the roots of Nazism and the blaming of the Jews. She shows how the antisemitism that fueled Nazism was built on a broad and well-rooted system linking a range of beliefs and prejudice against a "Jewish world conspiracy." It built on various preconceptions against the Jews that had sedimented since the eighteenth century. In this sense, we could map out a network of conspiracy theories on the basis of the groups and stakeholders they target and negatively evaluate.

The philosopher Karl Popper (1971/2012) was one of the first intellectuals to theorize conspiracy theories. For him, all conspiracy theories grow and spread because of the natural tendency to refuse that things happen by accident. Individuals want to believe in conspiracy theories because they offer coherent and straightforward explanations to outcomes that would otherwise be considered as purely unintended. In addition, they connect seemingly unrelated events or phenomena, thus giving believers the impression that they have made sense of a complicated situation. Oliver and Wood (2014) also found that beliefs in Manichean narratives directly correlated with beliefs in conspiracy theories. They remind us that conspiracy theories are not only left to poorly educated and marginalized individuals. They also form coherent systems of ideas that even the smartest can embrace when those they connect with (in real life or on social media) provide them with a "sound box" amplifying the message.

There are also evident characteristics shared by individuals believing in conspiracy theories: they lack trust in others, they fear the future, and they are highly critical of the societies they live in (Goertzel 1994). The emergence of conspiracy theories is often linked to the concept of anomia, popularized in Durkheim's study of suicide as a social fact (1897/2005). Anomia reflects the lack of moral guidance in modern societies: citizens feel left out and without any clear norm to guide their behaviors, thus leading to clashes in belief systems. In anomic societies, individuals tend to focus on interactions with those sharing the same beliefs and withdraw from broader societal integration. They end up being isolated morally, feeling misunderstood, and thus are more likely to embrace systems of ideas that will give them a community and moral codes defined by the opposition to others' norms, and, more important, a common enemy. Conspiracy theories create a context of widespread paranoia and hostility within initially homogenous populations but also across countries and defined audiences.

While conspiracy theories are systems of beliefs based on negative evaluations, the motives in spreading them might be only remotely connected to the actual group or individual they target. In the case of the conspiracy theories around George Soros, Soros is the target, but the real objective is for the Hungarian president to find a perfect culprit to exonerate himself from blame for the economic and political difficulties faced by the country. By contrast, during the 2016 election in the United States, Trump supporters spread rumors on Hillary Clinton's health and sleep patterns, to attack her fitness for office. But in many cases, the targets of conspiracy theories can be elusive and mythical—conspiracy theorists blame many of today's issues on freemasons or illuminati. Freemasons and illuminati can be anybody, from the next door neighbor to the president of the United States. Audiences can "imagine" the enemy as it fits their own contexts. The more elusive the target, the better culprit it makes. The opinion can then be federated under the same banner against a common enemy. Like other forms of negative social evaluations, conspiracy theories are a tool of social control, which has the power to manipulate the masses.

Conspiracy theories are not left unanswered. Mainstream media have invested in debunking fake news—the issue is that the cost and the resources to deconstruct fake news is much higher than the production of the fake news. There are also many other challenges. Individuals embracing fake news are not necessarily consuming those mainstream media in which they can be exposed to counter-narratives. Conspiracy theories will always have a head start with regard to their velocity and their diffusion but also their numbers: individuals and groups attempting to debunk conspiracy theories will have to be selective and target those that are the biggest threats to social cohesion. Have you ever tried to argue with a moon landing skeptic, or any other conspiracy theorists (usually they believe in more than one)? Many of us have, without much success. Unfortunately, few of us have the technical knowledge to explain how rockets go through the atmosphere to land on the moon. Such a scientific fact is a lot easier to bust and disprove than to establish or defend.

What are the consequences of conspiracy theorists being busted? The lies end up being forgotten, and even when the rhetorical devices of conspiracy theories are taken down, implications for those who gave them life remain limited (Arendt 1973). Public opinion forgets more quickly about the false-hood of the conspiracy theory than the time it took to believe in it. Such a mechanism aligns with the phenomenon of cognitive dissonance we will explore in the next chapter—once individuals have adopted and embraced a system of belief and this system is proven wrong, they either stick to it or they have to cognitively eliminate the idea that they adhered to it in the first place.

Ironically, conspiracy theories can thrive because they are stigmatized (Barkun 2003/2013). In this case, negative social evaluations are spread and reinforced in their strength and effect because their sources are themselves adversely perceived. Those buying into conspiracy theories will give them even more legitimacy because those theories are discarded by a majority and by sources of authority—which, within a conspiracy theory, is usually looked at with suspicion and mistrust. When arguments are rejected by the majority and by legitimate actors, it supports the claim that the idea is vol-untarily kept secret by "those in power." Conspiracy theories are unique in the broader family of sources and origins of negative social evaluations, as they are negatively evaluated themselves, which paradoxically reinforces their ability to convince. There is a spiraling mechanism through which being divi-sive becomes more influential when it is being perceived as divisive itself. The power of a conspiracy theory resides in its ability to remain a closed system of reinforcing arguments.

Conspiracy theories unfortunately can have a societal impact. Conspir-acy theories are systems through which negative evaluations are generated and diffused to manipulate masses in the service of a minority. The nega-tive social evaluations they are fueled with are conducive to societal division, often threatening the fabric of our communities. Conspiracy theories thrive on hatred, and on the negative labeling of deviance, or on framing behaviors or characteristics of groups as deviant. In this sense, deviance seems to be in itself socially constructed but remains the key reason why actors might be negatively evaluated.

Deviance as a Source of Negative Social Evaluations

In the previous section, we explored why social actors, audiences, and media *issue* negative social evaluations and the social reasons for their existence. In this section, we will move toward an explanation of why social actors *receive* negative social evaluations. What do actors do to be negatively perceived? As we have seen when discussing negative evaluations as a form of social control, those evaluations are not necessarily deserved or sought after, and individuals and organizations have no other choice than to suffer them because of who they are rather than because of what they may have voluntarily done.

A large share of the research on negative social evaluations has looked at deviance as a broad and consensually accepted antecedent of negative social evaluations. Types of deviance include deviance from the normal—actors that are considered similar to the majority; deviance from the norm—what is considered right by the broader society; and deviance from expectations. The forms of deviance are quite diverse, but they have in common the idea that a deviant social actor is different or divergent from the crowd.

Deviance as a critical determinant of negative social evaluations is quite often an integrative part of the frameworks conceptualizing those evaluations and related processes. The early work of Goffman (1963) in some ways even collapsed the study of stigma and deviance, suggesting that they could not be studied apart from each other.

A number of typologies of deviance exist in the literature on negative social evaluations (Goffman 1963; Falk 2001). Falk, for example, differentiated between societal and situational deviance. Societal deviance is widely accepted as such. Generalized and broad audiences agree on an act being deviant. Alternatively, deviance can be situational and specific to a given cultural and social context. Refusing to queue would be a lese-majesty in the United Kingdom where I live but perfectly acceptable in France where I am born—I am situationally deviant when I attract hostile looks because I have failed to notice the queue to get my morning coffee on my way to work. In the same fashion, while homosexuality remains accepted by most, a share of the population even in the most liberal countries does continue to be hostile (cf Pew Research Center 2013). In addition, audiences can be extremely polarized with regard to their perception of deviance within a same cultural context. During the debate around the gay marriage bill in France, this antagonism was particularly apparent in the violence of the demonstration opposing the bill (Stenger and Roulet 2018).

By contrast with Falk's typology, as I stressed in the Introduction, Goffman (1963) distinguished three sorts of stigma and underlying types of deviance: physical stigma—usually visible, including inherited (such as deformities) and obtained (for example, tattoos; see Timming 2015); conduct or character stigma—a personality trait or a reprehensible behavior; and group identity or tribal stigma—belonging to a stigmatized collective such as a race, an ethnicity, or a political or religious group. Goffman's typology can be in some ways problematic, as the three forms of deviance significantly overlap. The stigmatization of homosexuality, for example, could belong to the two last categories (Ragins and Cornwell 2001). For some, being gay is being part of a tainted community, while for others homosexuality is mainly seen as a morally reprehensible behavior. The stigmatization of ethnic minorities also straddles the physical and the group identity categories.

In this book, I put forward a slightly different typology of deviance to explain negative social evaluations: I introduce the question of *agency,* making the point that some forms of deviance can be voluntary or chosen to some degree, and others might be experienced and suffered without any active involvement in that state, on the deviant actor's side. In the first case, a social actor is negatively labeled as deviant because his or her agentic power got him or her there. In the second case, the actor's label is passively obtained because of the very nature of the actor and his or her identity or innate behavior and practice.

As we will see, exploring this difference between genuine and voluntary forms of deviance helps in understanding the nature of the negative social evaluations they trigger.

Difference as Genuine Deviance

For sociologists, one of the primary sources of stigma is the possession of undesirable characteristics, and in most cases, social actors have very little agency over the possession of those despised characteristics (Goffman 1963; Link and Phelan 2001). In other words, they do not choose to be deviant. Sexuality (Ragins and Cornwell 2001), race (Loury 2003), national origins (Nath 2011), gender (Anderson-Gough, Grey, and Robson 2005), and physical differences (Goffman 1963) are included in those attributes that individuals cannot easily change and have not chosen (Link and Phelan 2001). As the pop star Lady Gaga would say in her well-known song, genuine deviance is about being "born this way." Her song, about empowerment for racial and sexual minorities, embodies this idea of tainted but unescapable deviance, with lyrics promoting self-acceptance. As evidence that the song resonated with the experience of a wide public, it holds the Guinness Book record for the fastest-selling song on iTunes, with one million downloads in five days.[4] For Falk (2001) and other stigma researchers, the existence of an outsider group creates a sense of community for the "normal." That is, social actors get a sense of their collective identity because of those they can visibly exclude from their in-group. The coherence of a group is thus partly built on the exclusion of those seen as deviant, which confirms the importance of the social role conferred to negative social evaluations.

Those negatively labeled attributes that are genuinely held by individuals can sometimes be concealed and revealed to limited audiences (Jones and King 2014). Among those, religious affiliation, sexual orientation, social class, values, and beliefs can remain hidden characteristics. Goffman (1963) stated, however, that hiding a stigmatizing attribute is in some way a sign of internalizing the perception of this attribute: when individuals hide a characteristic to avoid stigma, they recognize that this characteristic is a defect. In short, "they may come to believe themselves in the inferiority of their social identity" (Stenger and Roulet 2018, 259). In this qualitative study, we found that homosexual auditors would reveal their identity selectively when they were sure that they would not be negatively perceived because of this attribute. In particular, they would avoid revealing their sexual identity to partners and more senior colleagues, assuming these would be less tolerant of it. In fact, LGBT auditors tend to hide their sexual identity when they believe it may harm their career. To some extent, this phenomenon aligns with Foucault's hypothesis (1977/2012) that institutions and hegemonic organizations do not regulate individuals through physical threats. Instead, social control is internalized, in particular through evaluations or simply the impression of being evaluated.

In the same paper, we also showed how concealing a stigmatized identity can generate social discomfort. In several situations, homosexual auditors were interacting with peers and co-workers and discussing their everyday lives. We observed that when asked about Valentine's Day or their weekend plans, gay and lesbian workers would tweak the truth to avoid having to tell about the gender of their partners. In this sense, the stigmatized continuously have to reflect on the way they can be perceived, and in return, this reflexivity affects their behaviors and makes them more careful about what they share in social interactions. In fact, those holding a stigmatized characteristic are likely to see any adverse treatments they experience as due to this same characteristic: they will often suspect rightfully or not that they are being treated differently and sometimes discriminated against because of it. The management of a concealable stigmatizing feature depends on the timing and the situation (for example, has the individual become comfortable in his or her social environment? How is the characteristic perceived in this specific context?) but also on the characteristics of the concealable identity holder (for example, what are the other characteristics of the individual that might matter? How is the individual accepting this stigmatized characteristic?).

Stigmatization may not necessarily come from a deviance in the attitude of an individual but because of how his or her health influences behaviors. Some afflictions are not necessarily widely recognized or known as such and are stigmatized for this very reason. Audiences attribute behaviors to negative traits rather than to the affliction. One example is fibromyalgia, or chronic fatigue syndrome, because it does not always have immediately visible consequences for those who suffer from this illness: it is often misunderstood by co-workers (Åsbring and Närvänen 2002; Armentor 2017). Fibromyalgic individuals are often wrongly seen as slackers and thus suffer from a stigma triggered by the misunderstanding of their attribute. Co-workers are in disbelief, while at the same time they attribute the symptoms of fibromyalgia—such as falling asleep during the day—to the laziness of the person rather than to the sickness (Armentor 2017). For this reason, those individuals tend to hide their condition in the workplace (ibid.).

Genuine deviance also operates at the organizational and field levels (Hudson and Okhuysen 2009; Hudson 2008) with organizations whose very nature or *raison d'etre* are frowned upon by society. When collecting data for a project on the marginalization of refugees and international migration, we observed how the International Office for Migration (IOM), the transnational organization in charge of "regulating" migration, is negatively perceived by a range of stakeholders (Roulet and Salomons 2018). The IOM manages a range of programs in some countries, including those aimed at sending migrants back to their home country (assisted voluntary return or AVR). As a result, both pro- and anti-migration stakeholders, and the main audience—migrants—have a negative opinion of the organization. In this case, this activity is in the nature of the organization: the organization was founded to serve the purpose of addressing migratory issues, and this is what triggers the stigma. By contrast, in their study of Keystone, a social enterprise in the United Kingdom, Tracey and Phillips (2016) examine how the organization became stigmatized because of its actions in favor of migrants. In the Keystone case, the organization chose to engage in this activity among others. While this choice triggered hostility against the social enterprise, the decision can be seen as a positive form of deviance, or constructive deviance, as "behaviors that depart from the norms of the reference group such that they benefit the reference group" (Vadera, Pratt, and Mishra 2013, 1221).

In addition, organizations can be seen as genuinely deviant when their members are themselves perceived as genuinely deviant. The activist movement Black Lives Matter, campaigning against racism and violence, is a good example of an organization composed of individuals that are themselves stigmatized because of their race. The movement faced a significant backlash, and an alternative rhetoric was built to weaken the argument of the group—including "all lives matter," casting black activists as attackers.[5]

Those attributes signaling genuine deviance can be perceived in different ways depending on the cultural or organizational context. In the article cited earlier (Stenger and Roulet 2018), we explain how the masculine rhetoric around performance in audit firms is what contributes to the marginalization of homosexuality. Anderson-Gough and colleagues (2005) also showed that the very same organizational culture in this industry also partially excluded women. Contexts in which homophobia is commonplace are called heterosexist (Waldo 1999) or heteronormative (Ward and Schneider 2009). Among the most researched contexts in which minority sexuality is considered deviant are the military (Herek, Jobe, and Carney 1996) and also the police, because of a "sub-machismo culture" (Burke 1994, 192). In the same way that homosexual auditors are seen as deviant from the conventional image of the successful auditor (Stenger and Roulet 2018), homosexual military personnel are perceived as clashing with the stereotype of the "good soldier" (Herek et al. 1996). In all of those contexts, norms and rules play a notable role. The work of auditors is aimed at making accounts abide by the norms. The work of the military relies on discipline and order. In the context of police, Burke (192) notes the role of the profession as "regulator[s] of deviance."

While a range of social actors are considered deviant because of their very nature and have no other choice than suffering this negative perception, others behave in a way that makes them likely to receive negative social evaluations.

Voluntary Deviance: Those Who Do Not Abide by the Norms

This section will focus on social actors that *choose* to violate norms. This voluntary deviance is self-selected, in contrast with genuine deviance. Under this umbrella can be included wrongdoing (Palmer, Greenwood, and Smith-Crowe 2016) and, more specifically, professional misconducts (Muzio et al. 2016). Social actors usually have an interest in transgressing norms (Palmer and Yenkey 2015) and can strategically do so (Roulet 2019a). In their study of the 2010 Tour de France, Palmer and Yenkey (2015) investigated the use of performance-enhancing drugs among professional cyclists. Here the instrumental motive is pretty apparent—chances of winning are higher when cheating. In the same vein, the Volkswagen affair was also motivated by greed (Clemente and Gabbioneta 2017). In 2015, Volkswagen was found to have tweaked the engines of its cars so that they would hide their inability to meet U.S. emissions standards. Cheating on the emissions tests for its cars was a way to dupe customers while minimizing costs instead of investing in meeting the standards. Competitive pressures also encourage wrongdoers: when cyclists saw their cheating peers being unpunished but performing better because of doping, they would become more likely to do so themselves (Palmer and Yenkey 2015).

However, limiting voluntary deviance to misconduct would be a mistake. Some voluntary deviance can be more loosely connected to questions of ethicality. Body art or scarification are forms of deviance that are chosen by individuals and potentially contribute to their marginalization, and them being negatively evaluated, without being morally condemnable (Timming 2015). In his qualitative study on the impact of tattoos on the employment relationship, Andrew Timming notes that body art is prejudicially associated with a number of negative characteristics such as promiscuity, mental health issues, anger issues, and even drug consumption. Those mental associations are shortcuts due to biases of the audiences. In sum, voluntary deviance can be a choice made by social actors with reference to the norms of a defined group without being morally condemnable from a broader perspective. But it can also be an "in": the same study reports on the tattoos of prison guards, and how this helps them create a bridge with prisoners and a commonality that can support more harmonious relationships between two divided groups. Considering the growing number of tattooed individuals, in a decade, we might all need to get one to fit in!

As this example suggests, cultural contexts, at either at the national, field, or organizational level, are also more or less permissive of voluntary deviance. It relates to the eternal discussion between bad apples (individual characteristics drive misconduct) or bad barrels (the context at least incentivizes but in some cases forces individuals into wrongdoings) (Ashkanazy, Windsor, and Trevino 2006; Muzio et al. 2016). Cyclists from countries with the strongest hostility to corruption and the highest degree of transparency and legal norms were less prone to using performance-enhancing drugs (Palmer and Yenkey 2015). In contexts in which populations believe in the value of competition, firms are more likely to greenwash, to pretend they are socially responsible to look good; by contrast, in countries where beliefs in the virtues of individual responsibility are prominent, firms will favor concrete social and environmental actions (Roulet and Touboul 2015). In some fields, typical practices may be perceived as misconduct by the broader society (Roulet 2015a; 2015b; 2019a). In my doctoral work, I studied how excessive risk-taking, exaggerated variable wages, and opacity were considered the norms of the investment banking industry, but those norms faced a strong backlash after the financial crisis and became perceived as wrongdoing (ibid.). The question of bad barrels versus bad apples often comes up when we think about rogue traders: those front officers on the trading floors of investment banks who decided to bet astronomical sums of money without the approval of their hierarchy. Nick Leeson provoked the fall of his bank, the Barings, in 1995 with a hidden account dissimulating a loss of $200 million. Jerome Kerviel, a trader at Societe Generale, was responsible for a loss of almost $5 billion. In both cases, there was a limited perspective of personal enrichment. But in fact, existing work has pointed out the role of organizational features and the cultural context (Scholten and Ellemers 2016): wage disparities creating a competitive environment and an organizational culture in which morality is in the back row both contribute to the likelihood of misconduct. In this case, those rogue traders were negatively perceived by a broad audience because of deviance from social norms. But in their context, their behavior was likely to be seen as normal (Roulet 2019a). Even for voluntary deviance that would not be morally dubious, it would be perceived differently across contexts. The study by Timming (2015), for example, reveals that tattoos are considered more positively in the social work industry in contrast with banking, for example.

But voluntary deviance can have unpredictable consequences on the way those deviant actors are perceived (Entman 2012; Vaughan 1999). Enron and Arthur Andersen disappeared with the accounting scandal in 2001 and 2002. Another fraud knocked down WorldCom at the same time. However, despite losing considerable brand value, BP survived the oil spill in the Gulf of Mexico in 2010 and the public outrage that followed. Similarly, Union Carbide pulled through the Bhopal gas leak in the 1980s. By comparison, the gross misconduct of Deutsche Bank spying on its board members in 2009 almost went unnoticed. In this sense, voluntary deviance does not necessarily trigger negative social evaluations, and when it does, it may do so to different extents.

The perception of voluntary deviance depends on both the context and the characteristics of evaluating audiences. Norms at the contextual level may interact with audience-specific norms that are unrelated to the context. A recent study by Patrick Reilly in the *American Sociological Review* looks at which comedians are vulnerable to the accusation of theft jokes, building upon a participant observation of the stand-up comedy industry in Los Angeles (Reilly 2019). Joke theft can be seen as a coincidence, and thus there is variance in the legitimacy of such accusations and the way the community enforces them. Reilly found that those stand-up comics who are perceived as inauthentic to the community and mainly driven by their recognition outside the field are more vulnerable to joke theft accusation. In other words, commercially successful comics are the ones most often seen as joke stealers. Here the interaction between commercial success and lack of loyalty toward the community signals deviance from the norms of the field of stand-up comedy—but not necessarily deviance from broader social norms. However, once a comedian is accused of joke theft, the broader audience will start sharing the same negative perception of that person, already spread in his or her field.

As we have seen with tattoos, malicious intentions might not always be the motives for violating norms. When individuals face excessive power in organizations, limiting their autonomy and agency, they can experience frustration ultimately leading them to engage in deviance (Lawrence and Robinson 2007). This is quite paradoxical when it comes to voluntary deviance, which is by definition a form of deviance that is enabled by the agency of actors. According to Lawrence and Robinson, it can be the lack of agency within organizations that triggers the willingness to deviate as a form of resistance. Still, those resisting actors make the choice to deviate from workplace norms. In this case, we can talk about "positive deviance" (Spreitzer and Sonnenshein 2004). Although the very existence of positive deviance is often challenged in the literature (Goode 1991), Spreitzer and Sonnenshein define it as "intentional behaviors that depart from the norms of a referent group in honorable ways" (832). In sum, when norms are bad, deviating from the norms can be morally commendable—a typical example is when norms of an industry or a profession clash with social norms, meaning norms at a broader level (Roulet 2019a). The norms of the investment banking industry before the financial crisis, such as risk-taking and excessive variable wages, were questioned from a moral point of view, and any deviance from those norms could have benefitted clients or prevented some aspects of the financial crisis. So does positive deviance lead to negative social evaluations? That might be the reaction of some audiences, Spreitzer and Sonnenshein argue, taking what they call a reactive approach to deviance. In Chapter 4, on capitalizing on hostility, we will see how deviance can be seen as positive by some audiences and negative by others, thus triggering signaling mechanisms that make negative social evaluations beneficial.

In the same fashion as for genuine deviance, voluntarily deviant individuals tend to form organizations, collectives, groups, and communities that also engage in voluntary deviance. In this sense, the negative evaluations suffered by individuals for their deviance is transferred to the group or community they represent. I previously mentioned the Incel community—a group of individuals close to male supremacist values. Two terrorist attacks in 2014 and 2018 were attributed to Incel members, and those events put scrutiny on this community. The Incel might have remained unnoticed without it.

Alternatively, when an organization has one deviant member, there can be a risk of contamination to his or her organization or group, which can then be seen as deviant. And in this case, the organization might be tempted to get rid of the source of the stigma to avoid being affected by courtesy stigma. The story of Justine Sacco, a public relations executive, is particularly telling: she tweeted a profoundly offensive tweet mixing racial undertones and making fun of AIDS before boarding a plane for her holiday to Africa. As she landed in Cape Town, eleven hours later, her employer was writing the statement to announce her dismissal, although the statement mercifully read, "*We hope, however, that time and action, and the forgiving human spirit, will not result in the wholesale condemnation of an individual who we have otherwise known to be a decent person at core.*"

At the field or industry level, existing work has shaped the concept of contested industries (Galvin, Ventresca, and Hudson 2005), similar in some ways to the concept of organizational stigma brought up by one level (Hudson 2008). Industry legitimacy can fluctuate over time as the industry's activities are more or less accepted. Galvin and colleagues studied how the perception of the tobacco and gambling industries changes over time because of the variance in how deviant their activities were considered. Legitimacy fluctuates for those activities and thus for those industries as a function of the historical evolution of norms at the societal level. The tobacco industry, despite the inherent risk of consuming its product, presented itself as a "normal business" operating in a context of "free market, free choice" (72). Organizations in the gambling industry took advantage of the same rhetoric but also ensured they would diversify to show a mix of deviant and less deviant activities (Galvin et al. 2005). In fact, when mostly legitimate firms have some deviant activities, such as arms trading, any attention to such decoupling makes them likely to divest (Durand and Vergne 2015). The history of the investment banking industry follows a similar pattern to some extent (Roulet 2013). Ho (2009) reports that before the 1980s, investment banks had very little success luring young graduates onto the campuses of ivy league universities in the United States. This followed a long but sharp decline of the industry's standing after the 1929 crash (Fraser 2004). The industry rebuilt its legitimacy on the takeover movements in the 1980s, adapting its practices to closely follow the renewed focus on shareholder value maximization (Roulet 2013; Roulet 2019a). Graduates started being attracted by this industry and its prominent players—Goldman Sachs, J.P. Morgan, Merrill Lynch, and others—because of its strong culture and the prestige associated with those companies. This golden age lasted for decades until the financial crisis seriously questioned the alignment between the industry's values and society's values (Roulet 2015a). For those core-stigmatized industries (Hudson 2008), we can debate whether engaging in those reprehensible activities such as selling weapons or tobacco is voluntary or genuine deviance at the organizational level. Selling weapons or tobacco, getting people to gamble, encouraging systemic risk are well in the nature of those industries—they are their core activity, the reason why they exist. We can interrogate whether this is a deliberate choice or a position that is so anchored in the identity of the organization that it has become genuine and taken for granted. In the same vein, we can ask whether the members of those organizations have self-selected themselves into joining them or "ended up there" because they needed to make a living. In my work on investment bankers, I found that most members of those banks that are heavily disapproved of would deny potential issues with their activities (Roulet 2013; Roulet 2019a).

Deviance, however, is not the only antecedent of negative social evaluations. By focusing on deviance, we give more importance to the behavior of the evaluated social actor, and less to the conduct of the evaluating one. We did recognize that evaluation could be in the eye of the beholder and that deviance was by contrast to the norms of a reference group, but this does not fully explain the agentic power of the evaluating actors.

Upward Comparisons: If You Are Hated, You Might Just Be Doing Something Right

In this section, we will focus on how the situation of evaluating actors can be a crucial antecedent of negative social evaluations. Previously, we looked at the characteristics and behaviors of evaluated actors to explain why they received negative evaluations. Here we will focus on a motivation that can be found in the evaluating rather than evaluated actor. In particular, we will explore the role of upward comparisons in triggering negative social evaluations. I have already discussed social comparison as a motivation for the formulation of negative social evaluations, building upon the foundational work of Festinger (1954). The concept of upward social comparison expands social comparison theory and makes it more specific. Upward social comparisons—when someone compares him- or herself with someone who outperforms him or her—triggers a feeling of relative inadequacy and subsequent frustration. Smith and colleagues (2009, 530) explain how *Schadenfreude*, the joy of observing others' suffering, is reinforced when "misfortune befalls an envied person." Upward comparisons usually target those social actors who are visibly higher than the evaluator in established pecking orders or social ranking and often lead to feelings of jealousy or envy (Clanton 2006), ultimately resulting in the negative evaluation of this higher-ranked actor. In other words, high-status, high-performing social actors are often subject to upward comparisons. They bring other parties to consider their own performance in a negative light.

This adverse appraisal can be related to the performance itself but also to other characteristics of the target. For example, we love to hate reality TV celebrities: they get famous, and often wealthy, sometimes without deserving it. We might stress their absence of merits and how the situation lacks fairness. We will not, however, necessarily challenge their performance—whether it is about selling a crappy music single, an autobiography, or movies they have been invited to play in. We will stress the inequitable outcome in relation to their qualities. By contrast, if someone runs a marathon faster than us, we might be a "bad sport" and make an excuse for their high performance or our poor one. We will accuse them of cheating, being unfairly advantaged, having had more time to train, or any other justification that we can use to maintain our self-esteem. Thus this negative social evaluation is more about the performance and its antecedents than the performer him- or herself. Surprise, surprise, we are more likely to engage in bad sport behaviors when people around us are doing the same (Kavussanu 2008), in the same way we cheat when our teammates do it too (Palmer and Yenkey 2015)!

The Australians even have a name for the phenomenon of upward comparison and the subsequent negative social evaluation: the tall poppy syndrome (O'Neill, Calder, and Allen 2014). As reported by Feather (1989, 265), the *Australian National Dictionary* defines a tall poppy as "a person who is conspicuously successful and (frequently) . . . one whose distinction, rank or wealth attracts envious notice or hostility." In fact, the term comes from Livy's history of Rome, and the tale of the tyrannical king Tarquin. Tarquin's son asked him advice regarding a city he had conquered. Tarquin decided to answer symbolically by cutting all the tall poppies in his garden. The son understood that he needed to get rid of all the notables that might challenge his supremacy. The tall poppy syndrome is the tendency to maintain equality by cutting out those who think they are better and worthier than others (Feather 1989). As noted by O'Neill and colleagues, "high achievers in many fields are often subjected to negative criticism because their talents or achievements elevate them above or distinguish them from their less successful peers" (212). On the basis of experimental evidence, Feather found that we tend to be more pleased when it is a high rather than average achiever that falls from grace.

In our essay on the imposter syndrome in academia, we identify upward comparison as a continuous source of negative social evaluations (Bothello and Roulet 2018). In a hypercompetitive field such as social sciences, one will always feel surrounded by more successful researchers, concentrating the best publications and most of the media attention, and piling up awards over awards. This phenomenon can be highly frustrating in a work context in which individual performances are comparable on the basis of well-identifiable metrics such as citations or number of top-level publications. Thus we tend to envy and cast out those individuals. The megastars of academic fields regularly tend to be bad-mouthed. Upward comparison triggers negative social evaluations when "attributes or behaviors of others threaten the individual's own self-definition" (Clanton 2006, 412). In fact, those who threaten our own self-definition are by definition more visible because more threatening. In the academic field, we tend to see and focus on those at the top, which triggers a misrepresentation of our status within our field (Bothello and Roulet 2018).

Haters in the workplace are not attacking others' success, but rather their lack of it. Envy and jealousy are often driven by the false idea that successes, status, or achievements are finite resources, meaning those resources have to be shared, and social actors concentrating them prevent others from achieving the same. However, only the success that is in one's reach is likely to be targeted by upward comparison and followed up by negative evaluation. By contrast, a person who does not compete on the same level or in the same field, with a similar frame of reference as the one that can potentially be targeted, is unlikely to engage in that comparison (Clanton 2006). If we go back to the example of academics being jealous of each other, it is unlikely that individuals outside academia will envy academic publications because those publications have limited meaning for them. For example, I could not have been prouder when I announced to my friends that I had been offered my absolute dream job and that I was taking a tenured faculty post at the University of Cambridge—but for them, being French (and thus not as familiar with the prestige of the university as my British family) and outside academia, it did not mean anything special to them. By contrast, colleagues in my field were a lot more appreciative.

We saw that those engaging in upward comparisons do it to maintain their self-esteem. The negative social evaluations issued as a consequence, because they provide an excuse for the pecking order we observe, help protect the perception of self when threatened by the success of others. When this happens, we are also more likely to build social connections with others, to experience belonging as a way to compensate for the threat posed to our self-esteem (Park and Maner 2009). The experimental results obtained by Park and Maner only hold for individuals who already have high self-esteem, and thus see themselves as able to regain confidence in their value through the eyes of others who might appreciate it. By contrast, those with low self-esteem will withdraw from social interactions to focus on increasing their value itself, rather than the perception of their value. For example, physically attractive persons, when told they are ugly, will build new connections that may disconfirm the statement and reassure them. This response would be typical of individuals or actors facing an episodic negative social evaluation or an "event stigma" (Hudson 2008). By contrast, a person who is truly facing a critical mass of hostile evaluators will instead work on what is being singled out, or in other words "remedy personal attributes perceived to be deficient" (Park and Maner 2009, 215). A person facing "fat shaming" will focus on losing weight. This answer happens because of the stickiness of the negative social evaluation—what Hudson would call a core stigma.

For the target of upward social comparison, receiving the related negative evaluations can be harsh, but it also has positive aspects. Experimental research on this topic (Menon and Thompson 2007) has first shown that individuals underestimate their ability to cope with an external threat when targeted by upward comparisons. However, those comparisons also make them see themselves as stronger and more resilient than they are ("if they hate me, it is because they feel threatened by me"). In other words, having haters is good for the ego. Those who receive negative evaluations because of upward comparisons might realize that they are targeted because they are doing something right, not because they are doing something wrong. As we will see in the section on the benefits of negative social evaluations, in some cases they act as a confidence booster for those who receive them.

Scandals, or the Publicization and Diffusion of Negative Social Evaluations

In the previous two sections, we distinguished between two triggers explaining why actors receive—or are perceived as deserving—negative social evaluations: deviance and upward comparisons. We will focus now on critical mechanisms of translation to understand how deviance or upward comparison may or may not trigger negative social evaluations and to what extent.

There are fundamental differences in the way those sources of negative social evaluations translate into negative evaluations. Genuine deviance leads to long-term categorization processes (Jones and King 2014), that is, contexts in which some actors are grouped together in a stereotypical and simplified way. By contrast, misconducts are usually publicized via scandals (Kuhn and Aschcraft 2003; Puglisi and Snyder 2011; Entman 2012) and negative media coverage (Deephouse 2000): the misbehavior is made visible to a broad public. Looking at those mechanisms enables us to answer two key questions with regard to negative social evaluations: How do they stick? How and why do they spread?

Scandals and negative media coverage imply the spreading of negative social evaluations within and across audiences (Clemente and Roulet 2015). Some actors, called infomediaries, relay the information and publicize it (Clemente and Gabbioneta 2017; Clemente, Durand, and Porac 2016), whether this is the reporting of deviance or the reporting of positive features of organizations or individuals, leading alternatively to infamy or celebrity (Zavyalova, Pfarrer, and Reger 2017). The main infomediaries are in fact media actors, from newspapers to emerging social media and including TV Channels, radio, and online media. There is potential variance in the treatment that is made of a case of deviance by media outlets: for example, the *New York Times* was more critical of the role of investment banks during the financial crisis than was the *Wall Street Journal*, because of the proximity of the latter with the business world (Roulet 2015a; 2019a). Clemente and Gabbioneta (2017) examined how different German newspapers framed the Volkswagen scandal. As noted earlier, Volkswagen was revealed to have cheated on the test for its diesel engines in 2015. The following media coverage oscillated between attacking the reputation of the firm, attacking its breach of norms, or scapegoating it, depending on the media outlets. Some media outlets might blame a firm itself while others might attribute responsibility to the context or the competition. Media "frame" deviance in different ways, leading to different extents of negative evaluations. The various media outlets do influence each other when it comes to negative media attention: when one outlet reports on misconduct, other outlets are likely to do the same, even when there is variance in the opinion of those outlets with regard to the misconduct (Roulet 2019a).

Scandals in particular are one of the primary mechanisms through which misconduct and voluntary deviance translate into negative social evaluations. Scandals are defined as the publicization of transgressions (Adut 2008; Piazza and Jourdan 2018). In his study of the scandal over the homosexuality of Oscar Wilde, Ari Adut (2005) identifies the visibility and publicity given to the transgression as what prompted his fall, rather than the deviance in itself. Adut takes a resolutely constructivist approach to scandals, arguing that what matters is not the deviance but rather the perception of deviance. Deviance might not be perceived as such until it is singled out and made visible to audiences that will then engage in social control behaviors and try to curb it. Oscar Wilde's era was known for its puritanism, but Wilde's "sexual predilections had long been common knowledge in London before his trials without affecting the dramatist's wide popularity" (ibid., 213). In other words, Wilde's homosexuality was known but not pointed out, and his contemporaries consecrated him. However, once the scandal erupted, Wilde was pursued with considerable zeal. Indeed, once the transgression was publicized, a multiplicity of stakeholders wanted to be involved in the rectification of the deviance to exhibit their own rectitude. The publicity aspect of scandals is also crucial. Stakeholders and members of audiences cannot ignore anymore the deviance—they are forced to react to it. Oscar Wilde's homosexuality was not an issue when individual actors thought they were the only ones to know—when it was gossip or a rumor "keep[ing] information within bounds" (ibid., 218).

Other cases of downfalls illustrate the importance of temporality in the emergence and unfolding of scandals. As a critical mass of hostile stakeholders emerges, there are also temporal "windows" of opportunity during which individual actors can be singled out for misconduct. To illustrate this phenomenon, we can take the example of Harvey Weinstein, the infamous film producer (see the case study by Finney and Hadida 2019).[6] In October 2017, dozens of women, having collaborated with Weinstein, accused him of sexual abuse. As a consequence, he was kicked out of the Academy of Motion Picture Arts and Sciences. The Weinstein affair was at the origins of the #MeToo movement. In January 2018, in an interview, the actress Sharon Stone gave an awkward laugh when asked whether she knew about Weinstein's misbehaviors. The truth is that everybody had known for a while about the actions of the malevolent producer. However, victims remained isolated voices, or what Noelle-Neuman (1974) would call a "silent majority." All those abused women stayed silent, thinking about themselves as mostly isolated cases and thus afraid of being singled out and punished by the powerful producer if they were to denounce him. Reports of his conduct suggest that he indeed blackmailed the women he abused, threatening them with retaliation—a credible threat considering how powerful and central he was in the field—if they were to tell anybody about his "demands." Once a few fearless first movers had

exposed him, other victims felt more comfortable speaking up, thus triggering the critical mass needed for the scandal to take shape. In 2017, however,
Weinstein appeared more vulnerable, and as the peak of his career appeared
to have passed, the conditions were ideal for reports of misconduct to emerge
and be considered with the credibility they deserved.

The example of Oscar Wilde also tells us about how negative social evaluations stick—that is, why some actors remain negatively evaluated for long
period of time rather than episodically. Wilde was negatively perceived by epi-
sodes, but he was generally associated with his achievements rather than his
deviance—until publicization created a "critical mass" against him (Devers
et al. 2009, 162). As predicted by Hudson (2008), some actors face event stigmas—when the negative social evaluation is episodic—that might ultimately
translate into a core stigma—when the negative evaluation becomes naturally
and intuitively associated with the social actor, it sticks. Negative social evaluations as they consistently target the same social actor over time and from
different audiences become cognitively accepted and taken for granted (Scott
1995; Bitektine 2011). In such a situation, broad audiences stop questioning
whether behaviors or practices are transgressions and start *assuming* they are.
Within those audiences, individual actors become convinced that their belief
with regard to the negatively evaluated actor is widely shared. For those audiences, those beliefs become well anchored, unlikely to change, and will do so
very slowly if they do.

This phenomenon brings us to the question of how genuine deviance
becomes progressively stigmatized. In other words, how do categories of
individuals or organizations receive extreme and sticky negative evaluations? While it is hard to trace the emergence of stigmatized categories, those
related to sexual transgressions are almost universally established (Adut 2005)
although to a different extent depending on national cultures and historical
periods. Other stigmas have emerged because of new societal and economic
conditions. For example, the stigma of being laid off and unemployed is contemporary and has only emerged because of new economic practices (Karren
and Sherman 2012). The contemporary perception of work implies the marginalization of those who do not, as they are not seen as productive members
of the society. Instead of being seen as the victims of layoff—a passive experience—their lack of skills or performance is blamed instead, through a process
of attribution. Minorities or older workers suffer a double whammy, and the
two stigmas add to each other.

Scandals or categorization do not only spread within and across audiences as a perception of others, but also as a negative label that includes a growing number of targets. In a nutshell, the group of targets of stigma may progressively grow as additional actors become associated with this group. Stigma can be transferred from one actor to another, and across levels from individuals to organizations. Goffman (1963) talks about courtesy stigma, while others call it stigma by association (Barlow, Verhaal, and Hoskins 2018). After the Second World War, actors who had worked with peers or directors blacklisted for their membership of the communist party would subsequently suffer from this association, in particular with regard to their career outlook (Pontikes, Negro, and Rao 2010). And this mechanism also worked backward, meaning that actors were 13 percent less likely to find subsequent work even when their association with the stigmatized preceded the divulgence of their coworker's affiliation to the Communist Party. Hudson and Okhuysen (2009) showed in their work on men's bathhouses that organizations in this industry fear to taint the evaluation of their users, and reveal the fact those users belong to a stigmatized category. With regard to scandals as a process that spread negative social evaluations, Adut (2005) refers to the term *"contamination."* As scandals diffuse, consumers or stakeholders start switching to alternative non-tainted providers (Piazza and Jourdan 2018). In their study of sex abuse by Catholic clergy, Piazza and Jourdan showed how the Christian denominations that were enforcing stricter moral norms and were not tainted by the scandal benefitted from a boost in membership. This goes back to the core argument I have made with regard to the societal role of stigma: it guides resources toward the nonmarginalized actors, and inversely deprives stigmatized ones.

Do some characteristics protect actors from being affected by the diffusion of negative evaluations? Philips and Zuckerman (2005) found that higher-status actors are usually less penalized for violating norms. However, the negative social evaluation literature suggests that a high status does not necessarily protect social actors from contamination. For example, Pontikes, Negro, and Rao (2010) found that winning an Oscar did not minimize the stigma by association with communist co-workers. Adut (2005) argues that contamination is more likely when the scandal initially targets a high-status actor. A higher-status actor is more visible, which makes the taint also more prominent, and stakeholders are more likely to be hostile to the tainted actor to make a demonstration of their rectitude. According to Adut, scandals operate as a form of "popular justice" (220), as the collective feels forced to redeem itself from having hosted deviance by showing excessive zeal.

Finally, the diffusion of negative evaluations can be potentially nurtured or stopped by those individual actors receiving them. As we will see in the next chapter, the resilience of negatively evaluated actors plays a crucial role in the dynamics of evaluations.

CHAPTER 2

RESISTING HOSTILITY

Resilience to Negative Social Evaluations

Before diving into the counterintuitive consequences of negative evaluations, it is worth spending some time unveiling the intuitive ones. A wide range of work has already looked at negative consequences. The fact that there are negative consequences to negative social evaluations seems pretty obvious—intuitively it is normal to expect hostility to have adverse consequences on those targeted by resentment.

At the organizational level, negatively labeled firms and companies see their social relationships decay. Stakeholders usually take their distance from stigmatized organizations, begin to avoid interactions (Devers et al. 2009; Hudson and Okhuysen 2009), and more generally withdraw their support. Bruyaka and colleagues (2018, 446) distinguish between "*relational uncertainty*, which is the nonstricken partner's doubts regarding the trustworthiness and commitment of its stricken partner and apprehension regarding the current and future state of the [relationship]" and "*stigma anxiety*, which is the nonstricken partner's fear of being stigmatized by association." This argument is reminiscent of the concept of "courtesy stigma" in the foundational work of Goffman, the risk of obtaining a negative label for being associated with an adversely perceived party.

Concretely, investors and firms tend to retrieve their capital from firms belonging to stigmatized categories: Durand and Vergne (2015) found in their study of the arms industry that when firms or their peers face media attacks, they divest from the stigmatized industry to limit their exposure to courtesy stigma. Alliances fall apart when one of the partners is negatively perceived (Bruyaka, Philippe, and Castaner 2018). For example, Haack and colleagues (2014) show how the United Nations Global Compact (UNGC) suffered from its association with PetroChina, a firm that was considered scandalous from the perspective of climate activists. The UNGC consequently was considered suspicious by future partners. Because of stakeholders' disaffections, firms are forced to reframe their practices and activities to attenuate the effect of stigma (Carberry and King 2012). Barlow and colleagues (2018) found, in a study of the craft beer industry, that stigmatized products also harm the firms that associate themselves with those products. When craft brewers are linked to a product that is stigmatized by their community such as the American lager (because it is mass produced), their other products suffer from stigma by association and are seen as less authentic. Those findings all suggest that actors that are being negatively evaluated lose crucial ties—with partners or customers—because of it.

The negative consequences of adverse evaluations trickle down from organizations to individuals. Members of negatively perceived organizations also experience a range of detrimental consequences. For example, employees are overall less satisfied when their firm is rightly criticized (Roulet 2017). Several organizational members also tend to disidentify from a stigmatized organization to avoid their own identity becoming contaminated (Tracey and Phillips 2016). The groups we belong to drive our perception of self (Tajfel 1978; Tajfel and Turner 1979), and as a consequence, being a member of a negatively perceived group is hurtful to our self-image. Elsbach and Bhattacharya (2001) studied disidentification with the National Rifle Association: they found that individuals would distance themselves from an organization that could taint the way they are perceived by others. Dutton and colleagues (1994) cite the example of the Exxon oil spill in Alaska in 1989, which embarrassed Exxon's employees and made them feel poorly about themselves. They felt "that the public regarded them in a negative light after the Valdez oil spill" (241). Similarly, Petriglieri (2015) investigated how BP's executives distanced themselves from their organization after the oil spill in the Gulf of Mexico. Individuals naturally seek to associate themselves with organizations that enhance their self-esteem. Inversely, high-status firms are more likely to attract top employees, but once they have gained this affiliation, employees are more valued by the market (Bidwell et al. 2015). Users of services provided by stigmatized organizations—such as the customers of men's bathhouses—are also affected by courtesy stigma and become themselves stigmatized (Hudson and Okhuysen 2009).

At the individual level, as one would expect, negative social evaluations have a range of unfortunate consequences. Being negatively perceived is directly related to a loss of status and, consequently, lower work evaluations and discrimination (Link and Phelan 2001). The disadvantage of the stigmatized is experienced through social interactions in particular, as discrimination is embodied by a differential treatment, which is itself motivated by a desire of social distance from audiences (Pescosolido and Martin 2015). Rege and Telle (2004) also found in an experiment that not only do individuals have a preference for social approval, the suspicion that they are socially disapproved of is also enough to bear social costs. From this finding, we can conclude that an important share of the consequences of negative social evaluations is internalized—a phenomenon Pescosolido and Martin label as self-stigma.

Early sociological work on race indeed identified one key negative consequence of suffering prejudice: it becomes internalized by those affected. The seminal work of the African American sociologist and philosopher W.E.B. Du Bois (1903/1969) explored the concept of "double consciousness." Du Bois conducted the first ethnographic work of the life of African Americans, which resulted in his landmark study *The Philadelphia Negro*, published in 1889 (Du Bois, 1889/2007). On the basis of this research and his own experience, Du Bois elaborated theoretically about the nature of racial stigmatization in his collection of essays *The Souls of Black Folk*. He wrote, "From the double life every American Negro must live, as a Negro and as an American, as swept on by the current of the nineteenth while yet struggling in the eddies of the fifteenth century,—from this must arise a painful self-consciousness, an almost morbid sense of personality, and a moral hesitancy which is fatal to self-confidence" (1903/1969, 221). According to Du Bois, those who are racially stigmatized experience an internal conflict—they want to perceive themselves in a positive light but are brought back to and always reminded of the way others perceive them. This creates a divergence in the identity of the stigmatized, between an idealized and aspirational perception of themselves and their selves as circumscribed and diminished by the prejudice of others. Du Bois showed that African Americans struggled to see themselves as Americans, but they were also estranged from their African origins. The stigmatized tend to accept the "assessments of lower value or worth" (Pescosolido and Martin 2015, 94) and see themselves through the eyes of the stigmatizers. Modern forms of stigma-tization are not exempt from internalization. Li et al. (2008), in their study of HIV in China, report that more people with HIV would report self-stigma than discrimination—whether it was expected or anticipated.

If negative social evaluations have such adverse consequences, the ques-tion of resilience—the "ab[ility] to react to and recover from [them] with min-imal effects on stability and functioning" (Williams et al. 2017, 740)—is vital. How do individuals, groups, and organizations build resilience to negative social evaluations? The answer is partly in the mechanisms through which they internalize negative social evaluations. Group and organizational identi-ties emerge among those targeted by stigma (Tracey and Phillips 2016). This phenomenon is due to the experience of prejudice and exclusion felt by those who receive negative social evaluations—this common experience creates a social bound that comes with a variety of benefits and defense mechanisms.

This chapter will thus focus on those mechanisms through which individuals, groups, and organizations can build resilience to negative social evaluations. Resilience implies shielding against or rebounding from adverse consequences. A large part of those processes focuses on internal processes of resilience—the mechanisms in our inner selves that enable individuals, groups, and organizations to adapt to hostility. A share of those internal processes rely on identity, but they take roots at differ-ent levels of analysis. The chapter will start by covering the link between facing hostility and one own's identity—whether it is an organizational, group, or individual identity. Then the idea of "inventing the enemy" will be presented as a collective mechanism through which groups enhance and refine their perception of selves by imagining a common adversary. We will continue by exploring foundational work on how individuals rely on their group memberships to react to disapproval. Building on the liter-ature on dirty work, the following section will show how individuals pre-serve their perception of selves in stigmatized occupations and use those conclusions to inform more generally how social actors resist negative social evaluations. In the next section of the chapter, we will define the concept of cognitive dissonance—a process of preservation of the self by realigning the understanding of reality with the group's identity. Finally, the chapter will detail how organizations can take into account nega-tive social evaluations to change when they manage to overcome cogni-tive dissonance. In the concluding section of the chapter, I will present an overarching model of how organizations, groups, and individuals coalesce to build resilience to negative social evaluations.

Those processes of building resilience to hostility in themselves might produce positive outcomes, which we will explore in Chapter 3.

How Facing Hostility Forges Our Identity

In this first section, we explore a common thread that will help us make sense of resilience to hostility: identity. Identity is a core definitional attribute for social actors and captures their self-perception. Identity is distinctive and relatively stable in time (Dutton, Roberts, and Bednar 2010; Tracey and Phillips 2016). I will defend the argument that individuals, groups, and organizations partly define themselves—who they are, what they want—through the reception of negative social evaluations and the way they deal with them.

In general, social actors hate being told what to do and tend to react very strongly to it. Brehm and Brehm (2013) call this "reactance." Seeing one's freedom being curbed generates strong arousal. In the United Kingdom, the Brexit vote of 2016 generated a strong reaction from the European citizens. They learned that going forward they would need to get documented to stay in a country in which they had made their lives. People who had never demonstrated inundated the streets to protest the threat to their freedom. In the same vein, the Yellow Vest movement in France in 2018 was a backlash triggered by pro-environmental measures. Those measures were seen as a limitation of many people's freedom, and they consequently felt the need to rebel and take to the streets. More important, in such a situation, those who are pressured will actually stick to their position as individuals and toughen up their views as a group. Individuals coalesce to face a threat. They become a group because of the threat. And negative evaluations can be this threat.

This resilience to negative social evaluations can be seen within organizations as well. In a similar vein as with individuals, organizations can manipulate and maneuver their identity when facing external threats (Kreiner et al. 2015). Identity at the organizational level is defined by the way members articulate the distinctiveness of their organization, and by the link between their own identities and this distinctiveness (Gioia et al. 2013). When facing negative social evaluations, organizations can react and resist in a variety of ways. Identification with an organization is usually threatened by public hostility (Petriglieri 2015): the members of a disapproved of organization struggle to maintain an alignment between their own identities and that of the organization. A qualitative study of how executives reacted to the BP oil spill revealed the ambivalence they experienced toward the organization and how they tried to resolve this ambivalence (ibid.). They tried either to repair their relationship with their tainted employer or to sever the ties. To repair the relationship, they involved themselves in BP's responses to the oil spill, to enact positive aspects of their association with the organization. This process can lead to a form of ambivalent or selective identification—members try to maintain their link with the organization but are ready to withdraw if the public perception of the organization further deteriorates.

However, when their association with a negatively evaluated organization threatens their identity, the members of this organization might also find ways to push back. First, they might try to deflect blame by putting it on specific individuals within the organization, as in the case of organizational failure and bankruptcy (Sutton and Callahan 1987). They will explain to whoever wants to listen that it's not them, it's someone else who is responsible. Second, the threat of negative social evaluations will trigger an organizational identity crisis in which the organization can be cornered as the hostility penetrates the boundaries of the organization and makes members doubt about their affiliation (Tracey and Phillips 2016). Organizations engage in reframing the negative evaluations and inject pride into their members to overcome such situations. Tracey and Phillips, for example, examined the efforts of Keystone, a social enterprise in East England, stigmatized because of its support of migrants. They show how senior management reconstructed the narrative around the organization's purpose to inspire a boost in self-esteem, but also to present it as "standing alone in the face of considerable pressures" and thus "valiant" (754). Instead of negating the stigma, this identity work is aimed at presenting it as a misunderstanding of external audiences. Firms might also commonly invoke "uniqueness" when members react to public hostility by trying to stress how distinctive their organization is from the group of stigmatized actors (Sutton and Callahan 1987): for example, when filing for bankruptcy, firms will claim that they made a conscious choice "that permitted their organization to proceed in a direction that would have been impossible otherwise" (ibid., 427). Those examples illustrate how disapproved of organizations reframe their identities to discard external criticism and present themselves in a positive light despite hostility. Part of this process of resisting negative evaluations builds up on organizational culture—the values and norms shared by the organizational members (Ravasi and Schultz 2006). Ravasi and Schultz explored the case of Bang & Olufsen, a Danish company that produces audiovideo systems. Under the threat of a fast-changing competitive environment between 1978 and 1992, the managers of the company used the company culture to reinterpret the purpose of the organization and rejuvenate its identity. We can imagine how organizations experiencing negative evaluations may try to mobilize their organizational culture—key beliefs, values, and practices of the organization—to address external pressures (Roulet 2017).

Let us take another example to illustrate how individuals, when targeted by negative social evaluations, build resilience. Celebrities, as more visible individuals in society, are very often targeted by hateful and hostile comments on social media. The entry cost for such online trolls is low, and because of anonymity, the consequences for them are limited. The recent work by Ouvrein and colleagues (2019) on how celebrities react to cyberbullying show that one of the most common reactions portrayed in the media is for celebrities to "bite back"—"to show they are at least as powerful as the bully" (10). Indeed, when facing negative social evaluations, both our self-image (how we perceive ourselves) and our self-esteem (how we value ourselves) are threatened, and we engage in behaviors to protect them. When receiving negative feedback, narcissistic individuals—those with a strong perception of self—will push back the most in a way that "provides for the protection and maintenance (even enhancement) of one's self-regard" (Kernis and Sun 1994). The cause of negative feedback is externalized and the source—the evaluator—is disregarded and despised (ibid.).

At all levels of analysis, social actors can shield themselves against negative social evaluations and resist them, through identity mechanisms. Many of the mechanisms explored above have been further fleshed out and refined in a variety of literature that we will explore in the rest of this chapter. In the following sections, and before moving to other literature, we will further unpack the different ways through which individuals, groups, and organizations reframe their identities to resist negative social evaluations and preserve their perception of selves.

"Inventing the Enemy"

Identity being about self-perception, one of the main mechanisms of identity formation is through the contrast with others' identities, as others help reflect our own image (Elsbach and Bhattacharya 2001). In his book *Inventing the Enemy*, Umberto Eco (2012) explains how he did not know what to answer when a taxi driver asked him who were the enemies of his country, Italy. As he states, "having an enemy is important not only to define our identity but also to provide us with an obstacle against which to measure our system of values" (89). Inventing the enemy, and demonizing him or her is, in fact, crucial for self-definition as we, as individuals or groups, define ourselves by contrast to others. Eco cites the Catiline Orations given by Cicero to show how the depiction of the enemy would help the crowd understand what they stand for by considering what they oppose. As it was for the Romans, a common enemy is the "foreigner" or the "immigrant": anti-immigration sentiments are often associated with nationalist and sovereignty claims, such as in the case of Brexit. As put by Elsbach and Bhattacharya (2001), it's about "defining who you are by what you are not."

What happens when the enemy is everybody else? When Trump supporters wear a "Trump vs. Everybody" shirt (yes they do exist and they sell well), they define themselves as if they were the "last of the Mohicans," by contrast to the majority of the crowd opposing their views and their leader. This process gives them a sense of community, although in this case, they have not invented the enemy, as the enemy is alive and kicking. What they did however is change the definition of the enemy—if the enemy is everywhere, and strong enough to be "everybody," then the resisting minority must exhibit bravery and fortitude. Such a twist results in a galvanizing message.

There are many more examples of groups who defined themselves by contrast with others. The Islamic State in Irak and Levant (ISIL) and its self-proclaimed caliphate—which took advantage of the civil war in Syria and chaos in neighboring countries to establish itself from 2014 to early 2019—galvanized its fighters in the same way, by letting them believe they would be fighting until the end of the world. In fact, the prophetic message of ISIL claimed that the "Christian" invaders from "Rome" would circle them around and that a final battle would take place in Dabiq. On Judgment Day, they would fight against the rest of the world but would ultimately be saved as true believers. Again, here ISIL did not invent its enemy (it poked so many other nations that enemies flocked to them) but did give it shape. It invented an elusive and overwhelming enemy labeled as Roman or Christian crusaders and an anti-Messiah labeled as Dajjal (Wood 2015). Having an elusive enemy fit the criteria to galvanize a wide range of members of ISIL. For those who left Western countries to wage war (the "foreign fighters"), their "Roman crusaders" would be the people they felt oppressed by at home, and that they wanted to take revenge upon. For the Iraqi or Afghan fighters, those enemies would be imagined as the British or U.S. military who came to throw down Saddam Hussein or the Taliban. Those ISIL fighters—a very heterogeneous crowd—were unified by a common and evasive enemy under the same banner.

When individuals see themselves as opposing a common enemy, they engage in overcompensation efforts to affirm their identity. The case of the "Trump vs. Everybody" t-shirts is a good example of how the invented enemy is used to reaffirm the identity of those who wear them. Those t-shirts are sold by a company called Nine Line Clothing, which boasts of $25 million annual revenues (Jaffe 2018). The founder of this clothing company summarized his business model in one sentence: "Polarizing topics create brands" (ibid.). Such a mechanism is possible because people use brands to make their identities visible, in particular by opposition to enemies.

What are the implications in the business and organizational world? There is nothing more helpful to unite organizational members than a common enemy. It creates cohesion and pride—two assets that are key to organizations, especially when they are challenged. Universities, for example, thrive on rivalry—London universities (King's College London (KCL), University College London (UCL), and London School of Economics (LSE)) are often engaged in actual or imagined tribal feuds. The rivalry of UCL and KCL is rooted in their history, as KCL was created as a religious reaction to the foundation of the University of London. The rivalry between LSE and KCL is mostly the result of the geography—they are literally across the street from each other. According to an urban myth, UCL students once stole the KCL mascot. LSE students call KCL the "Strand Poly," assimilating their rival university to a vocational college and discarding it as of lower academic standards. In the same way, the annual Oxford-Cambridge boat race serves to revive the rivalry between the two universities. For that short moment students and faculty feel a strong sense of identification with their university, because they are reminded of a common enemy, which in fact is only different in name. Such stratagems are driven by the desire of organizational members (here students and staff) to belong to an organization of higher status. Students' self-esteem is a function of how they perceive their university and how they feel it is perceived by others, because of mechanisms of identification (Dutton, Dukerich, and Harquail 1994). Thus inventing the enemy is a way to value one's own organization by engaging in flattering or ego-boosting forms of social comparisons.

Private firms also feel the need to invent an enemy to reinforce their identity and the identification of their members. Globalization often creates the opportunity for firms to invent enemies across frontiers, as barbarians at the gate ready to take over their home markets. In the current economic context, Chinese rivals are often mentioned in the rhetoric to justify the mergers of European firms. Firms from other countries have regularly been perceived as the enemy in previous waves of globalization, such as the Japanese companies in the automotive industry. Western firms often use those foreign and distant competitors as bogeymen to present themselves and their members as courageous and heroic, fighting waves that might threaten the constituents they serve in their home countries.

Marketing has also often capitalized on interfirm rivalry to trigger a sense of identification from their customers. Identity mechanisms are prevalent in pitching products to broad audiences. For example, firms often engage in comparative advertising—when products or services are compared to those of one of the competitors. Apple famously started their anti-PC and anti-Microsoft advertisements in 1984, fostering Apple users' attachment to their brand. Another famous corporate feud is the one between Pepsi and Coca-Cola. In 1975, Pepsi launched the Pepsi Challenge: the firm organized blind tests for shoppers to compare the two colas, and the overall result showed that most customers favored Pepsi. As a reaction, Coca-Cola distributed a pinback button to their customers on which one could read, "I picked Coke in the Pepsi Challenge." This rigid boundary erected between the competitors forced customers to be loyal to one of the two camps and triggered identification of customers to the brand. Nowadays, comparative advertising often involves mobilizing customers on social media to defend their brand. Finally, while most of those marketing wars involved firms in the same industry, they do not always involve firms of the same size. We have seen challengers using this technique as a marketing stunt: in 2007, Dunkin Donuts launched a campaign attacking the coffee giant Starbucks for alleged snobbism. This attack helped Dunkin Donuts's clients see themselves as definitely different from those of Starbucks, which ultimately supported their identification with the first brand and disidentification from the second one.

Inventing the enemy is a crucial mechanism through which individuals, groups, and organizations create bogeymen to strengthen identification and hype up their self-image. The hostile outsider is not always fully imagined, considering that the idea of inventing an enemy often presupposes the existence of negative social evaluations. The way the enemy is pictured to insiders would, however, rely on exaggerations and caricature. Besides, inventing an enemy will usually foster further polarization—whether we look at Trump supporters or Apple users in the 1980s, their radical position was fostered by the imagined enemy, which in turn boosted hostility against them.

As we have seen, identity mechanisms often create a bridge between individuals, groups, and organizations. In the following section, we will further unpack the multilevel nature of identity-based reactions to negative social evaluations.

From Stigmatized Individuals
to Stigmatized Groups

As individuals receive negative social evaluations, they might coalesce and form groups with similarly stigmatized individuals that provide them with a microcosm. This group then acts as an alternative reference category for its members, instead of using the broader society as a reference (Blume 2002). That is, individuals start comparing themselves to their peers within their groups rather than to the crowd of outsiders. In such "counter-communities" (ibid., 21), the stigma is ignored because it is normalized within the boundaries of this group. This process is fleshed out in empirical and theoretical research focusing on stigmatized occupations—those who carry out "dirty work." The dirty work research has shown that individuals in a variety of professions—from janitors to proctologists to exotic dancers—could build a positive identity and sense of pride despite doing less than desirable work (Ashforth and Kreiner 1999).

Before diving into the lives of dirty workers, let us take a step back and examine the first set of evidence linking stigma with higher self-esteem. While most research on stigma assumed that stigma had negative consequences for the self-esteem and perception of the stigmatized, the work of Crocker and Major (1989) challenged this assumption. Those two psychologists suggest that stigma has "self-protective" properties and identify a set of three mechanisms. First, when receiving negative evaluations, the receivers consider them to be a consequence of the stigmatizing audiences' biases. For example, early work on gender differences found that when women received negative evaluations from men, and they thought they were discriminated against, they ended up experiencing higher self-esteem (Dion and Earn 1975). In a similar study, but this time on race, Crocker and colleagues (1989) looked at the link between negative evaluations and feedback in the presence or absence of discrimination. They had black students receive negative feedback from a white evaluator. The impact of this negative feedback on those students was strongly influenced by whether they thought the evaluator could see them, in which case they thought the evaluator could discriminate against them because of their race. When the negative feedback was blind, the black students could not attribute this negative evaluation to discrimination, and their self-esteem was consequently negatively affected. On the contrary, when they thought they had been discriminated against, the black students experienced a boost in self-esteem—they could see themselves as part of a group suffering adversity and that should thus be commended. In short, the fear of having been discriminated against moderated the adverse impact of negative evaluations on self-esteem to the point that it inverted the effect of this adverse feedback: negative evaluation in the presence of discrimination can trigger a boost in self-esteem because it reinforces the sense of belonging to a group and discards the value of the feedback.

The second mechanism of self-protection for negatively evaluated individuals comes from social comparison. Negatively evaluated individuals compare their performance to those of the stigmatized group rather than the broader set of individuals they could evaluate themselves against. The usual assumption in the literature is that when the stigmatized stay together in the same group, they struggle to build positive self-esteem because they see themselves through the lens of the stigmatizing audience. This hypothesis was formulated early on by Du Bois with his concept of double consciousness (1903/1969). On the basis of such assumptions, negative social evaluations could become a "self-fulfilling prophecy"—being perceived as inferior can ultimately materialize in becoming inferior because of the process of internalization (Crocker and Major 1989, 610). The stigmatized switch to a different reference group, and they compare themselves to their stigmatized microcosm—which becomes the only set of "significant" others (ibid., 611). We observed this mechanism in our study of homophobia in audit firms: LGBT auditors internalized the discrimination they were facing and started losing confidence in their ability to do well at work (Stenger and Roulet 2018). They started thinking that there were legitimate reasons for them to be thought of as performing worse than others, because of their minority identity.

In short, social comparisons are inhibited by stigmatization. In stigmatized groups, fewer objects of comparison are available, thus reducing the range of actors a stigmatized individual can compare him- or herself to. Early work on segregation—and since then this result has been challenged—found that black children experienced higher self-esteem in segregated contexts rather than integrated ones because white advantaged kids were unavailable for comparison in their social environment (Rosenberg and Simmons 1972). Inversely, advantaged individuals experience higher self-esteem when they are mixed with less advantaged peers (Crocker and Major 1989): this empirical evidence aligns with the idea that in a peer group, individuals feel gratified when others receive negative social evaluations because they can compare themselves positively with them.

Finally, members of a stigmatized group will think higher of the areas in which their collective performs well. This hypothesis builds on the idea that the impact of performance feedback on self-esteem is mediated by how central the dimension evaluated is to the self-concept (Rosenberg and Simmons 1972; Crocker and Major 1989). In short, a dimension on which members of a stigmatized group are poorly evaluated will be considered as irrelevant to their self-definition. We see this happening in academic communities in the field of management: groups of scholars who do poorly in terms of internationally recognized publications and are marginalized because of it will present those publications as irrelevant to their role and work as academics. By contrast, they will present other activities such as engagement, pedagogy, or administration as central to their self-concept. They will define themselves differently, reconstruct the boundaries of their profession, to deflect stigmatization and marginalization.

There is also a range of moderating factors affecting the relationship between being stigmatized and engaging in group mechanisms to protect one's self-esteem. Crocker and Major (1989) note that the time since the acquisition of stigma reinforces the sense of belonging to a stigmatized group and thus the self-protection that comes with it. In the same vein, the less concealable the stigma, the stronger this sense of belonging and the defense mechanisms. In addition, for those negatively evaluated, feeling responsible for this negative evaluation will accentuate the adverse effect on self-esteem and potential disengagement from a group of similarly stigmatized individuals. For example, the employees of BP tried to distance themselves from what connected them to the oil spill within the organization (Petriglieri 2015). They would avoid referring to their employer or their work in public, by fear of suffering courtesy stigma.

This distinction accounts for the difference I made in the previous chapter between genuine deviance—individuals who have no choice other than to deviate from the norms—and those who engage in voluntary deviance—individuals who have some agency over deviating from the norms. In practice, the boundary between the two forms of deviance is quite blurry in the case of stigmatized groups: homosexuality was perceived as a choice, and an escapable condition in Victorian England (Adut 2005), and this impression could potentially be internalized by individuals stigmatized for this characteristic (Stenger and Roulet 2018). In such a case, negatively evaluated persons would refuse to identify themselves with a group because such identification would make them blame themselves for a condition they have not chosen to experience.

Finally, Crocker and Major (1989, 620) insist that the more "an individual has structured his or her self-concept around membership in a group that is devalued, deprived, or discriminated against, the better that individual feels about him or herself in terms of global self-esteem." In sum, those who commit particularly fully to their stigmatized group and make it a central part of their identity will realize the full benefits of the protective defense mechanisms detailed above. However, the ability for the member of a stigmatized group to identify with this category is not always straightforward. In fact, some stigmatized categories of individuals have internal boundaries that prevent some members from integrating and considering themselves as part of the group. In the case of LGBT individuals, while gay and lesbian individuals can fully identify themselves to the group, bisexual men or women can experience significant confusion with regard to their capacity to belong to this same group (Balsam and Kohr 2007). On the basis of survey data, those authors found that bisexual men or women were more confused about their identity and less likely to interact with LGBT groups. To the question, "How well-connected do you feel to the lesbian, gay, and bisexual community?" bisexual participants answered lower than lesbian and gay peers. In such a case, bisexual men and women cannot necessarily benefit from the affiliation and the identification with the LGBT group and they suffer a double whammy: they are stigmatized for their sexuality, but they cannot fully benefit from the support of a stigmatized group. Bisexuality is a case of category straddling—being a member of two categories can make you a part of none (Durand and Paolella 2013; Paolella and Durand 2016).

Negatively evaluated individuals can coalesce as groups to protect their self-esteem. While Crocker and Major's arguments (1989) were a first theoretical inquiry into the group mechanisms protecting stigmatized individuals, their arguments were empirically applied and enriched by looking at professions that were collectively facing hostility.

Self-Esteem for the Stigmatized: Lessons from Research About Dirty Work

Identity mechanisms might be triggered at the occupational levels, and entire professions can often face public hostility when their activity deviates from broader social norms. This section will draw on dirty work research—which focuses on how individuals experience stigmatized occupations (Ashforth and Kreiner 1999; Kreiner, Ashforth, and Sluss 2006). The way this literature informs the phenomenon of despised occupations can help us understand the social identity mechanisms triggered by negative social evaluations at other levels of analysis. This literature bridges the gap between the individual and group levels, building on what was discussed in the previous section. In addition, I will explain how those identity mechanisms can also apply to organizations, fields, and industries.

To start with, we can trace back the use of the term "dirty work." The foundational work of Ashforth and Kreiner (1999, 413) dates the term back to Everett Hughes (1951) "to refer to tasks and occupations that are likely to be perceived as disgusting or degrading." The dirty aspect can have physical, social, or moral dimensions. Physical taint is associated with what most would consider as "disgusting" activities because they relate to death, garbage, or effluent (including human effluent, sorry to be graphic!). Thus funeral directors (Cahill 1999) or gravediggers (Petrillo 1990) are associated with the taboo of death but also with the repellent idea of manipulating decaying human bodies. But the revulsion can be more straightforward when the disgusting element is self-explanatory, such as in the case of proctologists (Kreiner, Ashforth, and Sluss 2006) or butchers (Meara 1974). The social aspect of dirty work covers those professional activities that require contact with social actors who are themselves negatively perceived. Thus police officers (Dick 2005; Gill, Roulet, and Kerridge 2018), asylum workers (Goffman 1961/2017), prison guards (Jacobs 1981; Crawley 2013) or care workers for the disabled or the elderly (Stacey 2005) are considered as doing dirty work. Finally, the moral aspect of dirty work covers professions that are seen as sinful or ethically dubious because they "employ methods that are deceptive, intrusive, confrontational or that otherwise defy norms of civility" (Ashforth and Kreiner 1999, 415). The most common forms of dirty work involving moral taint are exotic dancing (Grandy and Mavin 2012; Mavin and Grandy 2013) and prostitution (Wolfe and Blithe 2015). Ashforth and Kreiner (2014) also remind us that the negative social evaluations faced by those occupations are socially constructed; they are not inherent to the work being carried out. In sum, we could imagine proctology to be highly valued in some societies, although it would be hard to cite any anthropologists to support this hypothesis.

Nonetheless, society projects a tainted label on the members of those professions. Because those very individuals accept tasks that are despised although crucial to the functioning of the society, they actually enable others to live without having to associate themselves with those "dirty" and despised activities. Because society despises those tasks, the collective allocates them to groups that they then stigmatize. They assign to those groups the same label as the one they gave to the allocated job. As a consequence, the members of those stigmatized occupations tend to make their job a part of their individual and group identity and "personify the dirty work, such that they become literally *dirty workers*" (Ashforth and Kreiner 1999, 413). Thus, at first glance, dirty workers face significant constraints and limits to developing a positive sense of self.

However, a body of scientific evidence suggests that the members of those occupations paradoxically manage to maintain high self-esteem. For example, Jacobs (1981) reports that on a sample of prison guards, a majority of them thought people were more sympathetic to prisoners than their guards, but half of them considered themselves proud of their occupation. To explain this phenomenon, the literature on dirty work (Ashforth and Kreiner 1999; Kreiner, Ashforth, and Sluss 2006; Ashforth et al. 2007) relies on social identity theory. According to social identity theory, our behavior is driven by a desire to build a positive definition of ourselves, as it helps to situate ourselves in our social context (Tajfel and Turner 1986). Self-definition, however, strongly depends on how others perceive us, and this is signaled through and reflected by our social interactions. Occupations, in particular, serve as useful "identity badges" (Ashforth and Kreiner 1999, 417) in the context of social interactions, and the stigma attributed to dirty work would be expected to create difficulties for those badge holders to build a positive self-definition.

The model developed by Ashforth and Kreiner (1999) indeed suggests that the salience of the stigma over one's professions generates some degree of dis-identification: members may want to feel less overlap between their own identity and the identity of the dirty work occupation. In the meantime, however, dirty workers engage in two mechanisms that counterbalance this process. Those mechanisms, by contrast, generate identification with the group and thus pride of being part of such a profession:

Building a group ideology by reframing the stigmatized profession's activity

Social weighting: discarding negative audiences, overvaluing supporters, and favoring favorable social comparisons

Dirty workers build a strong occupational culture in the same way as Crocker and Major predicted for stigmatized groups in general. As members of a stigmatized group perceive a shared threat to their identity, they start drawing a protective boundary differentiating "us" and "them" (Ashforth and Kreiner 1999). Such occupational cultures help dirty workers create a positive ideology around their activities, anchoring "why it matters—in a self-serving manner" (Ashforth and Kreiner 2014, 87; see also Dick 2005). In particular, occupational ideologies define the relationships between the members of the profession and other societal constituents and stakeholders. As an ideology becomes more widely shared among members of the group, those members also see it as increasingly valid. In short, "groups often can sustain beliefs that individuals cannot" (Ashforth and Kreiner 1999, 421).

Those ideologies are "self-serving," as they focus on aspects that will glorify rather than devalue the group—instead of presenting dirty work as their only option in life, they will reframe it as evidence of bravery. Such glorification enables positive identification. For example, exotic dancers convince themselves that they are not engaging in a socially despised activity because they had no other choice, but rather see it as a form of empowerment and self-discovery, despite the potentially degrading aspects of the job (nudity and sexual objectification among many others) (Mavin and Grandy 2013). The same authors report this quote from one of them: "I learnt so much about myself, so much about men, so much about, like, everything really. . . . I feel really strong, really above men: before I did not feel like that at all" (244). However, exotic dancers also stress the artistic nature of their activity, and the creativity it requires—they reframe the occupation by focusing on the positive skills needed to do well in that line of work (Mavin and Grandy 2013). Bolton

(2005) found similar patterns with gynecological nurses. They often introduce themselves as simply nurses to avoid referring to gynecology, because of the taboo around sexuality and the female sex. However, they build a positive self-definition by celebrating the unique qualities required for the job (how you must be "special," "different," and "caring" to do this work), and how it aligns with their womanhood—another part of their social identity (ibid., 169). This process is a recalibrating exercise in the sense that it stresses a valuable part of the work and puts in the background the parts targeted by audiences as dirty (Ashforth and Kreiner 1999; 2014).

A key tactic to create an occupational ideology in a stigmatized group is to reframe a negative aspect of the profession and "infuse" it with a positive value: the "dirty particulars are wrapped in more abstract and uplifting values associated with the larger purpose" (Ashforth and Kreiner 1999, 421). When their identity is threatened, individuals can look for "positive distinctiveness" (Petriglieri 2011). For example, instructors in the funeral industry convince their students that the negative perception of their occupation is due to the widely spread fear of death (Cahill 1999). They often present themselves as helping families and friends overcome a difficult moment. Gravediggers have to manage the negative aspects of their job by regulating their emotions but also by realizing their work has useful societal implications (Petrillo 1990). While their activity is negatively perceived by most, they start thinking of themselves as playing a unique role of supporting those who are stricken by the death of a friend or relative. Police officers are often accused of using coercive authority for personal and questionable motivation as a form of power (Dick 2005). They absolve themselves for using coercive authority by resituating this practice within a broader social order "to construct a credible and creditable humanitarian identity" (ibid., 1384). When reframing is not possible, the negative perspective on the profession is simply negated. Debt collectors, for example, claim that their job needs to be done and that debtors are only upset about their situation rather than at the collector (Sutton 1991). However, some condemnable aspects can also be avoided through "refocusing": for example, public defenders will voluntarily avoid thinking about whether their clients are guilty of a crime to try to win a case (Ashforth and Kreiner 1999).

The second defense mechanism for dirty workers consists of "social weighting" (ibid.). "Outsiders" (any audiences outside the group) are seen as a constant threat to the group members' self-esteem (Ashforth and Kreiner

2014). The central defensive tactics around social weighting consist of condemning *the* condemners and selective social comparisons (Ashforth et al. 2007). Members of negatively evaluated social groups will thus commonly discard hostile audiences by deeming them an illegitimate source of criticism (Ashforth and Kreiner 2014). This process is communicated to the members of the group, who usually will share a common disdain, if not hatred, for the hostile audience. We found this mechanism rather prevalent among investment bankers during the financial crisis: when reminded that their profession is seen as responsible for one of the worst economic disasters in human history, they would explain that society does not understand the positive role they have to play (Roulet 2019a). For most mainstream media, the financial process of securitization (slicing up and repackaging financial products to spread the risk) is identified as a process that caused the financial crisis. However, for bankers themselves, securitization is what creates liquidity on financial markets, and it thus plays a crucial societal role (Roulet 2014). Ashforth and Kreiner (1999) cite a variety of other examples, including janitors criticizing bad tenants for their lack of manners, and exotic dancers condemning their double-faced clients for being in a strip club during the weeknights and at mass with their families on Sunday morning. While clients or users are not always the condemners, dirty workers may also put some distance between themselves and those users and condemners (Ashforth and Kreiner 2014). In such cases, they would argue that they are not to be confounded with the actors they serve, mostly to protect their identity from the stigma associated with the consumption or usage practice.

Condemning the condemners also has a flip side: supporting the supporters (Ashforth and Kreiner 1999). Members of negatively evaluated groups will cognitively focus on (and support) the potential audiences that provide them with positive feedback. While investment bankers during the financial crisis felt condemned by the media, they were at the same time valued for their typical practices by key corporate clients (Roulet 2019a). If corporate clients, the hand that feeds them, continued to value the bankers' practices, why be sensitive to criticism? Without supportive outsiders, members of a stigmatized group will withdraw themselves into their group, engaging in the cognitive dissonance mechanism I detail in the following section.

Another aspect of the second defense mechanism used by dirty workers and initially documented as a central tactic by Crocker and Major (1989) is "social comparison." This strategy implies "comparing oneself or one's occupation to other actors . . . who are thought to be worse off as a means of drawing esteem-enhancing inferences" (Ashforth and Kreiner 2014, 97). Surprisingly, negatively evaluated groups do not struggle to find other groups to disdain—groups, professions, and organizations are all situated in a pecking order (Podolny 2010). Thus exotic dancers might express contempt toward prostitutes, investment bankers toward retail bankers, gynecologists toward proctologists. This mechanism also exists within the boundaries of the negatively evaluated group, as individuals will preserve their self-esteem by seeing themselves as "big fish[es] in a little pond" (Ashforth and Kreiner 1999, 425). A successful and recognized exotic dancer—the star dancer in a particular club, for example—would be more protected from the stigma faced by his or her group, as he or she can compare him- or herself positively to other exotic dancers. We have observed similar patterns among investment bankers as they were facing significant public backlash (Roulet 2019a). Individuals in the front office (that is, those able to sell and buy financial products at the interface with markets) tend to despise those in the middle and back offices (those in charge of controlling risk-taking) and even more those in the retail and commercial branches. Those occupations are considered as less noble by front officers. Ashforth and Kreiner (2014), however, note that the lower the status of a stigmatized occupation the harder it is to find other groups that can be the target of favorable social comparisons.

Individuals in dirty work professions cognitively shield themselves to ignore and discard how they are perceived. Discarding external perception (condemning the condemners and engaging in social comparison) also relies on the group ideology, and the two mechanisms are intertwined. The case of funeral directors reframing the perception of their profession around fighting the fear of death (Cahill 1999) illustrates the link between fostering a group ideology and engaging in appropriate social weighting to defend a profession from public hostility. A strong ideology will help members of the group stick together and thus provide a harsher condemnation of the condemners. In addition, it provides members with a more robust and coherent set of arguments to build upon. There is thus clearly a reciprocal link between the ideologies developed by the stigmatized group and the strategies they use to compare themselves with others (Ashforth and Kreiner 1999).

There is also heterogeneity within stigmatized groups or occupations in the way external threats to self-esteem are discarded. Building on an experimental study, Kernis and Sun (1994) show that narcissistic individuals are more likely to discard negative evaluations. By contrast with less narcissistic individuals, they would also evaluate those negative evaluators as both less credible and likable. The stronger our self-esteem and our self-image, the more narcissistic we are, and the more we engage in reframing, resisting, and ultimately pushing back against outside criticism. We can imagine that the individual variance within stigmatized groups, in particular with self-perception, hubris, or narcissism, can add an additional layer of protection. As noted, for example, highly successful exotic dancers (those who have achieved status, or work for high status organizations) will be more likely to experience positive self-image than their peers.

We have seen how those stigmatized occupations create a group culture that helps members maintain high levels of self-esteem, by rethinking the perception of themselves in a more positive light. This stigmatized group culture becomes integrated in the behaviors of its members, and it becomes a natural way of thinking and interpreting their environment.

In the same fashion, organizations can shield themselves from outside opinions and engage in social weighting and comparisons. For example, Elsbach and Kramer (1996) have studied the reaction of individuals when their organization is devalued: they look at the staff of eight business schools that had suffered a drop in one of the key rankings. The authors note that in this situation organizational members do question their own perception of the core attributes of their school.

However, in a process comparable to the members of a dirty work occupation, members of devalued organizations responded by highlighting more favorable aspects of their identity. In particular, they focused their attention on dimensions that were not picked up by the devaluing rankings. Elsbach and Kramer clearly link the level of dissonance between the evaluation individuals receive and their own perception as correlated with the extent to which they engage in coping strategies. Similarly, we have found that members of disapproved organizations, in their reactions, were very sensitive to the credit they allocate to hostile audiences (Roulet 2017). When the outside criticism is judged illegitimate, public hostility to an organization generates an increase rather than a decrease in job satisfaction: in the same way as members of a stigmatized occupation, members of a negatively perceived organization condemn the condemners to preserve their self-esteem. They consider whether the criticism their group faces is justified. In other words, organizations that face public hostility can sometimes benefit from a better internal cohesion and a more motivated workforce if they can prove to their people that the public hostility is unjustified or unfair.

At the industry level, we will explore how occupations and organizations reframe their values, beliefs, and identities to preserve their self-esteem. This mechanism is comparable to the construction of occupational ideology in dirty work professions. The negative reflection provided by the external audience is bent and reframed to protect the members of the group from a threat to their self-perception. The fact that entire groups hold those beliefs gives them strength and triggers positive identification processes (Ashforth and Kreiner 1999). This argument has a lot in common with the mechanism of cognitive dissonance—when the outside threat to a group's perception of reality is cognitively discarded—that we will explore in the next section.

Cognitive Dissonance as a Way to Face Hatred

This section will discuss the concept of *cognitive dissonance* and how despised organizations and their members undergo this phenomenon. The social psychologist Leon Festinger coined the concept in the 1950s (Festinger, Riecken, and Schachter 2008; originally published in 1965). He infiltrated a doomsday cult and showed how zealots dealt with the situation when they realized that the predicted doomsday did not happen: to avoid dissonance between their beliefs and reality, they created excuses and new beliefs coherent with the situation. How likely is it for members of a failed cult to accept and recognize they have been played? As likely as a case in which members of a group would discard external cues because these are at odds with their beliefs.

The main findings of Festinger postulate that cult members would stay loyal to their organization even after the tragic prediction failed to happen (Festinger et al. 2008). Such a result was especially true if they had committed to the organization in a way that cannot be undone (for example, by selling everything they had before joining the cult) and if the cult was providing them with significant social support (Keating 2017). As put by Jon R. Stone, professor of religion, cited in Keating's piece: "If people invest their livelihoods, their reputations, their time and their money to one cause, if the cause fails, they don't just say, 'Oh well, that was fun.'" A key issue with closed groups that are negatively evaluated is that their members also become negatively evaluated (Hudson and Okhuysen 2009), which ironically makes it harder for them to leave. If they were to leave, they would indeed be confronted with those negative evaluations.

The same phenomenon of cognitive dissonance happens with modern cults—which also rely on prophetic stances. Going back to ISIL: its self-proclaimed caliphate galvanized the fighters by letting them believe they would be fighting until the end of the world (McCants 2015). The prophecies predicting that ISIL fighters would be killed by thousands and cornered in an ultimate fight that would bring back the Messiah helped the caliphate maintain the motivation of its people despite suffering significant setbacks and defeats in the meantime. What is clever in the coherent system of beliefs shared by ISIL members is that the debacle of the caliphate and its fight until the last drop of blood is, in fact, a fulfillment of their prophecy. In this sense, the narrative and mythology of the organization, its clash with outside perspectives, and the cognitive dissonance mutually reinforce each other to preserve the enthusiasm and drive of its fighters.

Similar to the doomsday cult studied by Festinger, members of ISIL could not revert to the reality of their home countries, where the organization they had been a member of had been reviled. As the caliphate was collapsing at the end of 2018 and 2019, we started hearing the voices of individuals who wanted to come back to their home countries in the West. The rejection they faced from public opinion, opposed to their return, could, in fact, have incentivized them to stick to the dying organization they were part of. As the cognitive dissonance—the gap between reality and the prophecies put forward by ISIL—grew, the number of foreign fighters joining the caliphate steadily declined.

Employees of heavily disapproved of firms also experience cognitive dissonance: outsiders' criticism will be discarded or at least discounted if it enables employees to maintain the (usually positive) image they have of their firms and themselves (Roulet 2017). The moment they stop believing their organization is right, they will also stop supporting it (Petriglieri 2015). When the cognitive gap between reality and the narrative of the organization is too broad, then the organization will struggle—like ISIL or other cults—to get new members. As shown in my study linking disapproval of organizations and job satisfaction (Roulet 2017), presented in the previous section, the key is to convince members of a negatively evaluated group that their condemners are wrong in order to preserve them from a loss of self-esteem. In Chapter 4, on practical implications, we will consider what we can learn from the concept of cognitive dissonance for internal communication in times of crisis.

Employees identify with their organizations, providing that they feel their values are aligned with their employer (Petriglieri 2011; 2015). Disapproved of firms know this and do everything they can to make this alignment strong or recruit employees that already fit with their corporate values. In May 2015, there was the third march against Monsanto and genetically modified organisms (GMOs), in four hundred locations across the world. This global backlash was driven by a grassroots movement called March Against Monsanto and the Occupy Movement. Approximately three thousand protesters marched in Paris, mainly targeting the controversial herbicide Roundup and the consequences of GMOs for health.[1] On the same day, the TV talk show *Le Petit Journal* tried to talk with Monsanto employees in Paris. All employees used the same word: they were "proud" to serve as employees of the firm. The same word was found in the official press release and also on the Monsanto webpage detailing the culture of the organization.[2] Monsanto employees, despite the general and widespread hostility, were convinced that their firm was misunderstood and that it stood against hunger and in support of farmers across the world.

Groups can also experience cognitive dissonance, especially when they have less defined boundaries, for example political groups or supporters of controversial individuals. For example, it is interesting to observe Trump's supporters' reaction (or absence of reaction) when he is caught red-handed lying. Trump, however, has the capacity to present incorrect facts and arguments with confidence, suggesting he believes those facts and arguments to be truthful. Naturally, his supporters are more inclined to believe the leader they support rather than his opponents. Such situations are especially true if a leader discards outsiders' evaluations by arguing they are motivated by the willingness to harm him rather than expose the truth. Trump thus creates a "reality distortion field," as the *New York Times* labeled it.[3]

In the following section, we explore both a source and manifestation of cognitive dissonance at the industry or field level: industry mindsets, or the set of shared beliefs, limiting the ability of social actors to confront themselves with a harsh truth.

Industry Mindsets in Contested Fields

Building upon the dirty work argument, I have argued that industries as a whole can also foster a positive identity despite facing strong public hostility. Organizations and actors within a negatively perceived industry can create their understanding of the world based on a coherent set of values and beliefs—

this is similar to the process of group identity reframing and ideology building identified in the dirty work literature (Ashforth and Kreiner 1999). In many ways, this phenomenon can remind us of the concept of cognitive dissonance we just explored. Industry mindsets, however, go way beyond a process of cognitively filtering information, and include strong identity mechanisms. In this section, we will explore how this industry- or field-level mechanism can be a powerful tool to answer criticism and create internal cohesion despite hostility.

Existing organizational theory has already accounted for ideologies developed at the field or industry level, and used to resist public hostility. Abrahamson and Fombrun (1994, 728) talk about "macro culture," defined as "relatively idiosyncratic beliefs that are shared by managers across organizations." They use this concept to illustrate why entire industries fail to adapt to exogenously driven change such as new technologies or types of competitors but also external criticism. Phillips (1994) shaped a similar concept of industry mindset or culture—defined as a set of "broad-based" assumptions. Phillips postulates that those "shared mindsets directly underpin perception, thought, feeling, and behavior of people who are members of a group in ways that are not directly obvious to either themselves or observers" (384). Homogenous and widely shared beliefs across organizations can create insularity and reluctance to adapt to changes. Managers in those industries interpret the environmental context in similar ways because of their shared belief system. Because individual field or industry members are bombarded with potentially ambiguous information, Abrahamson and Fombrun argue that their attention is necessarily driven toward what reinforces rather than what contradicts their beliefs. For example, they might be exposed to the contradictory perspectives of two audiences—one providing a positive evaluation of the industry and the other one a negative assessment. In this case, they will focus their attention on a positive evaluation that would be more in line with their perception of their industry.

Historical research has looked into many contested industries to see how they built resilience to public hostility when they enacted norms at odds with broader societal expectations. Those contested industries tend to thrive on a solid macro culture or industry mindset to protect them from external hostility. For example, gambling and tobacco industries have established their identities by inspiring strong ideologies such as free markets and free choice, thus enabling employees to hold a coherent set of beliefs to oppose hostile outsiders (Galvin, Ventresca, and Hudson 2005). Here the broad-based assumption underlying the industry culture (Phillips 1994) is that consuming harmful products is an individual choice and therefore people selling those products should not be considered responsible for the harm. Quite the contrary in fact, as tobacco and gambling firms even went as far as describing themselves as enacting individuality and freedom of choice (Galvin et al. 2005).

The macro culture also helps employees deal with external criticism by providing them with an entire system of meaning-making and rationality— they can individually use this set of values and beliefs to defend themselves and their self-esteem. Have you ever met employees of British American Tobacco or Monsanto at a dinner party? As noted in the previous section, Monsanto employees are likely to tell you how proud they are to fight hunger and how outsiders misunderstand the importance and the danger of GMOs. Employees of British American Tobacco would probably struggle more nowadays to explain their choice of working for a tobacco company. Twenty years ago, they would have invoked the argument of free choice and the free market to explain how their firm enables free choice. In 2020, they will probably deflect external criticism by stressing the corporate social commitment of their firm, and how they counterbalance the potential harm caused by their products. Other controversial fields have also been flagged in existing social science research for having been able to build resilience through a consistent set of beliefs and values, such as brothels (Wolfe and Blithe 2015), bathhouses (Hudson and Okhuysen 2009), and pornography (Voss 2015). But one of the most interesting industries having a resilient corporate culture is investment banking.

Investment banks have long attracted controversy, and in a way similar to tobacco, gambling, or brothels they went through cycles of legitimation and delegitimation. At the end of the nineteenth century, banks were associated with the equity investment they were syndicating for big firms (Morrison and Whilhelm 2007). Because the broader public perceived equity investment as suspicious, it also remained apprehensive of the investment banking industry until the 1920s (Roulet 2013). During the two first decades of the twentieth century, investment banks presented themselves as creating wealth for both the private and public sectors to gain legitimacy. After the 1929 financial crash, the Glass-Steagall Act separated commercial and investment banks, putting under a harsh light the negative impact the downfalls of those institutions could have on average people. Investment banks started struggling to recruit Ivy League graduates, as they had difficulties in convincing students that they played an essential societal role (Ho 2009). They only became legitimate again as they adopted the code of free markets and libertarianism during the takeover movement of the 1980s (Roulet 2015a). The field of investment banking interestingly relies on a coherent set of beliefs that provide a strong rationale for bonuses and extreme risk-taking. Bonuses are believed to be rewarding efforts in proportion to the value brought back to the bank, and risk-taking is seen as crucial to success and value generation (Roulet 2015b). Americans first started considering investment banks as legitimate in the 1970s, then progressively they became perceived as high-status and prestige organizations. This change of mood was fed by what Madrick (2012) calls the "Age of Greed"— a period of overwhelming support for individualism and shareholder value maximization. In that context, the motto of Gordon Gekko, the fictional villain of the movie *Wall Street* and its sequel—"greed is good"—made perfect sense.

The way investment bankers discarded public hostility during the financial crisis is what got me interested in studying them. It was not only about cognitive dissonance—for the bankers to ignore their impact and role in the financial crisis. More than that, I was intrigued by the set of coherent beliefs they held, which helped them cognitively shield themselves from the blame they experienced. How many bankers told me that the "ordinary mortals" simply misunderstood their typical practices such as bonuses and risk-taking"? One "bible" of investment bankers is Michael Lewis's *Liar's Poker*. Investment bankers often mention the book as a story that motivated them to get into the industry. However, it paints a bleak picture of Wall Street brokers obsessed with money and power. Michael Lewis himself was surprised by the counterintuitive effect his book had on aspiring professionals. In an interview for *The Motley Fool* in April 2015, he noted,

> I just thought the book might demystify [Wall Street]. Make it seem more ordinary and cause people who had some other passion to say, "Well, now I kind of see what that is. I don't need to go do that now." And it had the opposite effect. Every now and then, someone says to me, "Thank you. I read the book, and I went and became an oceanographer." But usually what they say is, "You're the reason I'm working on Wall Street. I read that book, and I really wanted to get into that."[4]

A number of young graduates got into Wall Street because they were actually attracted by the corrosive culture Michael Lewis depicted in his book.

In a similar vein, Gordon Gekko, the fictional villain of the *Wall Street* movies, also inspired generations of wannabe bankers, despite being a reasonably despicable character. In the original movie and its sequel, he drags young financiers into the dark side of the force, showing a sheer ignorance of ethics or morality. For example, Jordan Belfort, the (nonfictional) stockbroker who inspired the autobiographical movie *The Wolf of Wall Street*, mentioned Gordon Gekko as a role model in a 2008 interview for *The Telegraph*.[5] *The Wolf of Wall Street* itself depicted a world of excess and low morality, but when released, was publicly celebrated by a variety of firms including some in the financial sector, who even organized dedicated fancy-dress screenings.[6] Moritz Erhardt, a twenty-one-year-old Bank of America Merrill Lynch intern, who tragically died from overwork in 2013, was also known to "model himself on the Gordon Gekko character of *Wall Street*."[7]

Solid corporate values and industry mindsets (Phillips 1994)—even more when they clash with social norms—can sometimes be desirable to potential applicants and used by insiders as a coherent defensive argument when the organization is under attack. People want to be part of this in-group, *because* it seems to be loyal to strong and well-identified values. In some ways, having field-level values that are at odds with broader norms gives members of the group a strong sense of identity and erects stronger boundaries between the in-group ("us") and the out-group ("them") (Roulet 2019a). It gives those insiders something to stand up for and a sharp divide, behind which employees feel protected from outside criticism. When there is an apparent clash of values between the industry and the society, being part of that industry can also help send a signal of differentiation (Roulet 2013). Such ability to differentiate oneself ultimately brings a valuable self-esteem boost (ibid.).

In his interview for *The Motley Fool*, Michael Lewis then went on to discussing how, in the aftermath of the 2008 financial crisis, Silicon Valley is now the new Wall Street. While the Silicon Valley entrepreneurs do believe in the superiority of their contribution to the economy as much as Wall Street bankers do, it is hard to see how the misbehaviors of the former inspired new joiners (Gillmor 2014). Entrepreneurs of the tech industry, from Elon Musk to Steve Jobs, are quirky to some degree, and often break the rules, whether they are societal or legal, but their values do not clash with broader societal norms like Wall Street bankers in *Liar's Poker*. There is, however, the start of a shift in perception, and tech giants are beginning to experience the same struggle as Wall Street banks before the 1970s in part because of ethical concerns from potential employees.[8] It might well be that those tech giants have not yet been able to build this macro culture to protect them—shared beliefs at the industry level may help employees justify the relationships the tech giants have with the minister of defense or the criticism they face with regard to workers' rights.

One of the other mistakes managers can make when they are subject to a strong macro culture or mindset is to wrongly categorize their organization and misrepresent the boundaries of their industry or field. Abrahamson and Fombrun (1994) cite this mechanism to explain why U.S. automakers ignored their Japanese competitors for so long—they just did not see them as competitors. In the same way, during the financial crisis, retail banks did not realize immediately that their reputation was tarnished, as they categorized themselves as different from investment banks while in fact they were associated with them for most audience members (Clemente and Roulet 2015).

A macro culture thus has a range of adverse consequences for industries. Industries with a strong macro culture more commonly experience strategic inertia (public hostility does not trigger any change), and they tend to become even more homogenous.

In the case of negative social evaluations, macro cultures practically enable and are fueled by cognitive dissonance. Members of a tightly connected network of individuals within a field or industry sharing a set of beliefs and values will be in the same sort of "reality distortion field" as Trump's supporters. First, their attention will likely be driven away from external criticism—they will just ignore the condemners. For example, they will consider themselves outside the categories targeted by public hostility. Second, they will hold their own beliefs as superior to those put forward by outsiders and thus tend to discard the message spread by those outsiders. The more their values and norms are at odds with societal ones, the more likely they will identify with their negatively evaluated group (Roulet 2015b)—in the same way investment bankers were attracted by the characters of *Liar's Poker* or Gordon Gekko.

Beyond stigmatized industries and dirty work occupations, stigmatized groups can act as tribes (Cova, Kozinets, and Shankar 2012) or "counter-communities" (Blume 2002). Those groups can be attractive to potential new joiners because their values and their identities are made visible and salient by public hostility. One group that has faced a strong backlash but also triggered fascination for many outsiders is the Incel community—a group mentioned in the previous chapter. In a recent journalistic investigation into the life of Incels,

Reeve (2018) notes that Joey, one of the members she identified, did not share all the same characteristics as other group members (inability to socialize, physically unattractive—from the journalist's perspective). Despite this lack of overlap with in-group members, Joey felt a strong sense of identification to the Incel group because they represented his tribe. What made them a counterculture also made them attractive to potential joiners in search of a community with whom they could identify. Joey refers to his attachment to the group as an "addiction," because merely being part of the group reinforces his self-esteem and gives meaning to his life. For those reasons, the public hostility faced by the Incels since the terrorist attacks conducted in 2014 and 2018 is pushed aside as a blip and discarded as a misunderstanding by the members of the community.

Crisis Management: Change and Mea Culpa Rather Than Resilience

Negative social evaluations may trigger a crisis for industries, groups, or individuals. In the previous sections of this chapter, I explained how those social actors could build resilience to those evaluations as groups. We have mostly focused on how those groups can build protection from public hostility through cognitive dissonance, which gives those groups the ability to ignore and discard this hostility, and how they can build on a common identity to preserve their self-image. There might however be cases when negatively evaluated actors genuinely want to react, change, and adapt for the best. If they feel that negative evaluations are a severe identity threat, and that they experience a strong sense of identification and proximity to what is being targeted, they might engage in justifying their behavior and their approach to the situation (Wang, Wezel, and Forgues 2016). In some cases, they will go beyond simple justification and operate a change to regain trust and obtain positive instead of negative evaluations from their audiences. In those cases, they often have to overcome cognitive dissonance to accept the external message as a useful cue and build on it to evolve to elicit more positive evaluations in the future.

We could start with three examples at three levels of analysis. At the field level: the Volkswagen scandal triggered an industry-level shockwave as a range of automotive companies became suspected of misconduct (Clemente and Gabbioneta 2017). At the group level: in June 2010, the French football team came back without a single win from the World Cup in South Africa.

They suffered a major backlash in public opinion in France, a country in which football is almost considered a religion. At the individual level: in March 2019, the former vice president of the United States, Joe Biden, was accused of inappropriate contact as he was thought to be considering a presidential run for 2020. What did those three cases have in common? Those three social actors targeted by negative evaluations might have been guilty of voluntarily deviating from social expectations, but more important, they all did a *mea culpa*. They recognized their errors, made a public apology, and tried to explain how they would change to address those external concerns (Hearit 1995; 2006). They engaged in crisis management.

The parallel between managing a crisis and managing negative social evaluations is particularly fruitful to understanding the latter. The literature on crisis management and resilience is considered as intertwined (Williams et al. 2017). Negative social evaluations and the crystallization of scandals and public controversies can be seen as a crisis that can trigger change and kickstart a process of ultimately improving the evaluations received by the focal actor through "bring[ing] back things into equilibrium" (ibid., 735). Such a process is what Petriglieri (2011) calls "identity restructuring" following an identity threat. Social actors can indeed rethink what makes them distinctive and what makes them cohesive as a collective.

The literature acknowledges the existence of phases from the triggering event to the resolving of the crisis (Williams et al. 2017). It also emphasizes the importance of catching "weak signals" (Ansoff 1975), which in our context means spotting negative evaluations as they spread or cascade from audiences to audiences (Bonardi and Keim 2005; Roulet and Clemente 2018). Crises, like social evaluations, may materialize through a "genealogy" as they are "cumulative" processes (Roux-Dufort 2016, 27): they accumulate and culminate into a peak point. At this stage, returning to normal is much harder, and treating the roots that caused the scandal or the crisis requires urgent tackling. While social evaluations as the trigger for a crisis may affect the targeted social actor through a process (the French football team became progressively tainted as defeats accumulated), they can also emerge as a specific outburst (such as a scandal in the case of Volkswagen) (Williams et al. 2017).

Restoring an "equilibrium" is the primary objective of crisis management (ibid.): in other words, social actors targeted by negative evaluations will attempt to go back to receiving neutral or positive evaluations. It suggests that the takeaways from crisis management can mostly be drawn for actors that are facing event stigma (stigma as punctual occurrences) rather than core stigma (stigma as a core feature of the actor) (Hudson 2008). The process of repairing the reputation of a brand after it has suffered from customers' blasts online is comparable in some way to the mechanisms of managing a crisis (Rhee and Kim 2012; Earl and Waddington 2013). In our three cases, the targeted social actors tried to admit guilt to regain their social capital. The automotive industry made extra efforts to be transparent about their own processes and made their stance on ecology even louder. The French football team went through significant restructuring, apologized to the nation it represented, and recognized its faults in the media. Joe Biden recognized he had maybe been too tactile and vowed to respect people's space and be more careful. Such strategies might work even in the case of the worse controversies: Bill Clinton and Silvio Berlusconi, despite highly publicized sex scandals, managed to maintain a high level of popularity (García 2011). When does dealing with negative social evaluations as crisis management work, and why?

Managing a crisis, like managing a negative social evaluation, starts with detecting the adverse signal and is followed by planning and a damage control effort (James and Wooten 2010). The literature stresses the roles of cognitive (perceiving the threat and analyzing the information) and behavioral (adapting to the threat) responses (Williams et al. 2017). Cognitive responding is impossible if the social actors are subject to cognitive dissonance—as we have seen that resilience to public hostility could imply selective attention and information filtering. In the meantime, building on Weick's sensemaking perspective (Weick 1993), Williams and colleagues (2017) explain the importance of a shared sense of meaning as collective actors try to solve a crisis. Paradoxically, while a group ideology can generate cognitive dissonance when the group does decide to address an external threat, the shared values and beliefs provide a common framework to identify the way forward. Shared values and beliefs will help the interpretation of the cues and their translation into concrete responses. When it comes to behavioral responding, Williams and colleagues stress the importance of consistency: the enacted solutions need to be aligned with the group's overarching ways of thinking. In the case of negative social evaluations, disapproved of actors can only change to some extent to conform to what audiences expect. Audiences' expectations are not necessarily aligned with how they perceive themselves.

Like for crisis management, context is also crucial in the way social actors may adapt to negative social evaluations. Hearit (1995; 2006) explains how apologies vary across cultures in their effectiveness. Apologies are aimed at "seek[ing] to distance [the targeted organization] from their illegitimate behaviors and then create identifications with the public values they are reputed to have violated" (1995, 6). Hearit (1995) also compares situations in which public hostility is triggered by the incompetence of the targeted actor (for example, the Exxon oil spill in Alaska in 1989) or by a conscious choice (what was defined as voluntary deviance in the previous chapter, for example, when a Domino's pizza employee died as he sped for a delivery, also in 1989). Incompetence can be blamed on an operational error (and thus it is easy for the organization to explain how they plan to improve). Conscious errors question the morality of the targeted organizations, and in this case, it will be harder to prove good faith, as this relies on more intangible cues. Reacting to negative evaluations with hostility and defiance would be more accepted in some contexts than others. For example, García (2011), by comparing the Clinton and Berlusconi sex scandals, also observes significant differences across cultural contexts. Both attacked the accusers, in a similar way to members of a dirty work occupation, but Clinton did rely more heavily on apologies and mortification afterward. Berlusconi, by contrast, remained in denial throughout the scandal and accused the media of bullying him. García explains that Berlusconi's resistance to change and resilience to the negative evaluation was due to the higher power distance in Italian society. However, expressing anger to counter negative evaluations has been shown to work in both cultures. In an experiment, Tiedens (2001) compared the effect of a video of Clinton reacting to the scandal with anger and another one with sadness—anger created a stronger impression of competence.

Finally, when it comes to reacting to social evaluations, there is a difference to make between the walk (what is actually done) and the talk (what is supposed to be done) (Roulet and Touboul 2015). Social actors might want to pretend they are changing as a reaction to negative evaluations but stay the same. Who knows whether Joe Biden will change his behavior or whether the automotive industry will definitely steer clear from manipulating the CO_2 emissions of their cars? Negatively evaluated actors might reframe their values and practices but not necessarily change in practice. There is for example suspicion that despite regulatory pressures and a hostile public opinion, the changes in the practice of investment banks after the financial crisis were only marginal (Roulet 2013; 2019a). When negatively evaluated, social actors might evaluate the benefits of conforming to audience expectations in contrast with the costs of sticking to their guns and staying the same. They might also assess whether they can mislead audiences and get them to *believe* they have changed—but such a strategy can backfire. U.S. investment banks engaged in a mea culpa to get bailed out in 2008, but in 2009, the Cuomo report revealed that public money was still used to pay excessive bonuses.

In the last chapter, we will explore in more detail the practicalities of managing a reputational crisis. But before we move on to those practical implications, we will unpack how negative evaluations affect social networks and in particular how we change our relations to others. While we previously explored the collective responses to negative evaluations, it is crucial to see how interpersonal links are affected and how those individual behaviors drive group-level consequences.

How Negative Evaluations Change
Our Relations with Others

Social actors' reaction to social evaluations mostly depends on how those compare with the ones others have received. In other words, reactions to social evaluations are a function of social comparisons (Festinger 1954). Social evaluations can be considered as negative when contrasted with more positive ones received by other actors.

After interacting with those who receive better evaluations than ourselves, we tend to restructure our own social network. Park and Maner (2009) thus found that high-self-esteem individuals threatened by the success of others (meaning those whose perception of self was contradicted by the fact others were better evaluated) tend to build social connections as a way to cope. When concerned about how competitive they are, social actors become concerned that they might end up socially rejected (Leary and Baumeister 2000). This assumption is one of the cornerstones of the sociometer theory laid down by Leary (2005). Sociometer theory asserts that "self-esteem is part of a psychological system (the sociometer) that monitors the social environment for cues indicating low or declining relational evaluation" (75), in particular, those relational evaluations implying disapproval. Leary explains how self-esteem is a gauge individuals use to evaluate the capital provided by their social ties. He stressed that success does not necessarily lead to self-esteem—for example when success leads to disapproval from others (see also Jones, Brenner, and Knight 1990). Take the example of school: kids who do well might be seen as "uncool," and as a consequence, they might do worse on purpose in order to improve the way they are evaluated and become part of the in-group.

The threat of others receiving better evaluations triggers a desire to connect with others, and this reaction is motivated by the search for critical resources that will help mitigate the risk of social rejection (Park and Maner 2009). In particular, the affiliation with a group reassures their members on their level of social acceptance. Connecting with others also helps individuals reaffirm their identity despite adverse social comparisons and obtain support to compensate for those comparisons. For example, Goldman and colleagues (2014, 820) theorize the identity and status benefits of joining a gang and how those benefits are particularly prevalent for individuals who are already socially marginalized: "People who struggle with feelings of marginalization have difficulty establishing an identity and tend to have lower levels of self-esteem [which is why] for marginalized youth, joining a gang can be appealing as gangs provide youth with an identity."

Low-self-esteem individuals, by contrast with high-self-esteem ones, will not seek network resources because connecting with others is seen as creating potential additional threats to their self-esteem. Low-self-esteem individuals are indeed "especially vigilant to the possibility of rejection and negative social evaluation" (ibid., 213) that could come to any new connections made as they grow their network. Their reactions tend to focus on improving what will get them more positive evaluations—their characteristics and their existing network. In some ways, this explains to some extent the phenomenon of young individuals staying home because of social fears and only interacting with members of their own self-constituted and self-serving communities (Reeve 2018).

However, social networks and relationships with others are also a resource to trigger positive change (Williams et al. 2017). Successful others can provide an aspiration for the less fortunate individuals they are connected with. For example, when receiving negative social evaluations, those who are connected with social actors receiving positive evaluations can evaluate and assess how they can improve the way they are assessed by mimicking the latter. This is why small fishes in a big pond—for example, good students in a very top university—are more likely to progress than big fishes in a small pond (Ashforth and Kreiner 1999). Such a process can also generate frustration when mimicking is difficult and does not produce the expected benefits in terms of social evaluation. In fact, Marsh and colleagues (2007) found that attending a highly selective high school negatively affects the self-concept for a significant amount of time after graduation.

A Model of Group Resilience to Public Hostility

In this chapter, I have detailed a number of mechanisms through which individuals when they coalesce as groups build resilience to public hostility (see

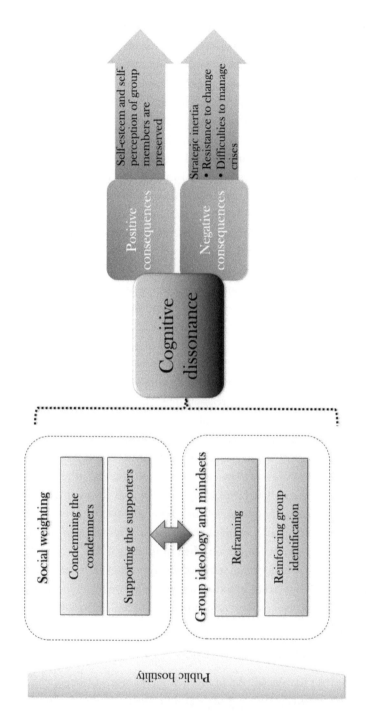

Figure 4. A Model of Group Resilience to Public Hostility. Source: Made by author.

Figure 4). We still need to articulate those different mechanisms. How do industry members use their shared beliefs and values to manage crisis and, inversely, how does crisis management rely on the platform of common understanding built within industries? In addition, how does the self-esteem boost informed by the dirty work literature reinforce industry mindsets, and vice versa? Cognitive dissonance mediates this process: it is triggered by the positive self-perception experienced by negatively labeled individual actors, and reinforces the strength of shared values and beliefs at the field level.

After being targeted by negative social evaluations, individuals engage in two types of defensive processes as groups—two mechanisms that were well identified in the dirty work literature (Ashforth and Kreiner 1999). First, we know that disapproved of groups engage in social weighting—they discard hostile audiences and overvalue the supportive ones. Second, groups build ideologies—a set of shared beliefs and values—to resist hostility, in particular by reframing and rethinking what is targeted by this hostility. Ideologies are basically what Abrahamson and Fombrun (1994) called a macro culture, and Phillips (1994) a mindset, at the industry level. Those ideologies reinforce group identification—individuals in those disapproved of groups will tend to focus their attention on the values that justify their activity, situation, position, and evaluation, and this will give them a sense of belonging. Those two processes interact and reinforce each other to some extent—with a strong ideology and sense of identification, it is easier to condemn the condemners. Inversely, by discarding haters and over-emphasizing supporters, disapproved of groups can create a more homogenous and self-serving ideology.

Social weighting and ideology building generate more cognitive dissonance: the groups experiencing those two mechanisms are more likely to ignore any external evaluation but also strategic information that does not fit their expectations or self-perception (Abrahamson and Fombrun 1994). Research on macro culture and mindsets reveals that cognitive dissonance leads to strategic inertia, lack of attention toward important signals, and resistance to change despite potential crises. At the same time, cognitive dissonance generates resilience to negative social evaluations for the group members—they will leverage on dissonance to protect their perception of self. In addition, the stronger the clash between the group values and the societal norms, the more the group is attractive to potential new joiners, as they can use their affiliation to the group to differentiate themselves and sharpen their social identity.

CHAPTER 3

GOING BEYOND RESILIENCE AND CAPITALIZING ON NEGATIVE SOCIAL EVALUATIONS

In the previous chapter, we looked at how organizations, groups, and individuals could resist public hostility and build up their resilience to negative evaluations. We mostly focused on a range of endogenous processes of identity reframing and changes in social relationships. We also explored how those negative social evaluations can be managed as a crisis. Those arguments explain how negative consequences are mitigated and already hint at how negative social evaluations can be turned into assets. This chapter will take an additional step to discuss the benefits of negative evaluations, going beyond just resisting them. Understanding the mechanisms through which organizations and individuals become resilient to disapproval is only the first step to understanding the advantage they can build for themselves. For some firms, facing hostility helped them access an entirely new customer base. Highly controversial individuals have used public hostility to build strong support groups.

Our perspective had so far assumed that social actors experience negative social evaluations despite themselves and consequently engage in a range of responses to preserve their self-perception. In this chapter, I relax those two assumptions. First, social actors may voluntarily seek negative social evaluations. Receiving negative social evaluations can be instrumental, and the consequence of an active strategy. In fact, being controversial on purpose seems to have become a relatively common political strategy since 2015, when I started writing this book! We will see that many organizations and individuals mostly exist on a political stage or in a field through being visibly contentious. Second, we have focused on the maintenance of high self-esteem as one of the main drivers in the management of negative social evaluation. By contrast, in this chapter, we will explore a range of benefits that are unrelated to self-esteem and self-perception and are, in fact, externally driven.

Stigma has mostly negative consequences for individuals, as I discussed in the previous chapter. However, stigma scholars have also identified benefits for the stigmatized. Those scholars share the idea of taking stigma as an audience-specific phenomenon, with evaluations potentially nested at different levels. Blume (2002), for example, building upon Goffman (1963), formulates the argument that individuals who receive the worse evaluations from outsiders will have a higher status within counter-communities that are themselves stigmatized. Norton and colleagues (2012) also found that stigma provided a targeted actor with persuasive power. In a series of experiments, they observed that white Americans struggled to ignore the demands (requests for donations) of people holding a stigmatized label such as disabled individuals or African Americans. Those demands were more efficient when made by stigmatized individuals, whatever the arguments used. This mechanism is at odds with the general expectations that we avoid stigmatized counterparts and that we are more influenced by people who are similar to us and are parts of our in-group. This result is fueled by the desire of nonstigmatized individuals to appear more pleasant. In sum, interacting with stigmatized individuals generates anxiety for the nonstigmatized, who want to be perceived favorably and as unprejudiced. Unsurprisingly, when the white participants would see an appeal on video and would not have to react to it in real life, they did not experience the urge to respond positively to the stigmatized individuals. This finding is explained by the fact that they feel no need to be perceived as pleasant and unprejudiced if there is no audience to judge them. In this sense, much of what we usually assume about our interactions with the stigmatized is at odds with more recent scientific discoveries.

At the organizational level, most literature has also assumed harmful or at best neutral consequences of stigma, in particular because of reputational risk and the possibility of losing the support of key stakeholders (Warren 2007; Hudson 2008; Devers et al. 2009). However, recent work bridges the gap between the way organizations build resilience to stigma and how they capitalize on it. Tracey and Phillips (2016) explain how organizational stigma helps targeted organizations rethink themselves. In some ways, this mechanism can remind us of the ideology building and reframing effort in dirty work occupations. As the dirty work literature would predict, the defensive strategy identified by Tracey and Phillips generates "increased confidence in the organization's identity, a clearer sense of its core purpose, and (for those who remain part of the organization) stronger organizational identification" (761). However, they also demonstrate that resilience to hostility is only a first step, as stigmatized organizations may benefit from being "mark[ed] out" in the eyes of crucial stakeholders. They note that "the withdrawal of support by a stakeholder group because the organization is considered by that group to possess a fundamental flaw that discredits and deindividuates it may be more than compensated for by increased support from other stakeholder groups that perceive the organization to represent a set of values that they seek to uphold or promote" (ibid.).

Those findings on the benefits of negative social evaluations, whether they are at the individual or organizational levels, stress the importance of the contrasts between the perception of different audiences. The existence of multiple audiences is a crucial factor in explaining the presence of coexisting continua of positive and negative social evaluations. While a stigmatized condition is often a tragedy, those authors pointed out the ways social actors might take advantage of it when they cannot avoid it but also might voluntarily seek it.

In the first section of this chapter, we will start at the individual level and look at how negative evaluations, such as the one triggered by failure, can put individuals in the starting block for a path of future accomplishments. This is what is called the "bouncing back" effect. We will then move toward discussing impression management and the "visibility advantage": how organizations and individuals engage in controversies to obtain visibility which they can then derive rents from. One type of actors are fond of impression management strategies: politicians. We will look at how they engage in controversies to gain visibility but also trigger further group polarization. They foster more precise demarcations between sets of voters to support their identification with their group and their loyalty to a particular positioning. We will then consider the networks through which negative social evaluations impact social actors. Negative social evaluations diffuse through networks and influence network members on the condition they convey a meaningful signal: I will thus take a signaling perspective to explain the benefits of negative social evaluations. The penultimate section will offer a comprehensive model of how negative social evaluations can be beneficial, linking up all the mechanisms we have explored.

At the end of this chapter, we will also explore the boundary conditions to the main argument that negative evaluations can lead to beneficial outcomes. First, we will consider the balance between the benefits and the drawbacks of negative evaluations. Organizations and individuals that engage in controversial actions may harm their reputations in the shorter term. It might, however, help them garner the support of loyal supporters, and they may ultimately benefit from being more visible. Finally, we will cover the dynamics of evaluation and how the returns on evaluations can fluctuate.

"Bouncing Back": The Frustration of Being Negatively Evaluated

In this first section, we focus on the positive path experienced by some negatively evaluated individuals. An interesting paradox inspires this section: a range of people who have received terrible evaluations at the start of their trajectory have ended up doing impressively well. While the two are not always related, there are countless examples we could draw upon to show support for this pattern. Walt Disney famously was fired from the local newspaper—the *Kansas City Star*—in 1919 because he "lacked imagination and had no good ideas" (Anshel 2016). In the same vein, Rudyard Kipling was sent back one of his short stories from the *San Francisco Examiner* newspaper with the following note from the editor: "I'm sorry, Mr Kipling, but you just don't know how to use the English language."[9] Funnily enough, my English high school teacher told me the same word for word when I was sixteen—a pity he never accepted my LinkedIn request so that I could show him where I ended up! In October 1954, a young Elvis Presley performed in Nashville. After his concert, he was told by the concert hall manager that he should go back to Memphis and his former career: driving trucks.[10] The naturalist and biologist Charles Darwin wrote that "[he] was considered by all my masters and my father, a very ordinary boy, rather below the common standard of intellect," which did not prevent him from graduating from Christ's College, Cambridge, and writing *On the Origin of Species*. Another Cambridge student, running one of the most followed Youtube channels, Ibz Mo, pinned a tweet on his profile stressing how he was told he was a terrible student at school but despite that made it to Cambridge. All of those were told they would never make it. Still, they persisted and bounced back.

A large body of research has examined how individuals react to information that threatens their sense of self (basically, anything that makes them lose self-esteem), and how they "regulate" themselves as a consequence. Regulation, here, covers a range of reactive and adaptive behaviors often involving self-imposed constraints. This literature takes root in self-affirmation theory (Steele 1988), a perspective explaining why individuals try to protect the positive perception they tend to have of themselves. This is what Sherman and Cohen (2006, 261) call the "psychology of self-defense" or "psychological immune system." While the mechanisms identified in the literature are aimed at coping with self-threats, some of them might also boost the target of negative social evaluations. In their meta-analysis of that literature, VanDellen and colleagues (2011) distinguish three broad responses to threats to self-concept: compensation, resistance, or breaking. Concretely, when experiencing "discrepancies between desires or expectations and reality, [individuals] attempt to reduce resultant negative affect by changing their expectations, reconstructing reality, or exiting the situation" (ibid., 52). Individuals *break* when they decide to take the negative evaluations on board and reevaluate themselves in a more unfavorable way consistent with those negative evaluations. *Compensation* and *resistance* mechanisms, by contrast, are aimed at bridging the gap between the desired perception of self and the evaluations received from others, in particular through self-enhancement. In the aftermath of negative information about the self, a number of individuals will react by doubling up on their effort to *show what they are made of.* Because the experience of receiving negative social evaluations hurts the self-esteem of targets, those targets may want to engage in extraordinary efforts to avoid experiencing this again in the future.

In academia, rejection and negative social evaluations are a daily experience. However, those setbacks may predict future successes and upward trajectories for both academics themselves and their outputs. Looking at the hidden prepublication trajectories of academic papers, Calcagno and colleagues (2012) uncovered some counterintuitive trends: they found that papers that were first rejected in their first outlet of choice received subsequent higher citation rates once published, everything else being equal. The authors hypothesized that the review process helps make those papers stronger, and thus the feedback obtained throughout the process of rejection ultimately improves the papers' reach. In a recent piece, Wang and colleagues (2019) study the link between early career setbacks and future academic success. They compared scientists who had grant proposals that were just below the threshold to be accepted (near misses), and those who had grants narrowly approved (near win). Here we can say that the difference in the quality of the grant is marginal by contrast with the difference in evaluation: in the first case, the applicants received a negative evaluation, while in the second case, they received a positive one. The study found that narrow rejection generated attrition, with around 10 percent of negatively evaluated scientists just giving up and disappearing from the radars. In the meantime, however, for those who stayed in business, this early setback was associated with superior performance in the long run with higher-impact publications in the ten years following, by contrast with researchers who had not experienced rejection. Wang and colleagues thus found support for the idea that "what does not kill us makes us stronger," as they suggest the existence of unobservable effort and a grit factor, ultimately leading to superior performance (8). Interestingly, as previously noted, some people do get discouraged by brutal rejections and give up. Such a result confirms that only a selected set of individuals will experience a "bouncing back" effect in the aftermath of receiving negative social evaluations. Negative evaluations may generate discouragement for a share of actors receiving them, but some others might experience fruitful frustration, pushing them to improve their performance.

One illustration of this mechanism can be found among entrepreneurs who experienced a boost in motivation because of the stigma they faced. While the negative emotion associated with stigma is usually thought to stifle motivation, many cases seem to contradict this assumption. Bacq and colleagues (2018) developed a model of "stigma entrepreneurship" in which they explained the soothing effect of being a successful entrepreneur but also how stigmatization fosters the motivation and the grit to become one. In his study of a social enterprise, Amslem (2013) studied how homeless people were so frustrated by the stigma they were experiencing that they threw themselves entirely into the work that was made available to them. Bacq and colleagues (2018, 13) mention a deaf Vietnamese entrepreneur for whom it was clear "that most people viewed him and others like himself as incapable of performing work to the same level of those who can hear." This anger and frustration are what motivated him to create his hair salon and train deaf employees. Two of them had already created their own salons in their province. Bacq and colleagues also present the cases of a transgender person who started a porn label and of former prisoners who ran a restaurant in Cleveland. The authors explain how one of the key triggers for those entrepreneurs was the shame and frustration experienced when they were being put down and belittled because of their stigma. Malheiros and Padilla (2015) studied how Brazilian women who immigrated to Portugal mobilized the stigma they faced as an entrepreneurial resource in the beauty sector. They were stigmatized and presented as sexually provocative because of racial and cultural prejudice. They flipped around those negative evaluations to build a form of aesthetic capital that they could economically exploit.

Those who are incredibly marginalized because of their opinion may also be more likely to make themselves heard than those with low or moderate confidence in their opinion. When it comes to voicing an opinion, the spiral of silence theory (Noelle-Neumann 1974) suggests that when an opinion is controversial, those who hold this opinion are silenced (Clemente and Roulet 2015). However, recent research on the hardcore minority shows that those who are triggering the most hostility because of their non-conformist belief also tend to keep voicing their opinion despite the negative evaluations (Mathes, Rios Morrison, and Schemer 2010). Because they are already rejected, they feel like they have nothing to lose, which gives them the confidence to speak out (Griffen 2009). Those hardcore minorities have the power to trigger a change in public opinion and potentially to practices, values, and beliefs (Clemente and Roulet 2015).

I have discussed how this positive "bouncing back" effect might only affect some of the individuals having received negative evaluations. Maybe there is a selection bias: we only hear about the stories of those individuals who were painfully rejected but ended up successful enough to be visible. In the meantime, we could imagine that a bunch of people who were up to a terrible start did also have a pretty anecdotal and unremarkable path when they also did not do poorly throughout the rest of their trajectory—but those are not necessarily the observations we would be able to capture empirically. In fact, Di Paula and Campbell (2002) found significant differences in how individuals bounced back after a rejection, depending on whether they were low or high on self-esteem. Taking stock of the research on persistence after a failure, McFarlin and colleagues (1984) note that high-self-esteem individuals were more likely to persist after being negatively evaluated. Research by Di Paula and Campbell also shows that people with high self-esteem were indeed more persistent. In other words, if the negative evaluations do harm the targets' self-esteem, they might not always trigger positive consequences. Vartanian and Shaprow (2008) looked at how individuals who were stigmatized because of their weight subsequently engaged in physical exercising. They found that stigma harmed motivation to exercise. This finding is explained by the negative impact the stigma had on the mental health of those overweight individuals. In addition, they were usually teased because of their weight, particularly when engaging in those activities.

Nevertheless, lower-self-esteem individuals tend to ruminate on failure a lot more, which potentially may help them plan for future success. In fact, in their experiment, McFarlin and colleagues (1984) found that if persistence is not correlated with performance, the persistence of high-self-esteem individuals pays off much less than for lower-self-esteem participants. Those lower-self-esteem participants engaged more selectively with the task at stake and consequently achieved better results. In short, if we go back to the case of overweight individuals, the less the ability to lose weight is correlated with persistence, the more those with high esteem will struggle to lose weight. Depending on the task and the performance assessed, when negatively evaluated, individuals might be motivated to "bounce back" to a different extent.

The "bounce back" effect could be assumed to hold for collective forms of organizing, whether they are informal groups or formal organizations. In our study of gamification and waste management, Cristofini and I (2019) studied how families are incentivized to reduce their waste when they are socially compared through game mechanics. Being shown to be at the bottom of a ranking—only created for the purpose of generating a competition around the practice of zero waste management—was a strong motivator for families to change their behavior. Similarly, we can imagine that organizations want to show their goodwill when they get negatively evaluated.

Receiving negative evaluation can generate creative frustration. For the individuals affected, it triggers energy to "bounce back" to rectify those evaluations. When someone tells us we are not good enough, we want to show them they are wrong. Several mechanisms are at stake here. First, as identified in the previous chapter, negative evaluations present a threat to self-perception and self-esteem. While in the previous chapter we focused on internal mechanisms through which individuals protected their self-esteem from those threats (by reframing their identity or discarding the outsider's evaluation), I showed in this section that those individuals might instead want to actively change the evaluations, and by themselves. Moreover, one way to change evaluations is to prove those evaluations wrong. Such a process relies on additional effort and grit caused by the frustration of receiving negative evaluations. Also, negative evaluations get people to rock bottom, and from there, because they feel like they have nothing to lose, they can find the confidence to take bolder moves.

Impression Management and the Visibility Advantage

Illegitimate actions and poor evaluations are usually expected to generate adverse results and harm the acceptability of organizations and individuals. Being poorly accepted by wider audiences might, however, be a negligible drawback next to the potential benefits of being visible and famous for selected stakeholders. Such benefits can be especially attractive if those latter stakeholders are "rainmakers" for the evaluated social actors—basically when the evaluated social actors depend on those stakeholders for support, resources, and survival (Elsbach 2003; Pfeffer and Salancik 2003)—in other words, when those stakeholders have a significant influence on the bottom line of the evaluated social actor (Frooman 1999).

Here I mobilize insights from impression management theory. This framework is rooted in the foundational piece by Erving Goffman, *The Presentation of Self in Everyday Life* (1978). Goffman's main argument is that the perceptions we have of each other are primarily the fruit of theatrical performances. In this play, the social actors perform on the front stage for an audience, where they can exhibit positive characteristics that will resonate with the audience and thus yield personal benefits. They present an idealized image that matches the objectives of the audience and potentially hides their intentions. There is also a backstage, where the social actor can prepare his or her strategy. Goffman stressed that each performance is dedicated to a specific audience and that performers, because they may play contradictory roles at the same time, often keep audiences separate. However, while one audience might be hostile to the performance and the performer, other audiences might be watching the first audience and appreciate this hostility, and consequently be positively inclined toward this performance and performer.

Since Goffman, impression management theory has been applied both to individuals (Leary and Kowalski 1990) and organizations (Elsbach and Sutton 1992). The mechanics of impression management have proven themselves useful in the understanding of negative social evaluations (Carberry and King 2012). At the individual level, impression management theory disentangles the motivation to manipulate audiences and the objectives of doing so (Leary and Kowalski 1990). When it comes to the objectives of distorting impression, individuals may try to get audiences' perception to match their image of themselves, or to match the expectation of those audiences (ibid.).

At the organizational level, impression management theory assumes that organizations and their members use several strategies to "influence audiences' perception" (Elsbach 2003, 298). Such an approach might include "regulating" those perceptions; that is, constraining or enabling the way they are shaped. In the meantime, the adage "there is no such thing as bad publicity" reminds us about one of the most common strategies of perception management: negative social evaluations can be voluntarily sought because they provide targeted actors with a visibility advantage. Berger and colleagues (2010, 816) postulate that bad publicity can have positive consequences because it increases "awareness" and "accessibility." Audiences only have "finite attention," and this attention can be channeled and manipulated. To test their hypothesis, the authors looked at nearly 250 books reviewed in the *New York Times* from 2001 to 2003, and they explored the link between the nature of the reviews they obtained and their sales. They found that good reviews expectedly led to an increase in sales ranging from 32 to 52 percent. Bad reviews did lead to a 15 percent drop in sales . . . except when the authors were unknown, in which case they found a 45 percent increase in sales. They picked one particular example of a book with terrible reviews and a surge in sales:

> The book *Fierce People*, for example, was written by a new author and received an unambiguously negative review (e.g., "the characters do not have personalities so much as particular niches in the stratosphere" and "He gets by on attitude, not such a great strategy if the reader can't figure out what that attitude is"), yet sales more than quadrupled after the review. (819)

Similarly, for organizations and individuals, misbehaving to get noticed is probably paramount to a dramaturgical performance as Goffman (1978) would have imagined it. There is no need to be a good actor to be noticed, as "putting on a show" is a dramaturgical exercise that does not require any particular talent. Seeking negative publicity implies a focus on the outcome rather than on the performance.

In the next section, we will review the contribution of impression management to understand how negative evaluations can be triggered and manipulated to position a social actor in an advantageous position in its relationship with audiences. At a simple level, we will see how negative social evaluations can make actors—otherwise unnoticeable—visible, and how those actors might leverage upon their newfound visibility.

How Organizations Shock Audiences to Gain Support

Management research looking at NGOs and other nonconventional organizations has observed how those organizations could gain visibility and legitimacy by engaging in illegitimate actions (Elsbach and Sutton 1992; Helms and Patterson 2014).

In particular, the AIDS Coalition to Unleash Power (ACT UP) has attracted the interest of social scientists as one of those organizations that engaged in shocking the public to gain visibility. This association, founded in 1987, campaigns for increasing public funds for medical research and raising awareness with regard to AIDS. In their heyday, they commonly engaged in unruly "direct" actions by occupying government offices or drug companies, painting themselves in blood red. Those direct actions relied on civil disobedience—members engaged in actions that put them at odds with the law and voluntarily disrupted society. ACT UP considered the issues at stake so crucial that the existing rules of society were secondary in comparison. They targeted a variety of institutions and organizations from the church to the financial markets, and including schools and the magazine *Cosmopolitan*.

The objective of such movements is to make their issue prominent in the public debate. To achieve this objective, their approach is to shock and make a lasting impression. In their first demonstration at the New York Stock Exchange in 1987, ACT UP members refused to evacuate and laid down on the Wall Street pavement, getting worldwide media coverage for their cause. One of the posters used for their second set of events showed an inverted pink triangle with the words "Silence = Death." The pink triangle was an apparent reference to the Nazis' marking of gays during the Holocaust. The imagery is aimed at shock and at associating AIDS with a death sentence comparable to those faced by the gay community during the Second World War. The idea is also to guilt audiences into supporting the cause by suggesting that their neutrality is equivalent to complicity. Another example mentioned by Elsbach and Sutton (1992) is that of Earth First!, which spiked a tree to protect it from a lumber worker and allegedly planned the sabotage of a nuclear facility in 1987 and 1989. Those two actions gained significant attention because they threatened human lives. They touched upon something that was consensually seen as sacred by audiences.

There are many examples of more modern social movements mimicking the ACT UP strategy. Extinction Rebellion is one of those modern movements. The group was founded in 2018 in the United Kingdom and is aimed at fighting climate change and the ecological crises via nonviolent but disruptive means. In November 2018 and April 2019, Extinction Rebellion engaged in large-scale and week-long actions of civil disobedience throughout London, aimed at generating as much disruption as possible to protest against the inaction of governments. For example, they blocked the bridges on the Thames. They also engaged in what were labeled bizarre actions by the media, as some participants glued intimate parts of their bodies to the road. The more peculiar those actions, the more headline-grabbing they were. Most members of the group have expressed having no fear of being arrested, knowing that their actions necessarily carry this risk.[11] Beyond blocking transportation, the protesters also glued themselves to walls, to trains, and to the London Stock Exchange, ensuring that the glue was strong enough to prevent removal. In April 2019, 1,130 members were arrested.

The mechanisms at stake are rather simple: when organizations conform to broader social norms, they are quite likely to go unnoticed. In contrast, when they do something at odds with what is socially accepted, they get a chance to stand out of the crowd and get noticed by crucial outsiders. They might also focus on contexts that will be prone to media attention. For example, one of the first campaigns of ACT UP took place at the post office as late tax-return filers crowded it. The group knew that late tax-return filing received every year a disproportionate (and not necessarily justified!) amount of media attention. The activist organization PETA (People for the Ethical Treatment of Animals) is also known for its controversial actions: in 2016, members got naked, covered themselves in blood, and wrapped themselves in giant meat packaging in the streets of Barcelona. As clearly and visibly stated on their website, PETA owns up to their strategy: "Unlike our opposition—which is mostly composed of wealthy industries and corporations—PETA must rely largely on free 'advertising' through media coverage. . . . Thus, we try to make our actions colorful and controversial, thereby grabbing headlines around the world and spreading the message of kindness to animals to thousands— sometimes millions—of people."[12]

By shocking audiences and by engaging in illegitimate actions, those organizations have generated considerable attention from crucial audiences. Extinction Rebellion targets policy making, but the best way to do so is to garner support from a broad range of citizens, who will ultimately be voters. Similarly, ACT UP wants to raise awareness for AIDS as a public policy issue. In a week of demonstration in 2019, Extinction Rebellion did quadruple its number of supporters, from ten thousand to forty thousand, and in the meantime raised 200,000 pounds.[13]

One drawback of attracting attention through illegitimate actions is that other selected audiences might be less likely to offer support when their comfort or even the basic rules of society are challenged or threatened. Extinction Rebellion did disrupt the commute of five hundred thousand Londoners according to estimations, leaving some of them upset by the situation. Some voices pointed out the excessiveness of the group's action. As noted by the media coordinator of Extinction Rebellion after the London demonstrations, "We've been really worried about pissing people off, but we have tried really hard to be very apologetic in that respect."[14] A YouGov poll asked, "Climate change protesters have been disrupting roads and public transport, aiming to 'shut down London' in order to bring attention to their cause. Do you support or oppose these actions?" Only 13 percent strongly supported the cause, versus 30 percent strongly opposing it.[15] Individuals may provide their support on the condition their everyday life is not affected, and the excessiveness of activists may sometimes harm their support.

That is when NGOs such as ACT UP start engaging in impression management: their spokespersons would stress the credibility of the claims and minimize the disruption caused *a posteriori*, after having however capitalized on the visibility obtained via their controversial actions (Elsbach and Sutton 1992). We also observed the same phenomenon with the media representative of Extinction Rebellion, minimizing the consequences of the organizations' actions while stressing, by contrast, the urgency of the ecological crisis.[16] Another strategy documented by Elsbach and Sutton is decoupling. Such organizations tend to distance themselves from the actions that they see as potentially turning the audiences against them. They weight the cons of their action by contrast with the visibility benefits. Thus Earth First! distanced themselves from the spiking of a tree that almost killed a lumber worker—they stressed how this was done by rogue "individuals" within their organization, not as an "organized group" (ibid., 717). ACT UP blamed some local actions on a specific chapter of the organization, stressing that if "an affinity group did it, this group [rather than the whole organization] is responsible" (ibid., 716).

At the same time, the attention given to organizations engaging in illegitimate actions can also help them garner support from prominent social actors that will provide them with even more attention and symbolic capital. Extinction Rebellion, for example, benefitted from the support of the mysterious graffiti artist Banksy.[17] The street artist produced a mural in Marble Arch, London, featuring the logo of Extinction Rebellion and stating, "From this moment despair ends, and tactics begin." In this case, Banksy is "lending" symbolic capital to the group and pointing out to audiences the importance of the highlighted cause. The word "tactic" does, however, stress the strategic approach used by Extinction Rebellion: their unlawful and disruptive actions have a tactical objective. Ultimately, illegitimate actions provided those organizations with legitimacy through the support and endorsement of a variety of social actors and a wider membership (Elsbach and Sutton 1992).

While the actions taken by ACT UP or Extinction Rebellion are illegitimate in the sense that they deviate from social norms, they might appear legitimate to the groups themselves. For such groups, their cause is seen as a worldwide emergency. Any action is "justified" by the extent of the risks incurred by the issue at stake. Thus, from those organizations' perspectives, the deviance is to not act on the issues at stake. Thus Elsbach and Sutton (1992, 720) concluded that "illegitimate actions by ACT UP and Earth First! members were justified as necessary to save human lives and the life of the planet since all previous actions had failed" and that "justifications of this kind . . . shift attention from means to ends."

The combination of engaging in illegitimate actions and shocking audiences to be visible on one side, and managing impressions afterward to limit the spreading of negative social evaluations on the other, is not only common among NGOs but also among other forms of organizations. For example, another study looked at the legitimation of mixed martial arts associations in the United States (Helms and Patterson 2014). As put by Tracey and Phillips (2016, 761), the study by Helms and Patterson showed "how organizations use stigmatization to 'correct' misperceptions about how they are viewed and gain broader acceptance among those who stigmatize them." Mixed martial arts involves fighting in cages, without protection. While it sounds like a fun hobby, this is not the sort of activity you would want to show to children. The practice and the associations involved consequently have been stigmatized, preventing the discipline from growing. The stigmatizers relied on legal but also indirect means (for example, pressurizing TV channels to keep them from broadcasting the events). To react to the stigma, mixed martial arts organizations coopted other stigmatized labels in concomitant fields to gather their support. They also stressed the stigmatizing characteristics that could help them gather further backing: they built upon the supposed lawlessness of the sport to appeal to individuals holding similar political beliefs. As we have seen in the previous section, broad-based hostility can help garner supporters in subsets of audiences, and those supporters might be a lot more vocal than opponents. Mixed martial arts refined its positioning to maintain its core component while deepening some aspects that could bring more support from vocal audiences.

Visibility and attention through controversial actions do not only generate cognitive legitimacy (Bitektine 2011), they can also be an entire business model. Infowars, the far-right news website created by the previously mentioned Alex Jones, carved a unique positioning by taking extreme positions and making controversial claims. In particular, it relied on hate speech, harassment, and conspiracy theories. The website generated revenues through the sales of a variety of branded products, including health and wellness items (for example, nutritional supplements or coffee), survival kits, and water purifiers. In sum, Infowars' value proposition is to attract attention and visibility through contentious actions, to build a niche with a loyal audience. Williamson and Steel (2018) describe this audience as "angry, largely white, majority male . . . [who] internalize the rendering of their worst fears: that the government and other big institutions are out to get them, that some form of apocalypse is frighteningly close and that they must become more virile, and better-armed, to survive." Infowars then uses this now captive audience to sell products that vaguely address those fears. According to Alex Jones's divorce court case in 2014, Infowars generated more than $20 million in annual revenues. However, Jones and Infowars did not stop there in their strategy to generate revenues from their controversial stances. After Infowars was banned by a range of social media websites (including Facebook and Twitter) and by Apple's podcast platform, the website appealed to its supporters to buy more products as an act of resistance (Williamson and Steele 2018). The reach of the website was notably reduced, but it started featuring a federating all-caps banner: "FIGHT THE BULLIES, SAVE THE INTERNET, SAVE INFOWARS" (ibid.). Alex Jones made on air the argument that the "globalist" agenda and higher-order forces were after him and wanted to shut Infowars down, and that the only way for his supporters to resist was to buy the now heavily discounted Infowars' products.

The media landscape is, in fact, particularly favorable to impression management and audience manipulation (Roulet and Clemente 2018). Biltereyst (2004), for example, explained how the whole business of reality TV was built on the moral panic it triggered: the controversial nature of the content generates debate which in turn makes this content visible, and then valuable because of the audience it captures. In France, the first reality TV show, *Loft Story*, was kickstarted in 2001 with contestants having sex live on air, which enabled the show to get more than ten million viewers during the first prime time episode.[18] Those types of TV shows attract crowds because of moral controversies, and the broad audience gives advertising value to the content. Eighteen years later, TV audience scores are in decline, and both public and private channels work twice as hard to attract viewers. For traditional and highly legitimate channels, selling trash TV is harder because it is at odds with the identity and the norms of the core audiences of those media. Thus traditional TV channels engage in actions that are not illegitimate enough to threaten their identities but sufficiently controversial to attract audiences. In France, talk shows have been pointed out for voluntarily inviting divisive personalities, to cause "clickbait arguments."[19] They want schismatic discussions with people opposing violent arguments to each other on air, so that the following day, the whole media landscape will make the story buzz. This echo chamber will ultimately benefit the next edition of the talk show where it happened.

Sometimes the fruits of bad publicity have not directly been sought. That is, some social actors might receive considerable but unexpected benefits from negative social evaluations that they initially tried to avoid. In recent work, we looked at the founding of Scottish whiskey distilleries from 1823 to 1940 and the effect of stigmatizing actors such as the Scottish Temperance League and the Scottish Permissive Bill Association (Lander et al. 2019). Our preliminary results show that in some cases, stigmatization of distilleries and whiskey drinkers accelerated the growth of this negatively evaluated industry. The effort to ban the industry gave it visibility and made it available as a business opportunity for potential whiskey distillery funders.

Another example of the benefits of bad publicity is the case of tourist destinations that get put on the map despite themselves, through negative social evaluations. Berger and colleagues (2010) report the example experienced by Kazakhstan after the parodic movie *Borat* was released. The film was clearly making fun of the country, making it look and sound like a retrograde and backward third-world country. After the movie, however, Hotels. com reported that the requests regarding the country had tripled. Kazakhstan was on the map! Iceland experienced a similar trajectory with the eruption of the Eyjafjallajökull volcano in March 2010. The strange name of the volcano was impossible to pronounce, but the situation was easy to remember. The airspace in Europe was closed for days, and the country grabbed the attention of the news across the globe, though not for the best reason. The volcano and Iceland were now seen as responsible for putting a stop to the ordinary course of travels. The country responded with an advertising campaign, "Inspired by Iceland." Photos of the beautiful Icelandic landscape and its geysers were widely shared. As a result, inbound tourism experienced an exponential growth starting in the autumn following the eruption. In 2017, Iceland welcomed more than two million tourists—more than six times its population, and it can thank its infamous volcano eruption for having put the country on the map.

How Individuals Find Their "Raison d'etre" in Controversies

In the previous section, we saw how Alex Jones used Infowars as a vehicle to position himself in the media landscape and obtain attention that he could then transform into sales. Similarly, we saw how TV channels were voluntarily inviting divisive personalities to participate in talk shows to garner wider audiences. Organizations draw on controversy to generate value, but individuals often mediate those controversies.

In fact, impression management does not only happen at the organizational level; it can also be an individual strategy. We are commonly exposed to such phenomena (whether a deliberate strategy or a genuine choice) coming from the arts and culture. Madonna built part of her fame on hijacking religious signs. The American rapper Childish Gambino (also known as Donald Glover) astonished the public with a music video titled "This Is America." The video was full of violence, with the assassination of an entire choir. Despite being shockingly graphic, it won four Grammy awards and was viewed fifty million times in only four days.[20] The artistic content might partly explain this success, but more probably, its content might explain the attention it received, which ultimately generated success. The video received more exposure and thus more opportunity to reach audiences with whom it would have a fit.

Artists do not only exist through the controversial content of their production. They might generate controversies based on their behavior. French rappers Booba and his former protégé Kaaris were involved in a public brawl (in two opposing camps!) at the Paris Orly airport in August 2018. They destroyed more than €50,000 worth of duty-free merchandise. The relationship had heated up online in the months leading up to this event, with the two rappers insulting each other on social media. To obtain forgiveness in the courtroom, the defense explained that "both rappers had cultivated aggressive public personas—something common in the rap scene—and could not back down from a potential confrontation while saving face."[21] After this brawl, and their time in jail, the two rappers decided to settle their dispute with a proper boxing fight in a ring. As part of this dramatization, they also met on talk shows. This affair got them both a tremendous amount of publicity for months. This story would have been a perfect illustration of Goffman's presentation of self in everyday life, considering its dramaturgic aspect. It is hard not to believe that the whole thing had been—even partly and implicitly—staged and thought through as a marketing stunt. Kaaris was mostly known only to rap fans, and both rappers benefitted from a reaffirmation of their identities—as members of a culture of violence and virility that allows them to sell their music and inspires respect from their fans.

Some individuals who see their visibility eroding or are frustrated by a lack of recognition can decide to create visibility for themselves by engaging in controversies. Such a process is helped by social media or other platforms that can give a voice to those who might not have had one otherwise. Thus some academics have specialized in being controversial on social media—and in this category, we can find both highly legitimate scientists and marginalized ones. The first group considers they should be more recognized by the broader public while those in the second lack recognition from both the broader public and their peers. In both cases, tweeting controversies or attacking others on social media (politicians, peers, practitioners, or even in some cases, entire professional associations) gives them additional visibility.

Individuals can build a social presence or even prominence by engaging in controversies. They can become "someone." They become professional trolls, known for their opposition to others rather than for their ideas, usually because they lack the latter. Divisive personalities invited on to talk shows are not invited because of their knowledge but because of their approach to knowledge. By contrast, some individuals have legitimacy in their field or robust expertise and use this expertise as a buffer when they engage in controversies to gain visibility. There are a few cases of recognized and esteemed academics who became prominent to the broader public by taking divisive positions outside of their domains of scientific expertise. For example, Jordan Peterson, an accomplished clinical psychologist at the University of Toronto, is mostly known to the broader public for the positions on gender he took in public and in his book *The 12 Rules of Life: An Antidote to Chaos*. Other academics in his field have struggled to discard him, because of his scientific legitimacy, while at the same time being infuriated by his schismatic opinions. Another scientist, Noah Carl, was elected as a junior research fellow at St. Edmund's Hall, University of Cambridge, in 2018, thanks to the scientific legitimacy he derived from a publication in the *British Journal of Sociology* and an Oxford doctorate. At the same time, he had taken controversial views on race in journals that had limited scientific credibility. He was finally removed from his post in 2019 after months of protest and inquiry, but not before having obtained a disproportionate amount of visibility and esteem from far-right audiences. In those two cases, those academics had a platform of scientific legitimacy, which helped buffer them against the negative evaluations they were getting because of their controversial positions. While there were significant drawbacks to the contentious positions they took, they slowed down the negative effect by building up their credibility by drawing from other sources. At the same time, they capitalized on those controversial positions to gain the visibility they would never have obtained if they had just stuck to their areas of expertise.

Individuals often engage in such strategies to trade controversy for visibility when they are themselves marginalized from a community. The Irish mixed martial artist and boxer Connor McGregor is an excellent example of how individuals can compensate for declining fame with attention-grabbing behaviors. Beginning in 2016 with his first loss within the Ultimate Fighting Championship (UFC) he started assaulting referees, fed religious and ethnic tensions, and attacked a bus in 2018 to promote his fight against another boxer—Khabib Nurmagomedov. Instead of punishing him, the UFC provided him with a new contract and decided to sponsor his whiskey brand.[22] In fact, both the organization and the individual benefitted from the mischiefs of Connor McGregor. As shown by Helms and Patterson (2014), the mixed martial arts industry is prone to impression management—and in this case, Connor McGregor is its cash cow. His controversial actions have made him a fighter of choice for mixed martial arts fans in search of a good show, and those same fans see him as charismatic, because of and not despite his misconduct.

A great example of an individual who owes his political career to a negative evaluation is Antanas Mockus, the former mayor of Bogota and president of the National University of Colombia. As put by the *Washington Post* in 1995, his "main claim to fame was having dropped his pants and bared his buttocks in public when, as rector of the National University, he was being heckled by rowdy students."[23] While he was initially condemned for such a radical action and forced to resign from his university post, he gained a considerable amount of publicity in the long run. His shocking action became quickly considered a bold move that served as a slap to unruly youngsters. He became associated with positive values such as courage, authority, and audacity . . . simply because he had shown his butt to an audience of his own students! Those values made him an instant political star in a country riddled by corruption and violence, although Mockus recognized in an interview for the *New York Times* that Bourdieu would see mooning as "symbolic violence."[24] Mockus did have to remind the voters about his out-of-the-box thinking by taking controversial decisions or political stances. In short, the visibility and unique positioning Mockus gained through his nonconformist approach was only short-lived and had to be revived regularly.

Within organizations, being controversial and being conflictual are also commonly rewarded. Sutton (2007), in his book on assholes in organizations, provides several examples to explain how the most vehement individuals are often considered to be the most competent. He mentions the culture of "destructive confrontation" at Intel, in which the nastiest individuals are considered to have higher status within the organization. Sutton provides an explanation for this phenomenon based on Teresa Amabile's study "Brilliant But Cruel: Perceptions of Negative Evaluators," published in 1983: Amabile found that negative reviews of books would lead the evaluators to be perceived as more intelligent, competent, and expert although, expectedly, less likable. Thus producing negative evaluations and being consequently perceived as an asshole can give status benefits within groups, especially for those who do not necessarily have other means to get a higher status. This argument goes back to our initial point that being overly critical on social media can send a positive signal to others. However, it also suggests that the negatively evaluated negative evaluator is "intellectually insecure" (Amabile 1983, 146). Thus Amabile adds that "subjects who are particularly concerned with others' perceptions of their intelligence will tend toward negative criticism as a strategy of impression management" (153). However, she also concludes that it works because those who judge the intelligence of those negative evaluators do not realize that a tactic is duping them.

In this section, we have seen how individuals can voluntarily deviate from the norm, shock audiences, and seek negative evaluations to acquire visibility. Such strategies are beneficial in a variety of contexts, within an organization and in a political context (more on that in the next section), but do not come without drawbacks. The visibility gained through controversial actions only lasts for a while and might generate some backlash from the audiences being mistreated. In addition, employing such strategies might, in some situations, signal the lack of another resource that would help the individual build more legitimate credibility.

Political Impression Management, Audience Polarization, and Identity Politics

Impression management is prevalent at the individual level, and one group of individuals have well understood its value as a strategic tool: politicians. We saw how the former mayor of Bogota capitalized on a controversy he created to launch a political career. However, for many individuals, their whole political trajectory has been fueled by contentious and polarizing claims. In the same ways in which individuals become "social media" famous, politicians capitalize on positioning rather than content. They position themselves by sending a signal through the content they share with audiences. Politicians commonly use impression management to appeal to audiences and attract votes—either broadly, or by targeting niches of voters. This is what Hall (1972) calls political impression management.

In the first instance, producing negative evaluations of a political opponent has become a common political strategy. The tactic of negative campaigning or rejectionist voting is often credited to the conservative political strategist Arthur Finkelstein. The idea is to attack opponents on their failings and flaws rather than praise one's candidate. Such a strategy ignores the content of political programs to offer a simple-to-interpret and easy-to-spread negative label. This strategy affects the voting intention by dissuading some of the voters on the other side so that they simply do not go to the polls. In this case, the negatively evaluated party might well not be the one benefitting from the strategy. However, some politicians also purposefully attract negative evaluations as a strategy to win elections.

There are two advantages to being negatively evaluated as political impression management: creating visibility and triggering polarization. With regard to the first advantage, controversies give politicians the attention of audiences, and the move might attract some audiences that are not directly targeted by the stunt and decide to provide support for the divisive politician. Racist slurs, for example, have helped politicians make it into the news, while at the same time alienating part of their audiences. This phenomenon implies polarization. Polarization is the mechanism through which two groups in disagreement progressively become more extreme and entrenched (Iyengar and Westwood 2015). Such a mechanism is due to confirmation bias—individuals cognitively focus on information that will reinforce their views. They also selectively process information to confirm their beliefs. As the gap between the beliefs of the two groups widens, group members confirm each other's' perspectives, as social interaction remains confined to the boundaries of their group (Mackie 1986).

Politicians rely on the mechanism of group polarization when they reinforce clear boundaries around the groups, supporting them. Those clear boundaries rely on social identity mechanisms: voters as they embrace an opinion tend to choose the one that is more clearly associated with a group they can identify with (Mackie 1986). At the same time, groups that are more extreme in their positioning also have more salient features that facilitate identification. Yardi and Boyd (2010) studied thirty thousand tweets to uncover how microlevel interactions accentuate polarization. They found that interactions on social media confirming each others' views strengthen the group identity, but interactions between two different sides also reinforce the boundaries between in- and out-groups. Controversial politicians purposefully demarcate the in-group of their voters from outsiders: through this strategy, they trigger voters' identification with the group. When voters strongly identify with their political group, it increases loyalty (they are less likely to change sides) as their group opinion drifts away with further polarization (Mackie 1986).

The phenomenon of group polarization can also be associated with the idea of identity politics (Bernstein 2005). Politicians appeal to the salient characteristics of voters that can segment them into clear groups they can strongly identify with. Culture, race, or religion are leveraged to play groups against each other. By triggering further identification with their groups among voters, politicians also further the gaps and the opposition between groups. While the term was initially coined to explain how oppressed and marginalized voters could coalesce to get their rights recognized, it has also been used to fuel nationalism. Identity politics can be used to blame the out-group and feed hate toward this out-group. This out-group of "others" is defined opportunistically, depending on what will help federate the in-group and what the in-group will be able to identify as notable differences. In other words, politicians rely on the production of negative evaluations against an out-group, ultimately feeding identity politics. In the short term, their hostile discourse might get them to be negatively evaluated themselves, but as they reinforce polarization, their hateful and divisive discourse becomes mainstream and more widely accepted. We can imagine that there are diminishing returns in playing social groups against each other, as those slurs become more common over time and, expectedly, politicians derive less value from instrumentally taking such divisive positions.

Nevertheless, the news is full of stories of politicians taking racially prejudiced positions. In August 2018, the former U.K. foreign secretary Boris Johnson compared Muslim women wearing the burqa with letterboxes and robbers in his column in the *Telegraph*, a national newspaper. It was reported by the *Guardian* that Tory activists had praised such "straight talking" and that Boris Johnson was "saying what everyone was thinking."[25] Ultimately this Islamophobic stance was seen as bolstering his grassroots support among the conservatives. This phenomenon is another example of politicians benefiting from being negatively evaluated for producing negative evaluations as a political strategy.

Political impression management is also a question of positioning and signaling. When politicians polarize audiences, they also strategically position themselves in the political landscape where they know they can gather voters. For example, the former governor of Arkansas, Mike Huckabee, took political advantage of the Chick-fil-A scandal discussed in the section on the antecedents of negative social evaluations. When the firm faced boycotts for its anti-LGBT positions, Huckabee called for a Chick-fil-A Appreciation Day (Crilly 2018). In his call, he referred to the Christian community and traditional values, reminding audiences of his second hat as a Christian minister. This strategy helped him reinforce his legitimacy as a defender of those values and to position himself for the 2016 Republican primary. Behind this move, Huckabee was also trying to signal his commitment to those traditional values. This is what has been trivially called "virtue signaling." Individuals engage in moral outrage to show where they stand, without necessarily having to take any action to provide evidence that they are committed to this position in practice (Spring, Cameron, and Cikara 2018). For Huckabee, the cost of setting up a Facebook event to support Chick-fil-A was close to zero: he did not even have to get out of his bed to do so. Public commitment to a cause on social media is usually seen as virtue signaling. While the term is usually mobilized by the conservative movement to attack the positioning of liberal politicians, the case of Huckabee shows that the strategy is standard on both sides of the political landscape. The governor of Arkansas framed his support of Chick-fil-A as a defense of freedom of speech and faith. Later in this chapter I will further unveil the signaling mechanisms through which social actors attract negative social evaluations, and will explain how those adverse evaluations can send a positive signal to more crucial audiences.

As I presented this book in a variety of universities, one example of an individual who leveraged negative social evaluation came up during every single discussion: Donald Trump. Anna Merlan (2019), a journalist specializing in conspiracy theories, explained that Trump was seen as a "'truth-teller' in a style that spoke to . . . many Americans. They liked his thoughts about a rigged system and a government working against them, the way it spoke to what they had always believed, and the neat way he was able to peg the enemy with soundbites: the 'lying media,' 'crooked Hillary,' the bottomless abyss of the Washington swamp'." Trump used the two mechanisms identified here. He first created visibility for himself by taking controversial stances when he was still one of the contenders in the race for the Republican nomination. Then, throughout his presidency, he kept making more outrageous and bold claims. He framed those claims so that they sounded like the truth nobody else wanted to express. His opponents continued to voice their antagonism more loudly. At the same time, his supporters finally felt part of an active group they could identify with. This ability to identify was particularly attractive for voters who had felt marginalized and ignored by mainstream politicians. Opinions on both sides became more and more polarized, but important for

Trump, his supporter base remains extremely loyal because of the identity benefits they derive from belonging to the group of his supporters. In fact, from 2017 to 2019, his approval ratings have kept going up. Trump's strategy has inspired other politicians, as illustrated by the cases of Boris Johnson and other nationalist leaders across the globe. But even if we expand beyond politicians, there are some commonalities with the behavior of activists: Greta Thunberg, the climate change activist, commonly used her "haters" (her own word) to federate her followers.[26] She created strong boundaries between her in-group and the out-group.

How does Trump sustain his controversial position? Is it possible to be consistently divisive on the longer term? We did suggest that there are diminishing returns to such strategies. In some ways, it is true that Trump had to find new ways to be noticed and gather his supporters behind what he frames as "straight talking." This strategy, as it becomes the new normal, might become less attractive to audiences, and less original.

Trump continues to rely on the use of culprits through increasingly hostile rhetoric—whether it is China, the Muslims, or immigration. For example, in April 2019, Trump incited hate toward the Minnesota representative Ilhan Omar by associating her with 9/11 because of her religion. At some point, he might well run out of culprits to blame, or audiences might get tired of those moving targets.

The stronger the critical mass of supporters in favor of a divisive leader, the easier it is for others to join the group (Clemente and Roulet 2015). Supporters of controversial leaders can be negatively perceived—Trump supporters were often labeled as "racist rednecks" (for example, by the rapper Cardi B.)[27] However, as the group grows, it is easier to identify with it, and its members appear as less marginalized and more of a central voice—it becomes more legitimate. The negative evaluation associated with belonging to the group fades away and is compensated by other benefits such as the potential for strong identification. That is how political support for extreme position builds up until it passes a threshold beyond which it has unfortunately become a natural part of the political landscape.

The Enemy of My Enemy Is My Friend: A Network Perspective

According to his biographers, Winston Churchill noted that "If Hitler invaded Hell, [he] would at least make a favorable reference to the Devil in the House of Commons." This quote shows that the perspective that one has on exchange partners is often conditioned by the social context and links in which one is embedded. Our position in this social landscape conditions our perspective on others. This section will introduce the role of networks in understanding the outcomes of negative social evaluation. Many of the cases of positive benefits of negative social evaluation that we have already explored can indeed be explained through network science. Gartrell (1987) argued that all social evaluations could be explained through the lens of networks. The science of social networks can be summarized as explaining how individuals and organizations connect and how the structure of their ties conditions their behaviors. Networks create "frames of references" (ibid., 60) so that a negative evaluation coming from one party may translate into either another negative or sometimes a positive evaluation from another party. This is how social theory explains the familiar adage, "The enemy of my friend is my enemy": when a distant social actor is negatively evaluated by another one with whom one has close ties, one is likely to evaluate this social actor too negatively. More interestingly for the content of this book, the adage can also be formulated as "The enemy of my enemy is my friend." Two negative links cancel each other: the enemy of the enemy is someone you can band with. With this enemy of your enemy, you can share a common cause and opposition against a third party. In this case, negative social evaluations can yield benefits for the target.

One phenomenon fleshed out by network science to explain the impact of evaluation is "social balance" (Antal, Krapivsky, and Redner 2005). Individuals' choices always tend to express consistency: if a social actor A and a social actor B have positive sentiments about each other, they are likely to share the same perspective on actor C but will have a diametrically opposite view if they dislike each other. This is the balanced state that enables both parties to express coherence in their choice. According to psychological research, this explains why A, being the enemy of C, the enemy of B, makes A and B friends. Both A and B derive benefit from getting support against C. Some recent research validated this basic phenomenon in the context of a sorority in a large public U.S. university. A sorority member who would dislike the same person as one of her friends would be more likely to engage in harming behaviors toward that common enemy (such as gossiping, being rude, or stealing) (Venkataramani and Dalal 2007).

"The enemy of my enemy is my friend" has been tested in many different contexts and different scientific fields, both in hard sciences such as evolutionary biology and in other social and political sciences. For example, Lee and colleagues (1994) modeled this adage in the arena of international relations, showing that negative bonds tend to balance each other over time. Maoz and colleagues (2007) empirically tested those propositions over 186 years of global relations. In the field of international politics, if making a harmless enemy (such as a small and developing country) can get you the support of a powerful friend (such as the United States or China) also opposed to this enemy, then it is worth getting detestation from this harmless enemy. Maoz and colleagues ultimately found that "enemies of enemies are three times more likely to become allies than is to be expected by chance alone" (108). They also paradoxically found that they are more likely to fight each other than by chance, everything else being equal. In short, there is a strong emotional reaction toward enemies of enemies, in both directions, although usually tilted toward a positive one.

In the context of the relationships between consumers and firms, individuals, and more specifically customers, can define themselves by what they dislike rather than what they like. This idea is crucial to understanding how to build a loyal customer base when products are defined by comparisons and are in competition with others. Customer "tribes" do not only define themselves by what and whom they like, but also by what they dislike (Cova, Kozinets, and Shankar 2012). Enemies can sometimes trigger such disgust that one can identify with someone they do not share anything in common with apart from a mutual disdain.

One case illustrates well that phenomenon: pretty much everywhere in the world, all taxi drivers hate Uber. Yes, Uber is the kind of market disrupter that the industry had been waiting for. Taxi drivers felt as though they were being robbed of their jobs. France experienced a peak of tension between taxi drivers and Uber during the spring of 2015. Taxis were seen as out of fashion, and even frankly uncool, and nobody was happy with the quality of the service provided by the drivers, but French people were at best indifferent about their destiny. When taxi drivers began to engage in violent actions against Uber drivers, and in turn, those actions became visible on social media, the population began to take a clear side in favor of Uber and spread the word about the taxi drivers' misbehavior. The customer base of Uber has only been growing since this time, and this feeling of sympathy has gained them some new customers but also the support they needed from the population to avoid having the government on their back.

Negatively evaluated social actors often make a bunch of new friends among those who hate their negative evaluators. Those new friends might well be new customers. Chick-fil-A, following its anti-LGBT position and the consequent support from conservative groups, significantly grew its customer base. The Chick-fil-A Appreciation Day, on August 1, 2012, launched by Mike Huckabee as a reaction to the boycott, showed record sales for the fast-food chain. In fact, there was a spike of almost 30 percent increase in sales on that day.[28] Citing customer research, Crilly (2018, 3) explains that "Trump supporters were 12% more likely to declare Chick-fil-A as their favorite restaurant than were Clinton supporters" and that "there [was] a clear upward in the aggregate revenue and per-unit revenue" after the scandal. It not only gave the chain free publicity, it also energized its core group of customers—Christian conservatives who share the religious commitment proudly displayed in the firm's values. Ultimately, the scandal made those customers more loyal because it made salient the firm's values that could trigger customers' identification to the brand. In the next chapter, on practical implications, we will explore more thoroughly the practical ways through which firms can use a network perspective on negative evaluations to reinforce their links with their customers.

Negative evaluators also often get the help of their friends in producing and spreading those negative social evaluations. In an experimental study, Bastiaensens and colleagues (2014) found that people were likely to join in cyberbullying when it was carried out by their close friends, especially if they shared a collective identity. That is, the more bullies you have in your network of close friends, the more you might start bullying others. When going back to political impression management, this finding reminds us that politicians might be able to trigger cascading effects of hostility against their opponents when they have a close network of supporters.

While the existence of networks can condition the benefits of negative evaluation, several other factors need to be in place for this to happen. In particular, social evaluations need to travel through this network. In fact, the adage "The enemy of my enemy is my friend" has been challenged by mathematical and network scientists (see in particular the work of Leskovec and colleagues, 2010). While friends of enemies are likely to be friends and enemies of friends are likely to be enemies, the idea that enemies of enemies can be friends is overall less supported. Such a mixed result suggests that a network is not enough for enemies of enemies to become friends. For networks to enable beneficial negative social evaluations, other elements are needed, in particular the publicity (is it salient enough?) and the valence (is it strong enough?) of the evaluations. Actors might not feel strongly enough about their enemies to embrace the enemies of their enemies. Thus, in cases of attitude polarization, the network of potential parties may present structural holes— gaps in the network that signal an absence of interactions between two sets of actors. During controversies, networks are highly segregated, with clusters that are barely connected (Garimella et al. 2018). In such a case, bridges are required to connect sets of actors that are disjointed, and those bridges can be formed of common enemies.

Signaling Mechanisms Between Audiences

The previous section established the importance of networks in delivering positive outcomes for the targets of negative social evaluations. I have also stressed that networks were a necessary but not sufficient condition. A key element for negative evaluations to spread through networks and travel across audiences is the willingness of those network members and audiences. Evaluations are not necessarily channeled through audiences when those audiences have low motivation to share them. In this section, we will focus on how evaluations are *interpreted* and how negatively evaluated social actors can leverage this. The reactive perspective on deviance (Spreitzer and Sonenshein 2004) postulates that deviance is nonexistent without the observation and the highlighting of deviance by audiences.

One essential theoretical framework to understand how negative social evaluations can be beneficial, complementary to a network perspective, is signaling theory. This perspective, popularized by the Nobel Prize winner Michael Spence (1974), initially focused on the functioning of job markets. The economist showed that employers consider education a signal of the superior ability of productivity, in the absence of better information. The main argument of signaling theory is that when critical characteristics of a social actor are unobservable (or difficult to observe), audiences rely on a proxy. Since then, signaling mechanisms have been identified in a variety of contexts from financial markets to consumer behaviors, but more broadly in interorganizational relationships. For example, in a piece on philanthropy, we showed that Russian theaters receiving corporate money are less likely to receive awards from their peers, everything else being equal (Shymko and Roulet 2017). Receiving corporate money is understood by the rest of their field as betraying fundamental values of authenticity. However, we showed that this signal could be manipulated by theaters. They can decide to hide those ties under the carpet, and mitigate the negative valence of their links with tainted organizations by showing how limited those relationships are in time and scope. In this case, a positive tie can send a negative signal to peers, but we focus here on the opposite mechanism: when a negative evaluation sends a positive signal to critical stakeholders.

Deviance has material implications when an audience reacts to it (Spreitzer and Sonenshein 2004), that is, when it is signaled. We previously explored the hypothesis of a visibility advantage by looking at the consequences of negative book reviews: when receiving negative publicity, unknown social actors can gain prominence and ultimately benefit from negative evaluations (Berger et al. 2010). Diverging from the arguments developed by Berger and colleagues, we could postulate that what mattered is the combination of the content and the sending of the message. The fact that *New York Times* critics, a set of evaluators with specific characteristics, provided those reviews, helped sell those negatively evaluated books. Customers may have thought that if fancy and posh critics from an elite newspaper outlet despised those books, it might well suggest that they are easy and enjoyable reads. An excellent example of such a phenomenon is what happened to the *Final Destination* franchise. The critics absolutely slammed the first movie. *Time Out* called it a "nasty piece of work," *USA Today* presented it as "stupid, silly, gory," and it was a "mediocre TV movie" for the *Chicago Tribune*. For the *New York Times*, the movie was "dramatically flat," and the *Washington Post* told its readers "[The] final destination . . . might be the box office, to demand your money back." The movie was an incredible success in cinemas, making more than $100 million in revenues, four times more than what it cost. It might be that audiences did not take critics at face value, and interpreted their negative perspectives as a sign that *Final Destination* should be seen as a light-hearted and easily accessible horror movie. Personally, I would be the first to run into theaters to see a "stupid, silly, gory movie," and I might indeed occasionally be tempted by "mediocre" and "dramatically flat" entertainment, after a week in the classroom! Negative critical reviews might convey information about the nature of the target that might make it attractive to audiences.

A body of empirical evidence indeed suggests that negative evaluations by some stakeholders might be interpreted as a positive signal by other groups of more crucial stakeholders, and vice versa. In my research on investment banks during the financial crisis, I have shown many positive signaling effects of negative social evaluations. In one of my first papers, I looked at the negative press on investment banks in the print media (the *New York Times*, the *Washington Post*, and the *Wall Street Journal*) and showed that it was positively correlated with how prestigious the bank was perceived as by other field members (Roulet 2015b). In this case, hostility from a broad audience generates cohesion at the field level (what was identified in the previous chapter as resilience to hostility through the building of an industry macro culture). However, media disapproval targeting specific banks signals to peers how much those particular actors are suffering from being part of a contested industry, and thus how prominent those banks are within this group. As a consequence, negatively evaluated banks attract the esteem of field members as particularly contested actors. In a much more sophisticated paper, I isolated the coverage of banks' misconduct in the same news outlets and looked at how it related to typical practices of the field (following Roulet 2015a). I showed that what is considered as misconduct by the media can be interpreted as adherence to norms of the field and thus valued by key stakeholders such as corporate customers (Roulet 2019a). Those corporate customers value adherence to norms and regard it as a signal of the quality of the service. The more banks are negatively perceived for engaging in those field-level norms, the more they are perceived as close to the core values of their field.

This body of work shows that there are signaling mechanisms between audiences. A negative social evaluation by one audience can lead to a positive one by another—potentially more crucial—audience. From an instrumental perspective, social actors may manipulate audiences that will give them bad press to receive positive evaluations from the stakeholders who matter.

An Integrative Model of How Negative Social Evaluations Can Be Beneficial for the Target

In this chapter, I have developed the idea that social actors could benefit from negative social evaluations. Figure 5 summarizes the model of how negative

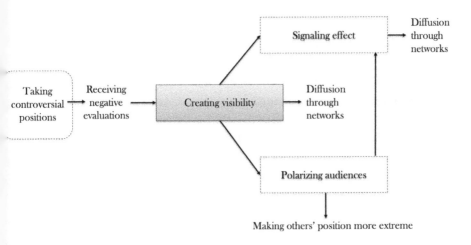

Figure 5. A Model Articulating the Benefits of Negative Social Evaluation.
Source: Made by author.

evaluations can be leveraged and how the different benefits are linked to each other. The idea is to link the different mechanisms identified in this chapter.

In the left side of the model, I acknowledge the possibility for social actors to voluntarily or involuntarily trigger the negative social evaluations by being divisive and taking controversial positions. As we have seen, politicians, but also cultural products such as movies or advertisements, often try to shock audiences. Such a contentious position is instrumental, in contrast with objects or actors that are confronted with negative social evaluations without having sought them. Whether it is the consequence of a strategic move, or passively received, a chain of consequences is triggered by the reception of negative social evaluation—whether it is widely shared, or specific to a particular audience. The first consequence of negative social evaluation is to provide the targeted actor with visibility—which spreads through the network of audience members.

Negative social evaluations make the targeted actor stand out: this is the first benefit, as actors leverage this visibility. Marginal voices become central and gain a wider audience, especially in the era of social media, where every individual actor has access to a communication channel. It also conditions and enables a variety of other beneficial levers and outcomes. Social actors can use their visibility to reinforce the boundaries between the in-group and the out-group, reinforcing identification mechanisms, and support from in-group members. I have stressed the importance of this strategy for political actors, but we can imagine that polarization can also happen as a consequence of divisive leadership within organizations. One risk of polarization is to transform audiences and generate further divergence—not to say extremism—in the opinion of members. By widening the gap between the in-group and the out-group, divisive actors take the risk of feeding unrest.

In parallel, the visibility of negatively evaluated actors enables them to send a positive signal to other audiences. This mechanism relies on the contradiction in the interpretation of multiple audiences: the characteristics or the behavior of the targeted actor will be negatively perceived by one audience, which will help another one make a favorable inference about this actor. In addition, the process relies on the ability of this evaluation to travel from one audience to the other. Again, the value of the signal is contingent on the diffusion through a network.

Boundary Conditions: When Is Being Disapproved of Better Than Having a Good Reputation?

Building upon the previous sections, I will use this section to discuss the boundary conditions under which negative social evaluations are beneficial. There are two critical potential boundary conditions to the arguments I have developed in this book. First, there are well-documented adverse consequences of negative evaluations, and thus we need positive consequences to counterbalance the negative ones. Second, an overlapping requirement is the heterogeneity of audiences. If audiences are homogenous, a negative social evaluation will be widely shared, through an echo chamber, without the potential for a divergent interpretation.

As previously discussed, negatively evaluated actors are most commonly rejected, isolated, and discriminated against (Link and Phelan 2001). An unfavorable reputation can deter applicants and partners, and adversely affects performance (Piazza and Perretti 2015; Durand and Vergne 2015; Hudson and Okhuysen 2009). Basuroy and colleagues (2003) found that negative and critical reviews adversely affected box office performance—and they affect them negatively a lot more than positive reviews boost performance (although

having a few celebrities in the film limits the damages of critical reviews—
Final Destination had none). More generally, contrary word-of-mouth
significantly damages the net present value of a firm, even when coming from
a small group of disgruntled customers (Goldenberg et al. 2007). Moreover,
although Berger and colleagues (2010) show that negative evaluations can
increase visibility and awareness, it would work the opposite way for targets
that are already visible: they show that for books that consumers are aware of,
the negative evaluations have a very negative impact on sales. Thus, in most
cases, negative evaluations harm their recipient, and it might well be that
the examples of the movie *Final Destination* and the book *Fierce People* are
exceptions. The visibility advantage might only pay off for initially invisible
actors, while established ones might suffer more from the negative evaluation
than they gain from the additional visibility.

In fact, some empirical evidence suggests that the effect of a negative reputation mostly carries a positive impact on competitors rather than for the
focal target. For example, Paruchuri and colleagues (2019) analyzed the consequences of the E. coli outbreak in Chipotle restaurants in Seattle. Through
a natural experiment, they found that when the crisis was most salient other
Mexican restaurants in the same area experienced an increase in sales. This
might be due to the salience of the category—audiences are cognitively sensi-
tized to Mexican restaurants, and even negative attention to the category can
be translated into success.

So, more generally, when are the drawbacks of negative social evaluations
canceling their benefits? The positive link between organizational reputation
and financial performance is empirically robust (Roberts and Dowling 2002).
In short, there is a competitive disadvantage but not necessarily a cost in not
having a good reputation. On the other side of the spectrum, it is difficult
to evaluate the exact cost of a bad reputation, for example, regarding sales,
recruitment, and retention. It is, however, possible to identify ex-ante the
stakeholder groups that will be affected and how those stakeholders impact
the organization's bottom line. By conducting an assessment of stakeholders'
salience and importance, organizations can evaluate the pros and cons of
having a bad reputation. In the case of investment banks (Roulet 2013; 2015a;
2015b), the surge of public hostility may only have affected them marginally
because of their relatively hermetic industry mindset. It was possibly
counterbalanced by the positive impact it has had on their ability to attract

corporate customers. Because the bottom line of the banks' profit is with those corporate customers, media disapproval is only marginally significant.

We have seen how negative evaluations from negligible audiences might lead to positive evaluations from influential stakeholders, via a ricochet effect. When theorizing social evaluations, I highlighted the potential co-occurrence of positive and negative social evaluations (Hudson 2008). As stressed by Helms and colleagues (2019), actors can be both stigmatized and legitimate. On the basis of this argument, I suggest that the cost of stigma might be negligible in comparison with the benefits of legitimacy gained *because of stigma*. This hypothesis is conditioned by the dependence the focal actor has over the two audiences. Social actors depend upon their stakeholders for resources to ensure their performance and ultimately their survival (Pfeffer and Salancik 2003). If negative evaluations are received from stakeholders that do not provide crucial resources to the actor, the downside risks of being divisive are limited. In the meantime, the signal to other more crucial stakeholders needs to reach them, with limited noise, for it to yield beneficial outcomes. In some cases, there might not be an audience either to attribute the negative evaluation or to interpret it. In the experimental study by Norton and colleagues (2012), they initially found that stigmatized individuals were more likely to get their demands accepted because of the self-presentational needs of their counterpart: people are more likely to accept the demands of a person in a wheelchair because they are afraid of being negatively perceived if they misbehave toward a stigmatized person. However, they found no persuasive power of stigma when there is no audience to judge how counterparts interact with stigmatized individuals.

I do acknowledge that in a large share of cases, being negatively evaluated has substantial adverse consequences. However, for individuals or organizations to be considered as breaking away from social norms, negative evaluations are inescapable. Industries that are questioned on ethical grounds, such as the tobacco or the weapons industries, will always be negatively perceived—they may be legitimate and survive while remaining stigmatized (Galvin, Ventresca, and Hudson 2005; Vergne 2012). The argument I develop in this book is that they will be able to cope with those negative evaluations and even potentially turn them to their advantage. In particular, I stressed both the internal advantage—in terms of organizational culture, internal cohesion, and identification from their members—and the external stakeholders they are dependent upon.

Because the lack of reputation may make social actors less competitive (Roberts and Dowling 2002), negative evaluations are to be avoided when they come from audiences that can affect the social actor's bottom line or *raison d'etre* (Pfeffer and Salancik 2003). Firms that receive positive and negative press tend to use investors' relations' firms to amplify their positive news in contrast to their negative views because of the negative effect those can have on their stock prices (Solomon 2012). Impression management, as was pointed out, relies not only on triggering the right information to reach the appropriate stakeholder, but that this information is framed in a way that will be interpreted positively. In a nutshell, impression management—the way the evaluation is managed—will often be the lever and the mediating mechanism that explains when a negative evaluation harms or benefits a targeted organization.

Finally, I previously pointed out the potential diminishing returns of negative social evaluations, and this might be an additional boundary condition. There is clear recursiveness in the way social actors seek negative evaluations for their own benefits and then reevaluate the attractiveness of such a strategy. When social actors capitalize on negative social evaluations, they may start seeking more of them (for the benefit of it). At the same time, they become more prominent, more powerful, and consequently may also paradoxically receive a greater extent of positive evaluations because they attract more attention. Nevertheless, their excess might be perceived as a new norm, and be much less likely to signal deviance. So far politicians like Trump have been able to push the boundaries of outrage one tweet at a time—but for how long? Infowars, the highly controversial conspirationist media, ended up being banned from the leading social media websites, finally harming its bottom line. If the strategy of triggering negative evaluations for instrumental reasons becomes mainstream, the competitive positioning it enables will stop being unique, and it will become a crowded space in which payoff is uncertain.

CHAPTER 4

PRACTICAL IMPLICATIONS FOR INDIVIDUALS, ORGANIZATIONS, AND SOCIETY

In this book, I have built a theory of how social actors deal with negative social evaluations and approach them strategically. We saw how social actors could potentially build resilience to negative evaluations through a stronger sense of self and identity. Finally, we explored the different ways they could capitalize on negative social evaluations.

As this project matured and the ideas started taking shape, I got the ambition (not to say the self-importance!) to provide a social theory of negative evaluations. As the social psychologist Kurt Lewin suggested in 1943, "there is nothing as practical as a good theory." Thus, beyond the distinct practical arguments I made as I unfolded the model, I want to explore several additional practical implications of my arguments. How can you, reader, build on those arguments for yourself, for your organization, and more broadly as a citizen?

Dealing with negative social evaluations is the focus of an entire profession: public relations and communication advisors. In this sense, I hope that the arguments developed here can be of relevance for them. Those professionals of evaluations would usually advise against their clients—whether they are individuals or organizations—actively seeking hostility and adverse feedback from audiences. Dietrich (2014) notes that Egyptians documented the achievements of the pharaohs, and the Romans wrote biographies of their emperors to gather political support from the masses. Pope Gregory XV invented modern propaganda as he sent missionaries to spread Catholicism in Europe and oppose the rise of Protestantism (ibid.). Dietrich also cites Edward Bernays as the father of public relations, who tried to persuade women to smoke in the 1920s on behalf of the cigarette brand Lucky Strike. Since then, the work of PR firms was made glamorous by TV shows such as *Scandal*, in which a communication advisor is in charge of protecting the reputation of the U.S. president (since then though, and by contrast with fiction, Trump decided he knows better how to handle his Twitter account). The fall of Bell Pottinger, one of the most prominent PR firms, in 2017, also put that industry in the front line. The firm fell into disgrace when it was shown to be fostering racial tensions in South Africa to deflect attention away from one of its clients. PR firms do not only manage negative evaluations for others, they also sometimes have to manage some of their own.

Existing work on reputation management, but also on those communication and PR firms, focuses on what Waller and Younger (2017) call the "art of changing how people see you." Many of my arguments suggest a similar objective—but formulate the hypothesis that sometimes social actors may not necessarily want people to see them in a positive light. Instead, I argue that sometimes one might want to obtain a bad reputation for instrumental reasons. Building on Hudson (2008), I argue that the reputation game can be played with two audiences having polar perspectives on the same actor or object. Once the potential divergence in audiences is acknowledged, there is a world of possibility to tread carefully in the realm of bad reputation and image. Sometimes, small nuances in framing can make a world of difference. On the basis of the different arguments developed in this book, I can offer a number of practical takeaways with regard to different stakeholder groups: customers, employees, and external stakeholders.

Playing with negative social evaluations to acquire visibility, reinforce an identity, or signal key characteristics to crucial audiences might not always be practically palpable. Yet there are ways to understand how negative social evaluations can be carefully managed—contained when they can harm, and leveraged when they can help. I acknowledged the possibility that negative evaluations might not overcompensate the loss of reputation that they imply. Overall, and everything else being equal, actors should seek to be positively evaluated in a majority of the cases—when there is no particular signaling effect, or when the evaluator is a crucial resource provider. In the first section of this chapter, we will look at how individuals can deal with negative evaluations at work, and more generally benefit from evaluations, whether they are positive or negative. Because evaluations are a common feature of the modern workplace but also subject to a variety of biases, it is crucial to understand the mediating mechanism between performance and evaluation.

In the second section of this chapter, we will come back to what I have identified as "divisive leadership": when leaders are purposefully contentious to be visible, and potentially signal virtue, play identity politics, and polarize audiences for their own gain. This leadership style has become widespread—inspired by politicians presenting themselves as "truth-tellers" and using new forms of media to spread their divisive message. But sometimes it can also be used for positive leadership in times of fast-paced change: the climate activist Greta Thunberg gained further support when gaining enemies.

Facing public hostility can also create a turning point for the organization, as I have stressed in the chapter on resilience to public hostility. Most of the academic research on organizational change points in the same direction: to engage in radical change, even when survival is at stake, a trigger might be necessary. What better trigger than a spark of public anger? An important point made by social scientists is that resistance from insiders and employees usually slows down organizational change. When the motivations for change are internal to the organization, employees may see the initiative as political or self-serving. By comparison, outsiders can be accepted as providing an objective point of view motivating organizational change. Hostility generates creativity to reinvent oneself in a better light. In other words, facing disapproval is an opportunity to rewrite the story of the organization and put energy into reinterpreting its activity and purpose, and to create a justification for its existence.

We will then turn toward the management of hostile stakeholders, especially on new battlefields such as social media. In previous chapters, we tried to understand how scandals unfold and the process of diffusion of negative evaluations. In this chapter, we will capitalize on those frameworks to understand what social actors can do about it to defend themselves. Social media is like David against Goliath—any isolated individuals can pick a fight against multinationals or entire nations. An organization can have limited control over the conversation around its products or services (Earl and Waddington 2013). Etter and colleagues (2019) recognized several specificities to the processes of reputation formation on social media. They note that emotional and informational content, accurate and inaccurate arguments, are mixed all together. The content is coproduced and shared, which accelerates the propagation of the evaluation of the targeted social actors. Such an audience is particularly hard to address because it is fragmented but also acting as an echo chamber in which passionate messages are more likely to be propagated. Indeed corporate downfalls may now come from social media, as public outrage can go viral in a flash via Twitter or Facebook (Baer 2016). Any dissatisfied customer or evil-minded competitors can take their rage to social media, and the risk is minimal as it can be anonymous. Later in this chapter, we will take a concrete look at the role of disgruntled customers and the negative evaluations they produce in fostering positive change.

Beyond generating positive organizational change, we saw how negative evaluations of organizations can hurt employees, for example, decreasing their job satisfaction (Roulet 2017). This mechanism requires an adapted strategy of internal communication. External criticism needs to be questioned: is it legitimate feedback? Is it a fair criticism? Depending on the reasons and motives that triggered this criticism, disapproved organizations or individuals may find the arguments to discard the outsiders' perspective. We also saw how such a mechanism could foster greater cohesion and identification when external hostility is judged illegitimate (ibid.). Usually, hostility is met with a crowd, and support and understanding can be found among other social actors experiencing the same situation. Disapproval can thus trigger greater solidarity among individuals from the same field or the same condemned organization, and among companies in the same contested industry. We will discuss the implications of those findings for internal communication: should organizations convince their employees that they are in the right and that they should engage in social weighting discarding outsider criticism? How can organizations manage situations of reputational crises, from the employees' perspective?

In the following section, we will look at the management of reputational crises from the outsiders' perspective. We will investigate the practicality of having multiple audiences producing diverging evaluations and discuss how organizations can manage reputational crises.

Finally, we will explore the societal implications of the overproduction of negative evaluations. We will look into the divisions created by this overproduction and the latent hostility in public and social communication. It will be an opportunity to consider practical challenges associated with the production of "fake-news-like" negative evaluations and conspiracy theories.

Triggering Positive Evaluations and
Beneficial Negative Evaluations at Work

Evaluations are a common practice in modern organizations. We have extensively covered the ways evaluations are produced, in particular the negative ones. But we can take a much broader view, on how both good and positive evaluations are elicited and how they influence the career trajectories of their recipients. In professional service firms such as audit or law firms, performance evaluations are widespread, and often subject to several biases (Stenger 2017; Stenger and Roulet 2018). Auditors, for example, are often evaluated by both their peers and their superiors, conditioning their ability to be promoted. In the work context, how can individuals ensure they receive the positive evaluations they deserve?

High performance does not necessarily lead to high evaluations, and vice versa. Various mediating mechanisms explain how performance is translated into social evaluations. Biases are not only caused by prejudice—whether they are about sexuality, race, religion, or other characteristics (Link and Phelan 2001)—but also by several behavioral factors shaping the actions of potential evaluators. For example, Amabile (1983) hypothesized that overly negative evaluators are usually behaving in this way because they are intellectually insecure, and excessive criticism gets them to be perceived as more competent. More recently, the work of Cho and Fast (2012) elaborates on this phenomenon. Their experiments show that those at the top are more likely to produce negative evaluations of their partners and subordinates when they feel their competence is threatened. From this body of empirical evidence, we can conclude that being unthreatening to the evaluator is crucial to elicit more positive evaluation. Cho and Fast also found that an expression of gratitude from a subordinate can help his or her superiors feel more confident about themselves, and those superiors were consequently less likely to denigrate their work partners. In other words, thanking a supervisor can help him or her experience positive affirmation, which in turn will positively affect his or her evaluations of work colleagues.

While the feeling of being threatened biases our evaluations, another related driver is jealousy or envy (Andiappan and Dufour 2020). A jealous supervisor might negatively evaluate a subordinate when he or she experiences a rivalry to obtain the attention of a third party. Alternatively, an envious supervisor might want what one of his or her subordinates has (for example, the attention, the esteem, or the respect of other counterparts) and thus punish this subordinate with unjustified low evaluations.

There are also interpersonal dynamics affecting the formulation of social evaluations. A recent article on *Schadenfreude* (Li et al. 2019) suggests that individuals within organizations are more likely to support mistreatment (for example, unfair negative evaluations) when it targets competitors and out-group members. In the same vein, they would also contribute to the blame if they strongly identify with the negative evaluator (ibid.). For example, in professional service firms there are cascading mechanisms of evaluation (Stenger 2017). The way employees are perceived by the boss of their boss conditions the way their boss would evaluate them, especially if those two evaluators are themselves close to each other. Thus positive relationships at work can buffer against being a victim of *Schadenfreude*: when employees have good connections with their colleagues, potential audiences are less likely to jump on the bandwagons of producing unjustified negative evaluations. Those positive relationships might rely on small acts of kindness, mutual trust, and, more generally, social proximity.

What can we conclude on how to receive less negative evaluations, everything else being equal (in particular keeping the antecedent of the evaluation, such as performance, equal)? And inversely, how to elicit more positive evaluations? The first individual advantage we identified relies on the embeddedness in a network of positive relationships. Being kind with colleagues, even the ones you literally cannot stand, pays off. However, those positive relationships might also be fed by micro-interactions—being genuinely interested in colleagues at the coffee machine might get them to support you the next time your boss unfairly barks at you.

Divisive Leadership: A Double-Edged Sword?

In this book, we have explored how politicians and other social actors employed a divisive approach to leadership, although we did not formally define this style of influence. Yammarino and Dansereau (2008, 137) provide some formal definitions. Divisive leaders "focus on the differences among individuals and form a relationship with only some individuals based on the differences among them (leader within-group linkage)." They rely more extensively on the divide between the in-group and the out-group and reinforce this divide to create loyalty of the in-group members to their collective. Divisive leadership has unfortunately been increasingly trendy in recent years, as Donald Trump's inflammatory rhetoric paved the way. However, politicians have been increasingly inventive in fostering the divide with the out-group. Matteo Salvini, the deputy prime minister of Italy and extreme-right wing populist politician, has been labeling his political enemies the *buonista* or "do-gooders."[1] In his rhetoric, being too good is wrong, and excessive idealism is hurtful because it negates the reality of the in-group members. This argument gives his party in power an excuse to do bad things in the name of realism and by opposition to "right-thinking."

However, divisive leadership is also visible in other areas of our society—we previously noted how celebrities use social media to federate their supporters against outsiders. Nassim Taleb, the man behind the concept of Black Swan, benefits from a strong fan base on social media. When he is attacked, his fans come to the rescue to support him against outsiders. Such strategies also happen offline. Mark Cuban, the owner of the Dallas Mavericks basketball team, has been fined millions for ranting about opposing teams and referees. Despite his crude language toward outsiders, employees are split: some of them respect him as an inclusive and inspiring leader while others have raised concerns about the quality of interactions he has with his subordinates and the culture he created within his organization.[2]

There is also a long list of divisive leaders who did well in the corporate world. Sutton (2007) stressed the culture at Intel, in which nastier leaders were better perceived by their peers. Building on Amabile's work (1983), Sutton also makes the argument that divisive leaders can do well in organizations because they inspire fear and their behavior signals status. Employees who fear their leaders are also likely to respect them and potentially see them as more competent. This impression might work at least for a while. Sutton finishes his book by asking the readers whether they should become assholes as well (please don't!).

We will explore in the last section of this chapter the disastrous implications that divisive leadership can have for society. However, it can be risky for the divisive leader him- or herself. Divisive leadership creates an "us vs. them" impression, which will ultimately divide the organization. A polarized organization cannot be in a state of equilibrium. Only two options are possible: the clash between the in-group and the out-group leads to the exclusion of the out-group members to homogenize the membership of the organization or, alternatively, the organization struggles to operate as it is crippled by internal conflict. In this second situation, the out-group members serve their own agenda instead of serving the one of the divisive leaders they are opposed to. Such options might not happen if employees are stuck with their divisive leader and have minimal job mobility—in such a situation, they might stick around and suffer from the work conditions. Jeff Bezos, for example, is known for his reluctance to recognize the role of unions, and the pressure he imposes on the bottom of the organization—for warehouse employees in particular. While Bezos has had the support of top executives, who have the agency to offer or withdraw their support, employees who are barely above the poverty line are deprived of a voice to oppose their CEOs. Inspiring fear also harms psychological safety and questions the trust employees might have toward their leaders. In the meantime, if a majority—especially a majority holding power or resources within the organization—starts questioning the divisive leader, it will make his or her position precarious. In the case of Travis Kalanick, the former CEO of Uber, he was for a long time considered the brain of a successful company and the disruptor of transportation ecosystems in major cities across the world. As his controversial positions (such as being part of Trump's advisory council) and misbehavior (for example, a heated discussion he had with a driver caught on camera, an accusation of mismanaging cases of sexual harassment and corporate espionage) came to light, Kalanick started losing the trust of his employees. As noted by *Bloomberg* in a long read on this case, "You could go into Uber on any given day and half the T-shirts were Uber T-shirts. They disappeared overnight."[3]

One of the main styles of divisive leadership that might be conducive to good result consists in being divisive toward outsiders while maintaining a high level of support and proximity toward insiders. Mark Cuban has always been ruthless with opposing teams and referees but regularly brought up his effort to be empathetic toward his employees.[4] Attacking the opponents of the organization is similar to the strategy of social weighting identified in the chapter on resistance to hostility. Such a strategy can support the identification of organizational members and foster internal cohesion. In the meantime, when leaders direct their hostility toward outsiders, they make their organization take the risk of being negatively evaluated. Divisive leadership might get stakeholders to withdraw their support of the firm, threatening their resource relationships with those counterparts (Pfeffer and Salancik 2003). In short, internal members feel more loyalty toward their organization and its divisive leader, but a more complicated relationship with stakeholders counterbalances those benefits. Alex Jones, the founder of Infowars, has used his online media channel to fire off left and right. He, however, went too far in barking at his stakeholders. While he gave his followers the impression that they were up against everybody else, and that they should stick together, he also lost the crucial support of many stakeholders such as the social media powerhouses. The case of Alex Jones illustrates the impact of a divisive positioning or framing on the reactions of customers.

How Social Media Can Help Create Intimacy with Customer Groups

In this section, we will look at the effect of negative social evaluations on customer groups and how haters can be played to firms' advantage. Corporate downfalls may now come from social media, as public outrage can go viral in a flash via Twitter or Facebook. Considering the very low barriers of entry, any individual can take their complaints to social media. But as we have seen in previous chapters, hate can be related to positive identity mechanisms and distinctiveness. Customers are often compared to tribes (Cova, Kozinets, and Shankar 2012), and in this sense, the group dynamics they experience can be used to the benefit of the firms.

There is indeed nothing simpler for customers than to complain through social media rather than to call the support services or visit a store (Earl and Waddington 2013). The cost of entry for disgruntled customers is low, but the satisfaction of being able to vent on social media makes it an attractive venue. If customers complain about your product or their experience, it is also that they are passionate, and in that sense, they are customers that firms should care about. You may remember the example of Electronic Arts, which we discussed in the Preface. Electronic Arts became one of the most hated firms in the United States because of a post on the online forum Reddit. Baer (2016) calls those disgruntled customers, who attack on social media, the "onstage haters." Those "onstage haters," by contrast with those who will only take their complaints through a private channel such as the phone or via email, primarily want an audience. Buckels and colleagues (2019) found that online trolling was correlated with sadistic tendencies. Still, it does not mean companies should ignore customer complaints. Baer (2016) found, on the basis of survey data collected in the U.S., that 81 percent of those twenty-five to thirty-four years old had been onstage haters. Ten years ago, a customer who was unhappy with a product would just stop buying that product. Nowadays, the same customer will take his or her discontent on social media first, which allows the supplier to answer the concern (Schultz, Utz, and Göritz 2011).

In the number of evaluations produced on social media, one unhappy customer looks like a drop in the ocean, but one complaint can spiral out of control—in such a case, the targeted firm can completely lose control over its image and the perception of its products and services (Dietrich 2014). How should organizations react to this non-negligible reputational risk? They could do like the British author Richard Brittain, cited by Baer (2016), who received a one-star Amazon review for his book *The World Rose*. He chased the teenager who had posted the review and crushed her with a bottle of wine (by the way, I promise not to do that if you give me a bad Amazon review—as a good French person, I love wine too much). Baer instead makes the radical argument that firms should answer *all* online complaints and address the comments of *every single* disgruntled customer, even when they include the worse insults. Baer suggests *hugging your haters,* showing that you care, and increasing "customer advocacy" (5).

There are many examples of firms that have tried to take this strategy on board. Baer (ibid.) cites the example of the owner of Fresh Brothers Pizza, a thirteen-stores-strong pizza chain in Southern California. The owner personally (and makes the "personally" known) answers every single Yelp review of her restaurants. She acknowledges the client's impression, apologizes, and explores how the issue might be addressed. Answering those concerns online with well-crafted and targeted justification is critical in an era when evaluations are widely available. In a recent study looking at negative reviews of London hotels on TripAdvisor, researchers showed that organizations could actively manage their market identity by making their answers public, thus shifting the spotlight to their own sets of arguments rather than those of unhappy customers (Wang, Wezel, and Forgues 2016).

AT&T, as a major phone carrier in the United States, handles a massive number of customer complaints. In 2009 in particular, hostile hashtags against the carrier (#ATTfail) were trending on Twitter to illustrate the public discontent around the failure of AT&T to deploy all the functionalities for the users of the iPhone 3GS. Since 2007 and the first iPhone, the company had been lagging in terms of network capacity, but only the strong denunciation on social media led the firm to speed up its efforts. While at that time it was using social media solely for public relations, it started to build a team to answer customers' requests on social media. It set a trend for big corporate companies to start taking customers seriously on social media.

Another example of a pioneering firm that started taking online complaints seriously was KLM during the volcanic eruption in Iceland in 2010 (Baer 2016). KLM at that time received a considerable amount of online hate. They realized that they had the choice between leaving the complaints unanswered or addressing them all, but if they were to start doing so, they would have to commit to such an approach. And they did decide to answer all of those complaints.

There is a clear case for dealing tirelessly with *all* negative evaluations from your customers on social media (Baer 2016). While negative information can diffuse at a swift pace on social media, the same media can also play the role of a channel through which firms can create more intimate interactions with their customers. Taking control of the conversation is the first step. It is, however, not only about addressing the concerns. Engaging with online haters makes clear business sense despite the investment in time and resources. Even small organizations like Fresh Brothers Pizza or hotels have an interest in doing so. Baer (ibid., 17) notes three key advantages among others: what he calls "turning bad news into good news" by retaining unhappy customers instead of losing them, creating "customer advocacy" by generating intimacy in customer relationships, and, finally, obtaining customer insights. All those factors can help the firm build what strategic management scholars like to call a "competitive advantage"—a way to be in a more advantageous position than your competitors.

First, answering customers' negative evaluations can help spin those unhappy customers around. Research has proven that proper complaint management could convert hostile customers into loyal future buyers (Johnston and Mehra 2002). Baer (2016, 17) notes how businesses "plac[e] too much emphasis on outbound marketing and the attraction of new customers, with comparatively little attention paid to keeping the customers they have already paid to get." Addressing social media complaints, showing how they have been treated and how much effort has been invested in the improvement, is crucial to regaining the trust of the broader base of stakeholders. Throwing positive answers at negativity can turn an interaction around. If investments have been made into customer care, organizations might even want to encourage customers to provide them with feedback. Organizations can then be quickly aware if something is going wrong. The dissatisfied stakeholders are well identified, and there is less risk that they spread the word if their requests have been addressed.

Customer advocacy enables a form of intimacy in the firm-customer relationship. This unique proximity can help the firm create a competitive advantage. As put by Baer (2016, 21), "when people have a problem, and that problem is solved, they love you for it." Some companies that have haters also have the most loyal customers: a good example is Apple, which faces a crowd of hardcore haters, intensely disliking the identity of their product. In the meantime, this antagonism forced loyal customers to get out of the woods to defend the Apple culture. Apple is one of those firms that polarizes the audience: haters and supporters are two sides of the same coin, and to have a core of loyal defenders, haters might be required. When firms face haters, the best way to respond is to gather their supporters and defend their identity and culture. In the meantime, one of the best ways to create this intimacy is to build a strong narrative around the firm-customer relationship. Dietrich (2014) suggests building on positive stories about the company, the customer, or the product. Storytelling humanizes the company and enables a stronger link with its stakeholders.

Firms can learn critical insights from disgruntled customers. Complaints on social media might highlight some critical areas of improvement. In other words, haters might sometimes make a good point. Addressing those complaints, but even more important, showing how they have been addressed and how much effort has been invested in the improvement, can change customers' perception for the best (Johnston and Mehra 2002). Negative evaluations on social media are free intelligence to improve business and build a competitive advantage. It then takes some energy to listen to this feedback. One way to mobilize both the organization and those passionate but cynical customers is to create a call for action (Dietrich 2014), and thus a joint commitment to improve the organization. For those firms that have been able to build an active community around their product or service, negative feedback might progressively move to the offstage, lowering the reputational risk (ibid.).

There are however downsides in trying to address all customers' complaints and hug even your most hateful haters. As noted by Baer, onstage haters do not always have the most delightful intention, and their reaction to your effort to take back the conversation is not always positive. Sometimes, "brand vandals expect to prey on fear" (Earl and Waddington 2013, 175). They want to see your firm struggle in reacting to the complaints, and they want to see the situation spiral out of control. They want their minute of fame on social media by making their case buzz and an audience cheering for the bad publicity they generate. Sometimes, organizations may voluntarily accept stigma and disapproval, anticipating any negative social evaluations coming their way. As noted in the section on crisis management in Chapter 2, organizations often do their *mea culpa*, but they might do it preemptively. For example, the University of Cambridge, although not a for-profit service provider per se, recently recognized that they might have profited from the slave trade and colonization and launched an official inquiry into its history. The idea is to anticipate any criticism by identifying the existence and the strength of those links with the slave trade.[5] As an employee of the university (and we could expect students to feel the same), with shamefully limited knowledge of U.K. history, I was upset to hear about the possible existence of those links to slavery, and the possible risk of courtesy stigma. However, such a strategy would enable the university to deal with future bad press around the question. Thus accepting blame is a double-edged sword. Placing oneself in a negatively evaluated category may help deflect future blame, but it can attract the blame in the first place. This situation generates negative attention toward the organization and, ultimately, cognitive illegitimacy. The truth can, however, be used to stop the "snowball from being turned into an avalanche" (ibid., 180).

In this section, we have discussed the power of creating intimacy with disgruntled customers. In most cases, customers, as a key stakeholder, can be a dangerous source of reputational risk. For organizations or individuals, responding to all of their haters online can seem crazy. There are clear risks in doing that—especially as admitting blame can be a double-edged sword. We have seen however, that organizations might want to invest this time and energy to retain customers they have often struggled to get in the first place. In addition, customer complaints can help organizations build a competitive advantage. First, they can reinforce the relationship with customers. And second, they can generate insights that might orient organizational adaptation.

Those customer complaints, in a similar vein to external criticism, might negatively affect employees and organizational members. In such situations, organizations need to communicate internally to ensure that members can safely protect their self-image and apprehend those outside pressures,

Internal Communication: Managing Employees
in Negatively Evaluated Firms and Industry

We have seen in the previous section, and in the chapter on resilience to hostility, that negative evaluations of an organization could be an important catalyst for positive change. Negative evaluations of an organization—whether they come from customers, as we explored in the previous section, or other stakeholders—can directly affect its members (Roulet 2017). Employees of disapproved of organizations will perceive outside criticism as a threat to their self-perception and self-esteem (Roulet 2015b). They are likely to either leave an organization that does not enhance their identity anymore or change the organization from the inside so that it does. Bolton (2019) even argues that firms can "hitch . . . a ride" on a hostile social movement. Organizations can capitalize on hostility to create customer and brand value by realigning their values with those of the movements that opposed them in the first place.

Employees can serve as a bridge between hostile stakeholders producing negative evaluations of their firm and the firm itself. Organizational culture is a lens through which identity threats can be dealt with (Ravasi and Schultz 2006). Employees, because they are the central internal stakeholder, provide a mediating force and an opportunity to interpret what is happening outside the firm to ultimately incorporate it in the firm's strategy and purpose. A good example is the group of Google employees who protested against how the firm handled discrimination and sexual harassment cases (Etter 2018). The negative evaluation this time did not come from the outside; it came from the inside. Initially, one could expect such a phenomenon of insider hostility to trigger negative evaluations from outsiders and it might have. Those massive demonstrations—60 percent of the Google employees took a stand—did make the point that Google's organizational culture had considerable room for improvement. In the meantime, they signaled that insiders could challenge a poor culture, and that the firm had the power to change. They also suggest that the firm's "culture [is one] that empowers employees to stand up and participate" (ibid.). There is a human factor in mostly technology-based and focused firms. Google is not only computers; they are humans, after all! Employees' distrust with regard to their employers can build up over a long period and be driven by threats to employees' self-esteem. For example, Hewlett-Packard experienced a slowly rising level of distrust over a long period, from 1995 to 2010, as employees increasingly felt they were treated unfairly by the management (Elsbach, Stigliani, and Stroud 2012).

An important point made by social scientists is that resistance from insiders and employees usually slows down organizational change (Rousseau and Tijoriwala 1999). Employees care enormously about the way their firm is perceived, to the point that they sometimes pick firms as a function of their image so that those new joiners can then benefit from their employer's image (Turban and Greening 1997). In the case of Google, the employees' fear of suffering courtesy stigma—their concern that Google might be disapproved of, and consequently its employees too—might have motivated them to take a stand against their corporate culture. We often tend to think that the motivations for change are internal to an organization; it can be seen as political or self-serving by employees, and thus be discounted. By comparison, outside criticism can be accepted as more objective to motivate organizational change. However, sometimes the inside criticism is triggered for the preemption of outsiders' hostility. In the case of Google, the movement started by the employees might have helped trigger positive organizational change. The fear of negative evaluations yielded an opportunity to adjust before suffering the consequences of inertia.

The opinion of employees matters, and if a wave of outsider-driven criticism harms their self-esteem, they will be the first to jump off the ship. Moreover, organizations need everybody on board in heavy water. As Earl and Waddington (2013, 221) have noted, organizations facing a reputational crisis need to "rais[e] their army" and make their employees their advocates. The critical factor here is the organization's ability to foster and maintain a strong sense of identity during a crisis. If the employees identify with their firm, despite a storm of unfavorable evaluations, they are likely to stay loyal to it and in fact fight back against external hostility. This is why internal communication is crucial when facing hostility (Roulet 2017). Employees need to be convinced that their organization is in the right as much as outsiders need to be convinced. This is the only way to help them maintain a positive image of themselves in the wake of a crisis. Preemptively and to shield themselves against future reputational crises, organizations—consciously or not—tend to reframe their history to present themselves in the most flattering light (Galvin, Ventresca, and Hudson 2005).

Internal communication in times of reputational crises is essential, but it often relies on fostering an "us vs. them" divide. As we have seen, individuals in stigmatized occupations do not necessarily experience shame, and they might even hold themselves in high esteem because of it. What some take as arrogance is the firm belief of being right, and doing something that matters. In fact, during reputational crises, firms can play on their industry macro culture to help their employees respond to an external threat to their reputation (Roulet 2015b; 2019b): macro cultures provide coherent sets of values and beliefs to discount outsiders' criticism. For example, in the case of investment banks, the idea that risk is reasonable and should be rewarded helped employees justify practices that were heavily disapproved of by the public (Roulet 2019a). To a certain extent, other industries have already reproduced the strategy of investment banks of fostering a macro culture to make their companies attractive. Strategy consulting firms do rely on the same mechanisms. For organizational or industry culture to shield a company from a wave of hostility, it needs to be endogenously spread through the organization. Mechanisms that encourage mutual exchanges between employees, in particular at different hierarchical levels, such as mentoring (Gill, Roulet, and Kerridge 2018), can support the processing of negative evaluations of an organization by its employees. With mentoring or other processes of formal and informal peer support, employees can express their fears and their concern, and normalize them.

Organizations need to develop a sense of pride among their employees and applicants by playing the pedagogical role of documenting their societal importance. If employees are told they are the best, they will rightly believe so, and will feel more confident about their work and their broader contribution to society through the mediating role of their organization. In the same vein, maintaining typical work practices relies on explaining the rationale to those who will engage in those practices, so they can embrace this logic and make it their own. In such a context, the employees will be able to resist external hostility against those practices.

Still, the faith of employees might not always be enough to rebuild a broken reputation. It's when external communication kicks in: it takes careful positioning and framing to deflect a reputational crisis.

External Communication, Reputational Crises, and Stakeholder Management

Throughout the book, I have defended the idea that negative social evaluations could be beneficial. Still, I acknowledged the existence of boundary conditions. Negative social evaluations can spin out of control, and in a majority of cases they will deprive firms of a reputational advantage (Waller and Younger 2017) and harm their bottom lines (Roberts and Dowling 2002). There are piling-up mechanisms through which moral outrage grows exponentially as social actors join the movement to signal their virtue. Even when some aspects of negative social evaluations can be beneficial, they need to be managed so that the negative consequences do not overshadow the benefits. In this section, we focus on the implications of negative evaluations for stakeholder management.

Managing reputational crises does require evaluation of the stakeholder network in which the organization is embedded. As put by Earl and Waddington (2013, 7) "becoming closer to your audience can give you better protection." In this sense, stakeholders who identify with the targeted actors, who experience a sense of intimacy with it, are likely to support them in the wake of a controversy.

However, it is not always the case, and stakeholders might have no plan to collaborate. Stakeholders can engage in a memorable but also cost-effective campaign of denigration—for example, Friends of the Earth targeted BP with "BP rebranded" (Earl and Waddington 2013), distorting the logo of the firm to harm the firm's reputation in a memorable way. To manage a reputational crisis, Coombs (2007) suggests focusing first on attribution—who can be held responsible for the crisis? Was the crisis about something under or outside the control of the targeted organization? With the attribution of responsibility, the previous relationships with stakeholders and the organizational response to the crisis will determine the potential damage to the organizational reputation. The right organizational response to the crisis should shape this attribution mechanism by changing the perception stakeholders have of the organization's role in the crisis. For example, if an organization is not responsible for a crisis, it should deflect the blame and show evidence of who should be held responsible. By contrast, if the firm is responsible, it should immediately engage in fixing the situation to repair the relationships with stakeholders. In the case of the BP oil spill, the firm ignored for too long some peripheral stakeholders who had enormously suffered from the accident, such as the local fishermen. The firm should have assessed and recognized without delay the damages for a variety of stakeholders and tried to make amends.

A fundamental approach to understanding stakeholders' reaction to a reputational crisis is to look at their initial expectations with regard to the organization (Lee, Lim, and Drumwright 2018). Organizations are often adversely judged on the basis of either their competence or their morality. Lee and colleagues ran an experiment and found that the stakeholders' expectations regarding an organization strongly drive their evaluation. When organizations are judged highly competent, stakeholders' expectations with regard to the organization's ability will be high, and if the crisis is about the lack of competence, the reputational risk will be higher. In the same vein, socially responsible organizations create high expectations of morality among stakeholders. If such actors are caught misbehaving, the blow to their reputation is more serious. They also found that for morality-related crises, organizations that have both competency- and morality-based reputations fare better. The practical implications of their work are that such a hybrid reputation is a crucial asset. Favoring one form of reputation (competency- or morality-based) can create higher expectations and consequently higher reputational damages.

As I have stressed, attracting disapproval can be a deliberate strategy, and part of a well-crafted communication plan. In this case, triggering negative evaluations is counterbalanced with regular efforts to recalibrate the perception of the organization. For example, we looked at how ACT UP or Extinction Rebellion would attract negative evaluations because of their illegitimate actions and then would stress the positive objectives of the organization as a way to minimize the reputational damages from their actions. Beyond the ethical concerns of such a strategy in some cases, as I will discuss in the conclusion, such a tactic requires a careful evaluation of the weight of the different stakeholders involved. Organizations also need to identify potential supporters who might be attracted by some dimensions other audiences would disapprove of. There is, however, a porous boundary between illegitimate and criminal actions: by employing this strategy, organizations often take the risk of breaking the law.

Beyond the factual ability to survive fines and lawsuits, the key to understanding whether firms that faced disapproval are allowed to remain is their ability to convince the stakeholders that are both directly affected by the scandal and have a significant impact on the business activity. Firms might have more or less room to do so. Such a communication strategy directed toward a crucial stakeholder also includes the cosmetic side of things. For example, the French historic bank Credit Lyonnais was on the verge of bankruptcy in 1993, then survived in-extremis, but changed its brand to become LCL. The idea was to "put the past behind" while trying to rejuvenate the image of the company. Changing the name and the logo did help the firm change its evaluation by key stakeholders, but this can take a fair amount of time if the previous identity of the organization was cognitively well anchored among audiences.

While most of the organizations we discussed in this section suffered "event-based" stigma (Hudson 2008)—a reputational crisis limited in time—some others suffer persistent negative evaluations because of their core attributes. In such cases, there are tremendous efforts required of members of this core stigmatized category to distance themselves from negative evaluations. Kisha Lashley, for example, studied how the U.S. industry of medical cannabis legitimized itself to escape its stigmatized condition and ultimately survive (Lashley and Pollock, forthcoming). They contributed to shifting the public discourse: while initially they were considered to be supplying a drug, they presented themselves as focusing on patients' health and rights. Core-stigmatized groups can start by introducing a broad set of relatable moral values. This first step helps create a new prototype that actors can associate themselves with. In other words, stigmatized actors engage in decoupling: they still embrace stigmatized practices while at the same time trying to distance themselves from those practices in the eyes of an audience. In practice, stigmatized actors should find a way to link their activities to broadly recognized moral norms, and publicly exhibit ambivalence toward stigmatized practices.

Negative social evaluations and reputational crises can encourage stakeholder coordination. Moral outrage can indeed create opportunities for collective action (Spring, Cameron, and Cikara 2018). Moreover, moral indignation can spread fast, as joining in is made desirable by the opportunity to signal virtue. At the moment, it has become common for people to draw attention to the lack of gender diversity in whatever events are advertised or pictured on social media. Such outraged reactions are easy to express; they make the denouncer look like a war hero without much effort. And there are unfortunately plenty of opportunities to denounce gender imbalance in panels and debates—the problem is common and widespread. What is a real issue—gender representation—and deserves to be pointed out is regrettably used instrumentally—maybe not always consciously—by some as a way to gain visibility. This situation also does not mean those outraged people will necessarily engage in changing the status quo. They might well just enjoy the visibility benefit and the pros of virtue signaling but will not act beyond their effortless social media post. The attention it provides for the issue does, however, put it on the agenda of other organized stakeholders. This brings us to, more broadly, the societal implications of negative evaluations.

Societal Implications: How Negative Evaluations Divide Us and What Can Be Done About It

This book explored how the power of being divisive has been used for the worse. It looked in particular at the way politicians play on division to gain visibility and gather voters. It linked this phenomenon to the development of fake news and conspiracy theories supporting the formulation and the spread of negative social evaluations. Those phenomena could have devastating societal implications.

In the previous chapter, we discussed the Trump case extensively, but it is easy to understand how the mechanisms of visibility through controversies and group polarization can fuel political extremism. By taking controversial stances, extreme politicians erect strong boundaries between their in-group of voters and antagonized audiences. Their position will get them significantly negative evaluations from opponents. At the same time, they will be able to convince marginalized voters to join a group of supporters that they can identify with. The identity of this in-group is attractive because it is clearly defined and comes with the recognized voice of what wrongly seems to be a bold political leader, who "says things as they are." The more people feel marginalized in society, the more attractive the sense of belonging offered by groups supporting fascist political leaders. This will create an ever-expanding rift between opponents and proponents—people will have less and less in common, and division will make the two parties unreconcilable.

As noted by Amnesty International, the highly divisive political rhetoric we are currently experiencing is dangerous for social cohesion.[6] Extreme political narratives are aimed at shocking audiences. To do so, they are increasingly built on fear and blame. This hate speech usually targets minorities on the basis of their religion, race, culture, or sexuality. These dehumanizing discourses have enabled many populist politicians to access power by playing on their constituents' identities. Moreover, some politicians do not only divide, they also bend public perception to serve their purpose. Public relations companies, for example, have started engaging in "astroturfing" on behalf of political leaders. Astroturfing is the idea of making the appearance of broad public support for an issue by fabricating this support, for example, through rhetorical strategies but also fake social media accounts and content (Dietrich 2014).

This dangerous situation of growing societal divide is not only fed by the political sphere. As we saw in the previous chapter, anecdotal evidence suggests that TV talk shows tend to invite divisive personalities to attract more viewers. Such choices may give a voice to extreme views and potentially also polarize opinions of audiences, ultimately favoring those extreme political views. In an article from the newspaper *Liberation*, the journalist cited an anonymous producer of talk shows in which divisive debates are common: "Our society is on the verge of implosion. It is divided, fractured, dark, without perspective. Look at how people insult each other on social media: TV channels are quiet in comparisons. We offer clashes on TV because people argue with each other all day long in real life."[7]

The rise in populism is one phenomenon that I have linked to negative social evaluations throughout this book. In particular, I discussed those evaluations that take the shape of conspiracy theories—and their implications for society. While we looked at social actors who take advantage of conspiracy theories as a fairly recent phenomenon, as illustrated by the notable success of Infowars, we have not directly examined the potential threats to democracy that it can generate. Anna Merlan (2019) blames more fundamental issues: "our increasingly rigid class structure, one that leaves many people feeling locked into their circumstances and desperate to find someone to blame," a "rising disenfranchisement, a feeling many people have that they are shut out of systems of power, pounding furiously at iron doors that will never open to admit them." The pace of social change creates a fertile ground for people who are looking for a simple, straightforward but coherent set of answers. The issue is that those answers are not reflecting the truth and are themselves a lever that extreme politicians can use to rise to power—furthering the disenfranchisement of their people and potentially manipulating the media landscape to keep fueling hate and division.

So what can we do about such an increasingly worrying situation? What can we do to limit the alienating power of divisive arguments? One key driver that was identified is fake news and conspiracy theories. Because of divisive stories, malfeasant social actors can estrange some parts of the population. The role of social media has been acknowledged, with Facebook committing in 2019 to actively fight fake accounts spreading divisive news—which could be observed during both the Brexit and the Trump campaigns. They recognized the existence of billions of accounts manipulated to influence elections.[8] They mobilized forty people in the Dublin office for the European elections of May 2019. The methods of manipulation are sometimes subtle and involve creating Facebook groups revolving around topics of broad interest (such as sports or health) and then slowly transforming them into fake news and extreme political advocacy. Online activist groups such as Avaaz have also used their resources to support the movement against fake news on social media. However, most social media firms do confess to being overwhelmed by the task and the challenge they have created for themselves.

Because of the threat conspiracy theories and fake news represent for democracy, public resources and governments need to be involved in countering the issue. We need a public service against fake news—with an international reach but also an understanding idiosyncratic to the different national situations. Finland has taken this problem very seriously by launching a comprehensive initiative in 2014, to educate its citizens to understand and identify fake news.[9] If social media cannot address the problem, those who consume social media content may be able to do so. The move was a reaction to propaganda campaigns launched online by Russia, its powerful neighbor. Finland invited fake news experts and started rethinking its educational system to encourage critical thinking, especially with regard to online content. As put by one of the Finnish educators involved, reported by CNN, "The first line of defense is the kindergarten teacher." For example, they put children in a situation of looking for information online on a specific topic and needing to critically assess the content they can put together. The students are trained to think twice about sharing or liking on social media; to question who has written what, with what bias; and to determine whether the information can be confirmed with another source. Finland also fosters this effort by stressing the identity and the values of the country (democracy, the rule of law, freedom, social and gender equality) and how they can be at odds with the divisive news that is shared by malfeasant sources on social media. Other countries are now replicating this model to try to fight the pandemic.

Beyond educative means, a public service against fake news could engage in direct fact-checking, challenging items of fake news, and preventing their diffusion. In France, some services of mainstream media are focused on debunking fake news, including a department of the French Press Agency. The economic model for those services is, however, precarious, in an industry that is already struggling for resources and ultimately survival. Fake news checkers do not produce novel coverage per se; they cover existing news differently. Thus those services only share the pie of what remains of an audience that quickly moves from one piece of news to a fresher one.

For this reason, fact-checking services could strongly benefit from public funding.

Anti-stigma campaigns could also help fight the spread of divisive evaluations. Smith (2012) revealed how those who challenge stigma can be more or less active, in the same way as stigmatizers, and that their position at the center of social networks can help them fight stigma. Smith identified two strategies used to fight stigma: educating the stigmatizers (changing their perspective and informing them) or challenging stigmatization (confronting stigmatization with opposing new arguments). The public system put in place in Finland relies on educating the masses so that they do not join the stigmatizers and will question the information they are given. However, most of the strategies employed at the moment to fight fake news rely on confronting the stigmatizers—opposing them without fostering the critical thinking that would help them question their own beliefs in an autonomous manner. A team of social psychologists at the Interdisciplinary Center Herzliya in Israel has gone one step further. This research program is aimed at understanding the psychology of the Israel-Palestine conflict and solving it by encouraging paradoxical thinking. In the *Proceedings of the National Academy of Science*, the scientists leading the project show the result of a large-scale experiment (Hameiri et al. 2014). Instead of disagreeing with the participants, they took the same views, then developed them to an extreme point until it appeared totally absurd to those participants. Confronted with the absurdity, the participants would rethink their beliefs and change them. These findings highlight the importance of putting ourselves in stigmatizers' and fake news producers' shoes to better understand their motivation, their core underlying beliefs, and challenge them efficiently.

While I stressed the benefits politicians derive from blaming marginalized groups for the hardship faced by a country, I also concluded that as this behavior becomes a norm, it might, fortunately, become more marginal. I argued that there are diminishing returns to political impression management. The more politicians rely on divisive rhetoric, the less it will create a competitive advantage by contrast with other political leaders. One may hope that when we reach this stage, the pendulum might switch back and the opinion and voters might start valuing again positive rhetoric promoting inclusiveness.

Some recent empirical research is also more positive about the state of our political division. Yudkin (2018) and his colleagues collected data from a representative sample of eight thousand Americans. They asked them about core beliefs on policy issues, including abortion or immigration. As noted by Yudkin in a *New York Times* editorial, "differences in political belief are manifestations of deeply opposing visions—not just about what makes good policy, but also about *what makes a good person*." Those different perspectives on virtue get the two sides to misunderstand what motivates their stances. To enable a dialogue again between divided parts of our society, the different parties need to acknowledge the roles of their beliefs and establish a common language. This common language would rely on core ideas (for example, we should do good, we are all entitled to fair treatment, and so on) defined in an unequivocal way. On the basis of this common language, we can bring different parts of society back together. The main challenge, however, is that for some of the crucial obstacles our society is facing (climate change, inequality, and so on), it has proven very hard to build this common understanding.

CONCLUSION

Throughout this book, I defended the idea that negative evaluations could be beneficial, under certain boundary conditions. Integrating antecedents, re-actions, and consequences of negative social evaluations in the same frame-work can yield new contributions for the broader fields of organization theory, sociology, communication, and management. The book started by clarifying the definitions in the field of social evaluations and explaining why nega-tive evaluations exist—in particular, what motivates actors to produce those evaluations. Then a model in two parts was offered. First was fleshing out the processes through which social actors build resilience to negative social evalu-ations. There are two sets of processes—social weighting (discarding the out-siders, overvaluing the insiders) and group ideology (building unique values, beliefs, and practices at the group level to protect self-esteem and maintain a high level of identification). Those two sets of processes lead to cognitive dissonance, which ultimately cuts the in-group from the out-group—for the better (negative evaluations and their damages to self-perception are ignored) and for the worse (the need for change is ignored). In the second part of the model, we focused on the clear-cut benefits of negative social evaluations. One trigger is vital to explain those benefits: the visibility generated by negative evaluations. Only this visibility can enable signaling characteristics that will be valued by crucial stakeholders, through the support of networks that can bridge the gaps between those audiences. The risk of further polarization of audiences is obvious—which explains how politicians and other prominent agents have benefitted from being divisive, but also how they might further fracture our society.

Further research will be able to solidify this stream of work—investigating not only the counterintuitive ideas that negative evaluations are beneficial but also that positive evaluations can have adverse consequences for targeted actors. In addition, the negative consequences of negative evaluations, for individuals, groups, and society as a whole, are still not fully understood. An unfavorable evaluation is a particularly contemporary phenomenon, as we pointed out when linking it to the occurrence of fake news or conspiracy theories. It might well be that a different macro context will make the phenomena—in particular, their adverse consequences for individuals, organizations, and democracy—identified in this book less prevalent. For example, Sirola and Pitesa (2018) show that in a positive macroeconomic context, organizational members see themselves as having more control over outcomes and are thus harsher when they evaluate others, simply because the lack of performance cannot be attributed to bad luck or external factors. They also note that evaluators are more positive when able to observe the outcome of their actions, as they overestimate their contribution to the result because of the heightened sense of control caused by the positive macroeconomic context.

Nevertheless, future inquiry on negative social evaluations—whether it comes from organization studies, sociology, economics, communication, or management—will be able to ground itself in the comprehensive framework I have offered here. There are multiple theoretical contributions in this book. First, it provides a review of the literature on negative evaluations bridging the gaps between different fields. This framework offers some room to understand better how social actors react to negative evaluations. Second, it differentiates two forms of positive outcomes of negative evaluations—emerging from two processes: resisting and leveraging. In that sense, the model is comprehensive and covers the links between different levels of analysis. Finally, it builds on the role of audiences to understand the limitations and boundary conditions of our model. This focus on audiences also helps better identify when and how negative social evaluations can be more beneficial than damaging. From a practical point of view, without simplifying them, this work covers a wide range of concepts and empirical findings that can be useful to practitioners. In particular, I discussed how individuals within organizations could maintain positive evaluations and preserve themselves from negative ones. *Divisive* has unfortunately become one of the main adjectives we associate with leadership.

From a marketing point of view, negative evaluations on social media can be managed to the advantage of the targeted firm. Finally, the societal implications of new evaluative phenomena such as fake news and conspiracy theories was explored—and I discussed what can be done as a collective to tackle this threat to democracy.

This Conclusion will go back to some critical elements of discussion emerging from the arguments developed in this book. First is a discussion on negative social evaluations from an ethical point of view. In many ways, the production and reception of negative evaluations raises moral questions: Is it right to produce negative evaluations? To attract them voluntarily? To use them for one's benefit? The next section touches upon the methodological developments in the field of social evaluations from qualitative to quantitative approaches. I then discuss the prevalence of evaluations in modern society and the contribution of the economics of attention in understanding this phenomenon. And the final section looks into areas of future research that can build on the theoretical arguments offered in this book.

The Ethics of Negative Social Evaluations

In the last chapter, the fall from grace of Bell Pottinger in 2017 was mentioned. Bell Pottinger was one of the major PR firms, infamous for its list of despised clients. Bell Pottinger engaged in a campaign, relying on social media and fake news, to convince black South Africans that they were more miserable than they should be because of white-owned private companies. The campaign was aimed at supporting one of the firm's clients owned by businessmen of Indian descent. The numerous strategies used by politicians to manage the perception audiences have were then discussed. The strategies used by NGOs to gain visibility were also explored. In those situations, we can legitimately question the ethicality of those strategies. They are aimed at manipulating and duping audiences and stakeholders. Their consequences can sometimes be disastrous for society when they contribute to reinforcing divisions. In this book, we looked at the instrumentality of being divisive. But we have not properly questioned the moral and normative aspects of such a strategy. The book described a social phenomenon more than it advocated for those strategies.

While the cases of Bell Pottinger or divisive politicians are often clearly condemnable, the strategies of NGOs engaging in illegitimate practices raise additional questions when it comes to ethics. NGOs such as

Extinction Rebellion are unconsciously fueled by a utilitarian perspective (Mill, 1863/2016). Utilitarian ethics postulate that the moral decision is the one that maximizes the happiness of the highest number of parties. Extinction Rebellion believes in the urgency of the climate change threat, and their extreme actions are aimed at triggering a reaction as soon as possible. Considering the extent of the danger implied by climate change, the disruption they engage in is marginal in comparison. From a utilitarian perspective, disruption is justified. The end justifies the means—and in this case, negative social evaluations can help bring attention—and ultimately support—for important societal causes.

Beyond shifting the focus of attention to crucial issues, can negative social evaluations yield benefits for society? When explaining the very existence of negative social evaluations in the Introduction I went back to the early mechanisms of stigmatization in Ancient Greece. Stigmatization was aimed at casting aside some undesirable individuals, who could be considered as a threat for society. Ethically questionable motivations sometimes drive the very existence of evaluations. For example, Vidaillet (2016) argues that performance systems emerged as a tool of social control because of human drives for envy and social comparison.

According to Bayer (2008), stigmatization is usually considered dangerous because it erects a barrier between those who need help and potential supporters and caregivers. Taking the context of public health, one could indeed argue that the stigmatization of AIDS has prevented many individuals from accessing treatment for decades. However, we could wonder whether stigmatization, in some cases, does not effectively reduce the prevalence of risky behaviors. For example, smokers or drunk drivers may be stigmatized for the collective benefits of society. In our work on waste management, we observed that sorting waste had become a prosocial behavior, while not doing so could trigger stigmatization (Cristofini and Roulet 2019). As put by Bayer (2008, 469), we need to "distinguish between stigmatization that served to turn the offender into an outcast and shaming that held out the prospects for re-integration." In this case, being the target of stigma may have negative personal implications on the short term but positive ones for society by curbing potential deviance. This argument, however, relies on the idea that stigma can avoid being dehumanizing. Phenomena of exclusion tend to be contagious and spiral out of control—thus often having negative and unfair implications, whoever is targeted. Burris (2008, 475) adds that "[stigma] is arbitrary in that it is decentralized and unlinked to any explicit form of institutional authorization or accountability."

Manipulating social evaluations and impression management can be deeply unethical. They can create further division in our society. In some cases, however, some have argued that negative evaluations can play a decisive societal role. First, they can generate attention for critical issues. Second, they can marginalize antisocial behaviors. Those two arguments rely on a utilitarian perspective, and for this reason, can also be questioned. Does the end always justify the means? Stigma comes in degrees (Burris 2008), and not all negative social evaluations are barbaric—but as the title of this book suggests, they are divisive rather than inclusive. They antagonize different parts of our society and potentially threaten our social fabric.

Methods to Empirically Capture Negative Social Evaluations

The social theory developed in this book leverages a wide range of empirical evidence from qualitative findings, including case studies and ethnography (for example, Hudson and Okhuysen 2009; Helms and Patterson 2014; Tracey and Philips 2016; Hampel and Tracey 2017; Lashley and Pollock, forthcoming) to quantitative insights, coming from experiments (for example, Park and Maner 2009; Norton et al. 2012; Cho and Fast 2012) and large-scale datasets (for example Pontikes, Negro, and Rao 2010; Piazza and Peretti 2015). My work on negative social evaluations, for example, often combines qualitative and quantitative methods (Roulet 2015a; 2015b; 2019a; Shymko and Roulet 2017). I have bridged the gap between a variety of mechanisms, usually supported by very different forms of evidence. For future research, there would be clear benefits in articulating some of those mechanisms through unified empirical approaches. In addition, the operationalization of those concepts can help us consider the divergence between them (Pollock et al., forthcoming). Differentiating illegitimacy and stigma in practice could help advance definitional debates in the field of negative social evaluations (Hampel and Tracey 2017; Helms, Patterson, and Hudson 2019).

Qualitative work has already provided us with a wide range of comprehensive theoretical models. Tracey and Philips (2016) provide a detailed model of stigma management through identity work. Hudson and Okhuysen (2009) provide a rich account of how organizations and individuals manage courtesy stigma. Both those crucial pieces build on rich ethnographic data and participant observation. Participant observation in negatively perceived contexts and organizations does have implications for the researchers: it can require the researcher to take some liberty with his or her identity during fieldwork (Roulet et al. 2017). It might involve "covert" (or partly "covert") research during which the researchers selectively reveal their identity and purpose as researchers (ibid.; see also, for example, Stenger and Roulet 2018). This approach does not come without ethical questions: Humphrey's (1970) covert work on homosexuality is often questioned with regard to its moral implications. He risked revealing the homosexuality of the subjects he observed to their families. Studying the stigmatized has often involved investigating the margins of society. Researchers may not share the same identity as those they observe, but empathy can help them connect with their field of inquiry (Claus et al. 2019).

Historical perspectives are also vital to studying negative evaluations. Hampel and Tracey (2017) complemented existing qualitative work by looking at how organizations can purge stigma in the long term. Those historical models are extremely rich and solidly inform our understanding of how negative evaluations emerge and are managed. They build on historical narratives (Gill, Gill, and Roulet 2018), which can help negative evaluations scholars build a longer-term perspective on the construction of stigma (Galvin, Ventresca, and Hudson 2005). Such an approach requires a large amount of data from a variety of stakeholders and audiences to triangulate different perceptions. There might also be biases in the reporting and the style of evaluations, depending on the historical context. Nevertheless, historical studies of contested industries, organizations, or social categories would be incredibly welcome. Qualitative methods might yield positive contributions to the definition of concepts as we start comparing cases across different contexts, geographically and temporally distant.

Experiments are also a method of choice to study negative evaluations. However, they often focus on individual-level stigmatization or a dyadic level of analysis (for example, Park and Maner 2009; Norton et al. 2012). They do offer opportunities to evaluate network effects, which are prevalent in the diffusion of evaluations (Bastiaensens et al. 2014). Studies based on surveys have also yielded exciting findings at the individual level (among others, the ground-breaking research of Ragins and Cornwell in 2001 on workplace discrimination against LGBT employees). Nevertheless, they rarely bridge the gap between different levels of analysis. There are relevant mechanisms to unveil linking the evaluations of individuals and organizations, and outcomes at those different levels of analysis (Roulet 2017). Considering the importance of context in the formation of social judgments (Bitektine 2011), psychological experiments would benefit—like other methodological approaches—from an explicit assessment of the generalizability of their findings.

Research on negative social evaluations has also given birth to innovative big data approaches, relying on social media (Etter et al. 2018) or newspaper articles (Vergne 2011). Those two sources of empirical materials have been proven theoretically useful as well to understanding evaluative processes (Etter, Ravasi, and Colleoni 2019; Roulet and Clemente 2018). Most large-scale analyses of negative social evaluations have so far been based on newspaper articles (Vergne 2011; Roulet 2019a), usually focusing on significant outlets in the United States covering the range of the political spectrum, such as the *New York Times*, the *Washington Post*, and the *Wall Street Journal*.

There are various approaches to media content analyses. Some researchers of negative evaluations have for example advocated for counts of negative occurrences (for example, number of negative articles) (Vergne 2011; 2012) while others have investigated the content of items produced by the media (Roulet 2015b; 2019a), for example by relying on sentiment analysis (Etter, Ravasi, and Colleoni 2019). Some studies focus on a smaller amount of textual data but rely on more fine-grained analysis (Roulet 2015a; Clemente and Gabbioneta 2017). Usually those analyses take an industry as their level of analysis (Vergne 2012; Roulet 2019a) and look at the intra-industry variance in negative evaluations. Machine learning and topic modeling could yield exciting methodological advancement to understand how scandals unfold and the role of media in social evaluations (Hannigan et al. 2019).

Social media is an excellent empirical source to understand the diffusion of negative social evaluation because of the traceability of network mechanisms: actors are connected through each other, and the audiences can be easily mapped (Roulet and Clemente 2018). By contrast, existing work on traditional media has heavily focused on the tone of media content (Roulet 2019a) rather than considering audiences and their constituents as a network. This approach is partly explained by the fact that newspaper data do not present a lot of opportunities to capture networks. Complex approaches to controversies on social media in computer sciences consider both the tone of the content and the network structure. Those perspectives have enabled scientists to identify "conversation graphs" and—on the basis of those graphs—measure the intensity of controversies on Twitter (Garimella et al. 2018, 1). Conversation graphs capture users and the nature of their interactions—posts, comments, mentions, endorsements. According to those approaches, what makes a controversy is a "clustered structure." This hypothesis is based on the fact that a "controversial topic entails different sides with opposing points of view, and individuals on the same side tend to endorse and amplify each other's arguments (ibid., 2)." In other words, a controversy is made of clusters of actors opposed with each other in different sets of arguments. Future research could further uncover processes of polarization by using such data.

A "Society of Evaluations" and the Economics of Attention

Have we become over-reliant on social evaluations as a society? Have we entered an era when practically everything has become social evaluation? Social evaluations are regularly produced to assess service providers, whether they are restaurants, hotels, or exchange partners on eBay. This profusion of social evaluations emerged concurrently with the prevalence of platform businesses (among others AirBnB, Uber, Etsy). Beyond evaluating others, we are, in return, assessed regularly when using services. We now spend a considerable amount of time interpreting the evaluations of others to decide with whom to interact—what services or products to buy.

Foucault (1977/2012) predicted a society in which social control would be subtle: he explained how we would voluntarily submit ourselves to new norms. With the burgeoning of social evaluations, control is indeed decentralized and put in the hands of a crowd. Power relations are not exerted through top-down mechanisms—instead, power relations are exerted through a decentralized and distributed network. When riding an Uber, we are careful about our behavior to ensure we obtain a good rating from the driver. Hotel and restaurant owners are now incredibly concerned about how their actions toward clients might affect the production of their evaluations, which ultimately may threaten their future stream of customers.

We have not waited for this rise in evaluations of all sorts to use them as forms of social control. Stigma is commonly internalized by those it targets (Pescosolido and Martin 2015). This internalization is partly what makes stigma a mechanism of social control (Goffman 1963): because the stigmatized know they are negatively evaluated because of their identity or characteristics, they impose constraints on and changes to themselves. Now evaluations are publicly shared and constructed through online platforms or apps. Negative evaluations remain internalized, but they are also reflected in our interactions with others, as others can process this information before and during interactions. As consumers and producers of those evaluations, it is hard not to be complicit with the power relations generated by social evaluations. We feel judged continuously and observed, but we are also prompt to share those evaluations, to exist and have a voice. Uber, for example, has long been using ratings to exclude drivers who would not always be on their best behaviors with their clients. A recent announcement by the taxi-hailing firm suggests they will extend this practice to users as well.[1] Thus ratings, in fact, give power to both sides. Taxi drivers who lose good standing might be excluded from a source of revenue they rely upon for survival, which might have greater consequences than for clients being deprived of their ability to hail a taxi on an app. By producing and consuming evaluations, we, however, give power to the platform centralizing those evaluations and the firm behind it—Uber uses this information, provided freely by users and providers, to optimize itself and ultimately improve profitability. We could imagine some services and products being only available to an evaluated elite, with the majority being excluded from it.

What are the behavioral consequences of this "society of evaluation"? Even without direct control, we are trained to conform because of those social evaluations. We have already adapted our behaviors to internalize the new norms of our context of evaluation overproduction. Because of the fear of receiving a one-star rating from our Uber taxi, we engage in small talk. Hotels and restaurants comply with any demands of the most vocal customers, by fear those customers might retaliate by providing poor TripAdvisor ratings. Anecdotal evidence from online customer services suggests that firms are most concerned about the complaints of those with the most significant social media followership.[2] They focus their attention on those who are threatening to exercise their evaluative power.

Paradoxically, the control over this society of evaluations can also be more easily concentrated despite being decentralized because a few organizations manage the platforms where those evaluations are produced. In a nutshell, the content is produced through the effort of the masses, but a platform and those behind it then control its content and its exploitation.

One limitation for this society of evaluation to expand indefinitely is the limits to our attention. Attention is a resource we allocate (Davenport and Beck 2001). Simon (1971) has already noted that because of the amount of information produced, we have to spend more energy, time, and resources to filter it and interpret it. For this very same reason, particularly in a society of evaluation, attention of audiences has economic value. It will be up to customers to decide whether the work of interpreting others' evaluations is worth the knowledge they can derive from it. It is probable that with the inflation of evaluations, they will become less meaningful or costlier to filter until new tools help individuals make sense of large amounts of evaluation.

Producing negative evaluation is itself delivering economic value because it attracts more attention. As seen in the chapter on capitalizing on hostility, websites or TV channels bet on divisive content to attract and capture audiences. Those audiences are then sold derivative products or advertising. The economics of attention have been well understood, and entire business models such as the one of Infowars are based on those principles. There will certainly be a growing interest in how actors monetize attention and use negative evaluations to attract it. At the same time, it is hard to imagine an infinite growth in the quantity of evaluations we produce or consume, and we can expect platforms to increasingly compete for our production and consumption efforts.

Future Research on Negative Social Evaluations

I hope that this book will open new opportunities for researchers to empirically explore the power of being divisive and the positive implications of negative social evaluations. In this Conclusion, I have already paved the way for some relevant areas of new research. The ethics of social evaluations is a relatively unexplored field, and very little is known about the morality of producing and consuming evaluations. There has also been minimal moral questioning of divisiveness as an individual or organizational strategy. More work can also go into proper methods to explore negative social evaluations, on both the qualitative and the quantitative side. Finally, I stressed the attentional perspective on the inflation of evaluation. If we consider the economic value of attention (Davenport and Beck 2001), we can evaluate the individual benefits of relying on evaluations, and consider how controversies direct attention to generate an economic rent.

Beyond the topics presented in this Conclusion, there are many more opportunities for research on negative social evaluations. There are clear benefits in bringing different social and human sciences together to make sense of the concept, in particular, communication, sociology, economics, psychology, management, organization and social theories, and ethics. All of those fields have brought different perspectives on the same concept and could benefit from cross-referencing each other in a more meaningful way.

First, there is a whole field of research to develop around the *process* of evaluation. For negative evaluations, understanding how scandals and controversies unfold involves building a better understanding of negative reputation spillovers (Paruchuri, Pollock, and Kumar 2019). Such understanding must rely on a more precise grasp of how media frame issues (Clemente and Gabbioneta 2017; Roulet and Clemente 2018). Media, in the broader sense of the term, can explain how social actors can be both positively and negatively evaluated at the same time (Zavyalova et al. 2016). As we develop an understanding of processes behind evaluation, we will be able to identify how they can potentially serve as a means of social control. How is control exerted through social evaluations? Is control exercised necessarily by audiences or by stakeholders interpreting the perception of audiences? Social media data are now commonly used to study scandals and evaluations in general, but future research could benefit from fleshing out the specificities of such echo chambers (Roulet and Clemente 2018).

Research on negative social evaluations at the individual level, in particular, focusing on the concept of stigma, is already extensive (see Pescosolido and Martin 2015; Link and Phelan 2001). Still, there is much to explore with regard to microlevel interactions and negative social evaluations. Future work could further unpack the process of resilience to negative evaluations through identity mechanisms. How do individuals relate to stigmatized groups but at the same time benefit from such membership?

In addition, we do not know yet how people categorize themselves with regard to stigmatized groups and how they decide on the nature of their relationships with them. The typology Goffman (1963) put forward—the stigmatized, the wise, and the normal—suggests complex relationships not only between evaluated and evaluating groups but also with third parties. Smith found that those three categories correspond to a network structure. It would however be useful to understand better how support for the stigmatized is built to support anti-hate campaigns. Helms and Patterson (2014) also stress the importance of "wise" audiences in supporting stigmatized individual actors and potentially helping make stigma beneficial. However, we have minimal comprehension of what makes an audience "wise" and how it emerges.

Beyond stigma, as I have suggested, negative social evaluations often provide feedback to the target. While we know it is difficult to benefit from negative feedback, because of the way we appraise this feedback (Audia and Locke 2003), we know little about how social comparisons affect our processing of such information. More research is needed to understand under which conditions "bounce back" mechanisms may occur.

At the occupational and group level, research on negative social evaluations has pointed out the subtlety of segregation (Tilcsik, Anteby, and Knight 2015). If members of the stigmatized group select themselves out of opportunities, there is a whole world of negative consequences we have not been able to observe. Segregation can have a spatial dimension, as stigmatized actors may be physically isolated (Rodner et al., forthcoming). In that sense, looking at negative social evaluations from a geographical perspective might be particularly fruitful. From a more positive point of view, the stigmatized may also develop unique skills in specific and secure contexts in which they can thrive. Research on self-esteem for stigmatized groups would benefit from being revived to unveil the benefits of negative social evaluation further. The theoretical piece by Crocker and Major (1989) is a comprehensive theoretical paper but does not study and unpack the three mechanisms empirically: discarding negative feedback as biased and illegitimate, social comparisons limited to a smaller group, valuing the dimensions on which the group excels. We have a limited empirical understanding of how those mechanisms interact with each other, and how they unfold at the individual level depending on the relationship with the stigmatized group.

Finally, more work is needed to understand the negative evaluations of organizations and entire fields or industries. We know that those evaluations shape the interactions individuals have with those fields (Piazza and Jourdan 2018), but the analysis of the dynamics of evaluations over a long period, as pointed out by Galvin and colleagues (2005), remains to be fully explored in future work. Historical work on negative social evaluations has already helped us understand how they unfold and affect stakeholders over the long term (for example, Hampel and Tracey 2017). Future research could also continue developing multilevel perspectives on how individuals and groups manage identity within stigmatized organizations (Tracey and Phillips 2016).

Overall, focusing on the benefits of negative social evaluations should yield further opportunities for research, in particular as we bridge the gap between different levels of analysis. Also, furthering our apprehension of audiences—their heterogeneity, their links to each other, their boundaries—can help us connect evaluations with both their antecedents and outcomes.

Thank You, Reviewer 2

The latest album of Eminem, *Kamikaze*, received an avalanche of negative reviews. It was labeled as his worse work. Despite those negative evaluations, the album sold four hundred thousand copies within a week of its release. Eminem bought a full page of advertising in the *Hollywood Reporter*, where he mocked his critics and concluded with, "Thank you for your support ass-holes."[3] Ironically, the *Hollywood Reporter* produced one of the worse reviews of his album, labeling Eminem as an "aging artist, trying, and failing to remain relevant."

Like Eminem (whose album I'm listening to as I write this conclusion), academics could append to their work the negative reviews they received because of it. In a fashion similar to the "bounce back" effect, negative reviews can frustrate the target to the point that those targeted actors try to outdo themselves. But sometimes, instead of helping individuals bounce back, negative reviews may instead discourage them.

Feedback certainly has value. But in looking at the effect of feedback, we too often focus on the content of the feedback rather than the tone and the way it makes the recipient *feel*. The feeling of the recipient is partly a function of how the feedback affected his or her perception of self. And the perception of self is also strongly influenced by other audiences—negative feedback received in front of an audience might hurt more. Many of us have seen fellow academics receiving nasty feedback in conferences and reproducing this behavior against other (usually, more junior) colleagues.

Receiving negative evaluations changes us. Yes, in some situations, it might be beneficial. In others, it might not. One key moderating mechanism is the way we *process* negative evaluations—as an individual, as a group, as an organization, or as an entire field. And there is a learning curve in the way negative evaluations are dealt with—learning how to gain from them and leave behind the blow to self-esteem.

This book hopefully contributes to making us rethink about how we handle negative evaluations. First, by helping readers look at the brighter con-sequences of negative evaluations when they are in the line of fire. But also, bringing them to be more skeptical about the way organizations and individu-als can feed on controversies. The trap of division is wide open in front of us, and it is hard not to fall into it. However, by showing how it is used to defend critical social causes, and empower marginalized voices, I want to believe the power of being divisive can be used for good.

NOTES

INTRODUCTION

1. "Parliamentary porn consumption laid bare in official figures," BBC, accessed November 10, 2019, https://www.bbc.co.uk/news/uk-politics-23954447.

2. Aaron Smith and Monica Anderson, "Social media use in 2018," Pew Research Center, accessed November 10, 2019, http://www.pewinternet.org/2018/03/01/social-media-use-in-2018.

CHAPTER 1

1. For a positive manner in regarding the treatment of this minority, see "Stand up as an ally," Stonewall, accessed November 10, 2019, https://www.stonewall.org.uk/come-outforLGBT/stand-up-as-an-ally.

2. Warren St-John, "Sorrow so sweet: A guilty pleasure in another's woe," *New York Times*, accessed November 10, 2019, https://www.nytimes.com/2002/08/24/arts/sorrow-so-sweet-a-guilty-pleasure-in-another-s-woe.html.

3. "TripAdvisor users threaten to leave bad reviews to 'blackmail' owners into giving refunds over unfair complaints," *The Telegraph*, accessed November 10, 2019, https://www.telegraph.co.uk/news/2016/12/13/tripadvisor-users-threaten-bad-reviews-blackmail-owners-giving.

4. Gil Kaufman, "Lady Gaga's 'Born This Way' is fastest-selling single in iTunes history," MTV, accessed November 10, 2019, http://www.mtv.com/news/1658317/lady-gaga-born-this-way-itunes.

5. David Smith, "The backlash against Black Lives Matter is just more evidence of injustice," *The Conversation*, accessed November 10, 2019, https://theconversation.com/the-backlash-against-black-lives-matter-is-just-more-evidence-of-injustice-85587.

6. This example was spelled out to me by my Cambridge colleague Dr. Allegre Hadida, a specialist of strategy in the motion picture industry. Allegre also referred me to the Sharon Stone interview.

CHAPTER 2

1. Agence France Presse, "Tens of thousands march worldwide against Monsanto and GM crops," *The Guardian*, accessed November 10, 2019, https://www.theguardian.

com/environment/2015/may/24/tens-of-thousands-march-worldwide-against-mon-santo-and-gm-crops.

2. "Our company culture," Monsanto website, accessed November 10, 2019, https://monsanto.com/careers/working-at-monsanto/company-culture.

3. Peter Baker and Linda Qiu, "Inside what even an ally calls Trump's 'reality distortion field'," *New York Times*, accessed November 10, 2019, https://www.nytimes.com/2018/10/31/us/politics/fact-check-trump-distortion-campaign.html.

4. Morgan Housel, "An interview with Michael Lewis," *The Motley Fool*, accessed November 10, 2019, https://www.fool.com/investing/general/2015/04/02/an-interview-with-michael-lewis.aspx.

5. Tom Leonard, "The wolf of wall street: Meet the real bad guy," accessed November 10, 2019, https://www.telegraph.co.uk/culture/film/film-news/10560364/The-Wolf-of-Wall-Street-meet-the-real-bad-guy.html.

6. Guy Adams, "Our hero, the wolf of wall street! City traders dress up to go to the cinema in honour of the sleazy 80s crook whose story is now a hit film (So does this mean they think greed is good again?)," *The Daily Mail*, accessed November 10, 2019, https://www.dailymail.co.uk/news/article-2543619/How-Wolf-Wall-Street-folk-hero-Britains-bankers-City-traders-dress-honour-sleazy-crook-story-hit-film.html.

7. Christian Gysin, "Bank intern, 21, who died after working 'eight all-nighters in just two weeks' had modelled himself on ruthless trader Gordon Gekko in film *Wall Street*," *The Daily Mail*, accessed November 10, 2019, https://www.dailymail.co.uk/news/article-2399336/Moritz-Erhardt-death-bank-intern-modelled-Gordon-Gekko-film-Wall-Street.html.

8. Caroline O'Donovan, "Clashes over ethics at major tech companies are causing problems for recruiters," *BuzzFeed News*, accessed November 10, 2019, https://www.buzzfeednews.com/article/carolineodonovan/silicon-valley-tech-companies-recruiting-protests-ethical.

9. Adam Bielenberg, "'I'm sorry Mr Kipling, but you just don't know how to use the English language'," *The Independent*, accessed November 10, 2019, https://www.independent.ie/entertainment/books/im-sorry-mr-kipling-but-you-just-dont-know-how-to-use-the-english-language-26700798.html.

10. "Elvis played the Opry only once and was told by the Opry after the show he'd be better off driving a truck," *Offbeat Tennessee*, accessed November 10, 2019, http://offbeat-tenn.com/elvis-played-opry-told-opry-show-hed-better-driving-truck.

11. Bruno Rinvolucri, Irene Baqué, Christopher Cherry, Adam Sich, and Katie Lamborn, "We can't get arrested quick enough," *The Guardian*, video, accessed November 10, 2019, https://www.theguardian.com/world/video/2018/nov/22/we-cant-get-arrested-quick-enough-life-inside-extinction-rebellion-video?CMP=share_btn_tw.

12. "Why does PETA use controversial tactics?" PETA website, accessed November 10, 2019, https://www.peta.org/about-peta/faq/why-does-peta-use-controversial-tactics.

13. Matthew Taylor and Molly Blackall, "Support for Extinction Rebellion soars after Easter protests," *The Guardian*, accessed November 10, 2019, https://www.theguardian.com/environment/2019/apr/24/support-for-extinction-rebellion-soars-in-wake-of-easter-protests.

14. Nadine White and Isabel Togoh, "1,100 arrests, three demands: What did Extinction Rebellion achieve?" *The Huffington Post*, accessed November 10, 2019, https://www.huffingtonpost.co.uk/entry/extinction-rebellion-revealed-in-numbers-as-demonstrations-draw-to-a-close_uk_5cc304a0e4b08170696842cb.

15. Yahoo Staff Writer, " Climate backlash: Majority of Brits oppose Extinction Rebellion protests in London," AOL, accessed November 10, 2019, https://www.aol.co.uk/news/2019/04/18/climate-backlash-majority-of-brits-oppose-extinction-rebellion/?guccounter=1andguce_referrer=aHRocHM6Ly93d3cuZ29vZ2xlLmNvbS8andguce_referrer_sig=AQAAAKlFDrE9AoB2nw7wbzoVHyCciKPtURcvDwgkJ5a5nPRar2RjEYz3_cOrCLGtI1xxdPNThDnhW-maFDdf8sgdvwa_toG3BPoL4ZGHMZhI8oHoVyB-3CWs0WM8jFvUPmJk2nkdmXGVF-EpJTP3LedHAL4ziKRnG3EHjrCsYUrgKTVmG.

16. White and Togoh, "1,100 Arrests, three demands."

17. Lanre Bakare, "London Rebellion mural is a Banksy says expert," *The Guardian*, accessed November 10, 2019, https://www.theguardian.com/artanddesign/2019/apr/26/london-extinction-rebellion-mural-is-a-banksy-says-expert.

18. S. C., "DANS LE RETRO. Il y a 15 ans, 'Loft Story' bouleversait le petit écran," *Le Parisien*, accessed November 10, 2019, http://www.leparisien.fr/espace-premium/culture-loisirs/dans-le-retro-il-y-a-15-ans-loft-story-bouleversait-le-petit-ecran-25–04–2016–5744621.php.

19. Jérôme Lefilliâtre, "Rentrée télé : Disputes à clics," *Libération*, accessed November 10, 2019, https://www.liberation.fr/france/2018/09/21/rentree-tele-disputes-a-clics_1680406.

20. Cameron Holbrook, "Childish Gambino's 'This Is America' racks up 50 million views in four days," *Mixmag*, accessed November 10, 2019, https://mixmag.net/read/childish-gambinos-this-is-america-racks-up-50-million-views-in-four-days-news.

21. "Booba and Kaaris: French rappers sentenced over airport brawl," BBC, accessed November 10, 2019, https://www.bbc.co.uk/news/world-europe-45796254.

22. Karim Zidan, "Incredibly, Conor McGregor may profit after farcical Nurmagomedov scenes," *The Guardian*, accessed November 10, 2019, https://www.theguardian.com/sport/2018/oct/07/conor-mcgregor-khabib-nurmagomedov-fight-ufc-229.

23. Douglas Farah, "Mayor who mooned finds his star rising in Bogota," *Washington Post*, accessed November 10, 2019, https://www.washingtonpost.com/archive/politics/1995/06/14/mayor-who-mooned-finds-his-star-rising-in-bogota/86acff6d-bce9–4dff-b715-ce47e0foe44c/?utm_term=.f22a987dc330.

24. Simon Romero, "A maverick upends Colombian politics," *New York Times*, accessed November 10, 2019, https://www.nytimes.com/2010/05/08/world/americas/08colombia.html?_r=0.

25. Pippa Crerar, "Boris Johnson's burqa comments bolster his grassroots Conservative support," *The Guardian*, accessed November 10, 2019, https://www.theguardian.com/politics/2018/aug/08/boris-johnsons-burqa-comments-bolster-his-grassroots-conservative-support.

26. Tim Baker, "Greta Thunberg hits back at adults 'mocking and threatening teenagers' in scathing Twitter thread," *Evening Standard*, accessed November 10, 2019,

https://www.standard.co.uk/news/world/greta-thunberg-hits-back-at-adults-mocking-and-threatening-teenagers-a4246691.html.

27. Reason Report, Cardi B, "Trump voters are racist rednecks," Youtube, accessed November 10, 2019, https://www.youtube.com/watch?v=IOAmNhhBHQw.

28. Jan Norman, "Chick-fil-A's controversy fallout," The OCR, accessed November 10, 2019, https://www.ocregister.com/2012/08/12/chick-fil-as-controversy-fallout.

CHAPTER 3

1. Gaia Panigiani, "In Matteo Salvini's Italy, good is bad and 'do-gooders' are the worst," New York Times, accessed November 10, 2019, https://www.nytimes.com/2019/04/13/world/europe/italy-do-gooders-buonisti-matteo-salvini.html?fbclid=I wARoUdzqY3E9oQ6GNzqFqBtBTXltZkwC8Y-9lolVFrSENqRNRLK8QH7Qwy_c.

2. Barri Segal , "Employees say working for Mark Cuban is a nightmare," Showbiz Cheatsheet, accessed November 10, 2019, https://www.cheatsheet.com/money-career/employees-say-working-mark-cuban-nightmare.html.

3. Eric Newcomer and Brad Stone, "The fall of Travis Kalanick was a lot weirder and darker than you thought," Bloomberg, accessed November 10, 2019, https://www.bloomberg.com/news/features/2018-01-18/the-fall-of-travis-kalanick-was a lot-weirder-and-darker-than you-thought.

4. Benjamin Snyder, "Mark Cuban: 7 ways for leaders under 30 to get ahead," CNBC, accessed November 10, 2019, https://www.cnbc.com/2017/05/05/mark-cuban-7-ways-for-leaders-under-30-to-get-ahead.html.

5. Eleanor Busby, "University of Cambridge to investigate how it benefited from slave trade," The Independent, accessed November 10, 2019, https://www.independent.co.uk/news/education/education-news/cambridge-university-slave-trade-profits-colonisation-inquiry-a8891911.html.

6. "Divisive political rhetoric a danger to the world, Amnesty says," BBC, accessed November 10, 2019, https://www.bbc.com/news/world-39048293.

7. Jérôme Lefilliâtre, "Rentrée télé : Disputes à clics," Libération, accessed November 10, 2019, https://www.liberation.fr/france/2018/09/21/rentree-tele-disputes-a-clics_1680406.

8. Emma Graham Harrison, "Inside Facebook's war room: The battle to protect EU elections," The Guardian, accessed November 10, 2019, https://www.theguardian.com/technology/2019/may/05/facebook-admits-huge-scale-of-fake-news-and-election-interference.

9. Eliza Mackintosh and Edward Kiernan, "Finland is winning the war on fake news. What it's learned may be crucial to Western democracy," CNN, accessed November 10, 2019, https://edition.cnn.com/interactive/2019/05/europe/finland-fake-news-intl.

CHAPTER 4

1. Shubham Sharma, "Now, Uber will ban riders with poor ratings: Here's how," NewsBytes, accessed November 10, 2019, https://www.newsbytesapp.com/timeline/Science/46795/212003/uber-will-ban-riders-with-low-ratings.

2. Lucy Wallis, "Why it pays to complain via Twitter," BBC, accessed November 10, 2019, https://www.bbc.co.uk/news/business-27381699.

3. Nick Reilly, "'Thanks for the support, assholes!': Eminem takes out full-page advert to mock 'Kamikaze' critics," NME, accessed November 10, 2019, https://www.nme.com/news/music/thanks-for-the-support-assholes-eminem-takes-out-full-page-advert-to-mock-kamikaze-critics-2382032.

REFERENCES

Aadland, E., G. Cattani, and S. Ferriani. 2019. Friends, cliques and gifts: Social proximity and recognition in peer-based tournament rituals. *Academy of Management Journal* 62 (3): 883–917.

Abrahamson, E., and C. J. Fombrun. 1994. Macrocultures: Determinants and consequences. *Academy of Management Review* 19 (4): 728–755.

Adut, A. 2005. A theory of scandal: Victorians, homosexuality, and the fall of Oscar Wilde. *American Journal of Sociology* 111 (1): 213–248.

———. 2008. *On scandal: Moral disturbances in society, politics, and art.* Cambridge: Cambridge University Press.

Albert, S., and D. A. Whetten. 1985. Organizational identity. *Research in Organizational Behavior* 7: 263–295.

Allcott, H., and M. Gentzkow. 2017. Social media and fake news in the 2016 election. *Journal of Economic Perspectives* 31 (2): 211–236.

Amabile, T. M. 1983. Brilliant but cruel: Perceptions of negative evaluators. *Journal of Experimental Social Psychology* 19 (2): 146–156.

Amslem, T. 2013. *Le rôle des outils de mesure de la performance dans la gestion des conflits identitaires dans une organisation hybride: Le cas de l'entreprise d'insertion ARES.* PhD diss., Université Panthéon-Sorbonne-Paris I.

Anderson-Gough, F., C. Grey, and K. Robson. 2005. "Helping them to forget . . .": The organizational embedding of gender relations in public audit firms. *Accounting, Organizations and Society* 30 (5): 469–490.

Andiappan, M., and L. Dufour. 2020. Jealousy at work: A tripartite model. *Academy of Management Review* 45 (1): 205–229.

Anshel, M. H. 2016. *In praise of failure: The value of overcoming mistakes in sports and in life.* Lanham, MD: Rowman and Littlefield.

Ansoff, H. I. 1975. Managing strategic surprise by response to weak signals. *California Management Review* 18 (2): 21–33.

Antal, T., P. L. Krapivsky, and S. Redner. 2005. Dynamics of social balance on networks. *Physical Review E* 72 (3): 036121, 1–10.

Arendt, H. 1973. *The origins of totalitarianism.* New York: Harvest Books.

Armentor, J. L. 2017. Living with a contested, stigmatized illness: Experiences of managing relationships among women with fibromyalgia. *Qualitative Health Research* 27 (4): 462–473.

Åsbring, P., and A. L. Närvänen. 2002. Women's experiences of stigma in relation to chronic fatigue syndrome and fibromyalgia. *Qualitative Health Research* 12 (2), 148–160.

Ashforth, B. E., and G. E. Kreiner. 1999. "How can you do it?" Dirty work and the challenge of constructing a positive identity. *Academy of Management Review* 24 (3): 413–434.

———. 2014. Dirty work and dirtier work: Differences in countering physical, social, and moral stigma. *Management and Organization Review* 10 (1): 81–108.

Ashforth, B. E., G. Kreiner, M. Clark, and M. Fugate. 2007. Normalizing dirty work: Managerial tactics for countering occupational taint. *Academy of Management Journal* 50 (1): 149–174.

Ashkanazy, N. M., C. A. Windsor, and L. K. Trevino. 2006. Bad apples in bad barrels revisited: Cognitive moral development, just world beliefs, rewards, and ethical decision making. *Business Ethics Quarterly* 16:449–473.

Audia, P. G., and E. A. Locke. 2003. Benefiting from negative feedback. *Human Resource Management Review* 13 (4): 631–646.

Bacq, S., I. Ajunwa, J. Ormiston, M. Toubiana, and T. Ruebottom. 2018. Stigma entrepreneurship: Theorizing the role of stigma and negative emotions in entrepreneurship. EGOS Conference Proceedings, Tallinn.

Baer, J. 2016. *Hug your haters: How to embrace complaints and keep your customers.* New York: Portfolio/Penguin.

Balsam, K. F., and J. J. Mohr. 2007. Adaptation to sexual orientation stigma: A comparison of bisexual and lesbian/gay adults. *Journal of Counseling Psychology* 54 (3): 306.

Barkun, M. 2003/2013. *A culture of conspiracy: Apocalyptic visions in contemporary America.* Vol. 15. Berkeley: University of California Press.

Barlow, M. A., J. C. Verhaal, and J. D. Hoskins, J. D. 2018. Guilty by association: Product-level category stigma and audience expectations in the US craft beer industry. *Journal of Management* 44 (7): 2934–2960.

Bastiaensens, S., H. Vandebosch, K. Poels, K. Van Cleemput, A. Desmet, and I. De Bourdeaudhuij. 2014. Cyberbullying on social network sites. An experimental study into bystanders' behavioural intentions to help the victim or reinforce the bully. *Computers in Human Behavior* 31:259–271.

Basuroy, S., S. Chatterjee, and S. A. Ravid. 2003. How critical are critical reviews? The box office effects of film critics, star power, and budgets. *Journal of Marketing* 67 (4): 103–117.

Bayer, R. 2008. Stigma and the ethics of public health: Not can we but should we. *Social Science & Medicine* 67 (3): 463–472.

Berger, J., A. T. Sorensen, and S. J. Rasmussen. 2010. Positive effects of negative publicity: When negative reviews increase sales. *Marketing Science* 29 (5): 815–827.

Bernstein, M. 2005. Identity politics. *Annual Review of Sociology* 31:47–74.

Bidwell, M., S. Won, R. Barbulescu, and E. Mollick. 2015. I used to work at Goldman Sachs! How firms benefit from organizational status in the market for human capital. *Strategic Management Journal* 36 (8): 1164–1173.

Biltereyst, D. 2004. Media audiences and the game of controversy. On reality TV, moral panic and controversial media stories. *Journal of Media Practice* 5 (1): 7–24.

Bitektine, A. 2011. Toward a theory of social judgments of organizations: The case of legitimacy, reputation, and status. *Academy of Management Review* 36 (1): 151–179.

Blume, L. E. 2002. Stigma and social control. *Reihe Ökonomie / Economics Series*, No. 119, Institute for Advanced Studies, Vienna.

Bolton, B. 2019. Hitching a ride on social or political movements can help firms profit, and change for the better. *The Conversation*. https://theconversation.com/hitching-a-ride-on-social-or-political-movements-can-help-firms-profit-and-change-for-the-better-105159.

Bolton, S. C. 2005. Women's work, dirty work: The gynaecology nurse as "other." *Gender, Work & Organization* 12 (2): 169–186.

Bonardi, J. P., and G. D. Keim. 2005. Corporate political strategies for widely salient issues. *Academy of Management Review* 30 (3): 555–576.

Bothello, J., and T. J. Roulet. 2018. The imposter syndrome and the mis-representation of self in academic life. *Journal of Management Studies* 56 (4): 854–862.

Bourdieu, P. 1977. *Outline of a theory of practice.* Cambridge, UK: Cambridge University Press.

Brehm, S. S., and J. W. Brehm. 2013. *Psychological reactance: A theory of freedom and control.* Cambridge, MA: Academic Press.

Bruyaka, O., D. Philippe, and X. Castaner. 2018. Run away or stick together? The impact of organization-specific adverse events on alliance partner defection. *Academy of Management Review* 43 (3): 445–469.

Buckels, E. E., P. D. Trapnell, T. Andjelovic, and D. L. Paulhus. 2019. Internet trolling and everyday sadism: Parallel effects on pain perception and moral judgment. *Journal of Personality* 87 (2): 328–340.

Burke, M. 1994. Homosexuality as deviance: The case of the gay police officer. *The British Journal of Criminology* 34 (2): 192–203.

Burris, S. 2008. Stigma, ethics and policy: A response to Bayer. *Social Science & Medicine* 67 (3): 473–475.

Cahill, S. E. 1999. The boundaries of professionalization: The case of North American funeral direction. *Symbolic Interaction* 22 (2): 105–119.

Cahill, S. E., and R. Eggleston. 1995. Reconsidering the stigma of physical disability: Wheelchair use and public kindness. *Sociological Quarterly* 36 (4): 681–698.

Cain, R. 1994. Managing impressions of an AIDS service organization: Into the mainstream or out of the closet? *Qualitative Sociology* 17 (1): 43–61.

Calcagno, V., E. Demoinet, K. Gollner, L. Guidi, D. Ruths, and C. de Mazancourt. 2012. Flows of research manuscripts among scientific journals reveal hidden submission patterns. *Science* 338 (6110): 1065–1069.

Carberry, E. J., and B. G. King. 2012. Defensive practice adoption in the face of organizational stigma: Impression management and the diffusion of stock option expensing. *Journal of Management Studies* 49 (7): 1137–1167.

Carter, W. C., and S. L. Feld. 2004. Principles relating social regard to size and density of personal networks, with applications to stigma. *Social Networks* 26 (4): 323–329.

Castelló, I., M. Etter, and F. Årup Nielsen. 2016. Strategies of legitimacy through social media: The networked strategy. *Journal of Management Studies* 53 (3): 402–432.

Cattani, G., S. Ferriani, and P. D. Allison. 2014. Insiders, outsiders, and the struggle for consecration in cultural fields: A core-periphery perspective. *American Sociological Review* 79 (2): 258–281.

Cho, Y., and N. J. Fast. 2012. Power, defensive denigration, and the assuaging effect of gratitude expression. *Journal of Experimental Social Psychology* 48 (3): 778–782.

Clair, J. A., J. E. Beatty, and T. L. MacLean. 2005. Out of sight but not out of mind: Managing invisible social identities in the workplace. *Academy of Management Review* 30 (1): 78–95.

Clanton, G. 2006. Jealousy and envy. In *Handbook of the sociology of emotions,* ed. J. Stets and J. H. Turner, 410–442. Boston: Springer.

Claus, L., M. de Rond, J. Howard-Grenville, and J. Lodge. 2019. When fieldwork hurts: On the lived experience of conducting research in unsettling contexts. In *The production of managerial knowledge and organizational theory: New approaches to writing, producing and consuming theory,* ed. T. B. Zilber, J. M. Amis, and J. Mair, 157–172. Bingley, UK: Emerald Publishing.

Clemente, M., R. Durand, and J. Porac. 2016. Organizational wrongdoing and media bias. In *Organizational wrongdoing: Key perspectives and new directions,* ed. D. Palmer, R. Greenwood, and K. Smith-Crowe, 435–473. Cambridge, UK: Cambridge University Press.

Clemente, M., and C. Gabbioneta. 2017. How does the media frame corporate scandals? The case of German newspapers and the Volkswagen diesel scandal. *Journal of Management Inquiry* 26 (3): 287–302.

Clemente, M., and T. J. Roulet. 2015. Public opinion as a source of deinstitutionalization: A "spiral of silence" approach. *Academy of Management Review* 40 (1): 96–114.

Coombs, W. T. 2007. Protecting organization reputations during a crisis: The development and application of situational crisis communication theory. *Corporate Reputation Review,* 10 (3): 163–176.

Cova, B., R. Kozinets, and A. Shankar. 2012. *Consumer tribes.* London: Routledge.

Crawley, E. 2013. *Doing prison work*. London: Willan.

Crilly, D. 2018. Chick-fil-A: Do conservative values trump liberal values? *London Business School Case*.

Cristofini, O., and T. J. Roulet. 2019. Let's play . . . with trash: Gamification and the micro-institutionalization processes of a socially innovative practice. *EGOS Conference Proceedings 2019, Edinburgh*.

Crocker, J., and B. Major. 1989. Social stigma and self-esteem: The self-protective properties of stigma. *Psychological Review* 96 (4): 608.

Crocker, J., K. Voelkl, B. Cornwell, and B. Major. 1989. Effects on self-esteem of attributing interpersonal feedback to prejudice. Unpublished manuscript, State University of New York at Buffalo.

Daudigeos, T., and T. J. Roulet. 2018. Open-access management research at a turning point: Giving relevance to a stigmatized object. *M@n@gement* 21 (4): 1178–1185.

Daudigeos, T., Roulet, T., and B. Valiorgue. 2020. How scandals act as catalysts of fringe stakeholders' contentious actions against multinational corporations. *Business & Society* 59 (3): 387–418.

Davenport, T. H., and J. C. Beck. 2001. *The attention economy: Understanding the new currency of business*. Brighton, MA: Harvard Business Publishing.

Deephouse, D. L. 1996. Does isomorphism legitimate? *Academy of Management Journal* 39 (4): 1024–1039.

———. 2000. Media reputation as a strategic resource: An integration of mass communication and resource-based theories. *Journal of Management* 26 (6):1091–1112.

Deephouse, D. L., and M. Suchman. 2008. Legitimacy in organizational institutionalism. In *The Sage handbook of organizational institutionalism*, ed. R. Greenwood, K. Oliver, C. Sahlin, and R. Suddaby, 49–77. London; Thousand Oaks, CA: Sage.

Devers, C. E., T. Dewett, Y. Mishina, and C. A. Belsito. 2009. A general theory of organizational stigma. *Organization Science* 20 (1): 154–171.

Di Paula, A., and J. D. Campbell. 2002. Self-esteem and persistence in the face of failure. *Journal of Personality and Social Psychology* 83 (3): 711.

Dick, P. 2005. Dirty work designations: How police officers account for their use of coercive force. *Human Relations* 58 (11): 1363–1390.

Dietrich, G. 2014. *Spin sucks: Communication and reputation management in the digital age*. Indianapolis: Que Publishing.

DiMaggio, P. J., and W. Powell. 1983. The iron cage revisited: Institutional isomorphism and collective rationality in organizational fields. *American Sociological Review* 48:147–160.

———, eds. 1991. *The new institutionalism in organizational analysis*. Vol. 17. Chicago: University of Chicago Press.

Dion, K. L., and B. M. Earn. 1975. The phenomenology of being a target of prejudice. *Journal of Personality and Social Psychology* 32:944–950.

Dougherty, D., and T. Heller. 1994. The illegitimacy of successful product innovation in established firms. *Organization Science* 5:200–218.

Du Bois, W.E.B. 1889/2007. *The Philadelphia Negro*. New York: Cosimo Classics.

———. 1903/1969. *The souls of black folk*. New York: New American Library.

Durand, R., and L. Paolella. 2013. Category stretching: Reorienting research on categories in strategy, entrepreneurship, and organization theory. *Journal of Management Studies* 50 (6): 1100–1123.

Durand, R., and J. P. Vergne. 2015. Asset divestment as a response to media attacks in stigmatized industries. *Strategic Management Journal* 36 (8): 1205–1223.

Durkheim, E. 1865/2017. *Les règles de la méthode sociologique*. Paris: Flammarion. For a translation, see Durkheim, E. 1982. *The rules of sociological method*. London: Palgrave.

———. 1897/2005. *Suicide: A study in sociology*. London: Routledge.

Dutton, J. E., J. M. Dukerich, and C. V. Harquail. 1994. Organizational images and member identification. *Administrative Science Quarterly*:239–263.

Dutton, J. E., L. M. Roberts, and J. Bednar. 2010. Pathways for positive identity construction at work: Four types of positive identity and the building of social resources. *Academy of Management Review* 35 (2): 265–293.

Earl, S., and S. Waddington. 2013. *Brand vandals: Reputation wreckers and how to build better defences*. London: A&C Black.

Eco, U. 2012. *Inventing the enemy and other occasional writings*. Boston: Houghton Mifflin Harcourt.

———. 2003. Organizational perception management. *Research in Organizational Behavior* 25:297–332.

Elsbach, K. D., and C. B. Bhattacharya. 2001. Defining who you are by what you're not: Organizational disidentification and the National Rifle Association. *Organization Science* 12 (4): 393–413.

Elsbach, K. D., and R. M. Kramer. 1996. Members' responses to organizational identity threats: Encountering and countering the *Business Week* rankings. *Administrative Science Quarterly*:442–476.

Elsbach, K. D., I. Stigliani, and A. Stroud. 2012. The building of employee distrust: A case study of Hewlett-Packard from 1995 to 2010. *Organizational Dynamics* 41 (3): 254–263.

Elsbach, K. D., and R. I. Sutton. 1992. Acquiring organizational legitimacy through illegitimate actions: A marriage of institutional and impression management theories. *Academy of Management Journal* 35 (4): 699–738.

Entman, R. M. 2007. Framing bias: Media in the distribution of power. *Journal of Communication* 57 (1): 163–173.

———. 2012. *Scandal and silence: Media responses to presidential misconduct*. Cambridge, UK: Polity.

Etter, M. 2018. How Google's employee walkout will strengthen the company's reputation. *The Conversation.* https://theconversation.com/how-googles-employee-walkout-will-strengthen-the-companys-reputation-106280.

Etter, M., E. Colleoni, L. Illia, K. Meggiorin, and A. D'Eugenio. 2018. Measuring organizational legitimacy in social media: Assessing citizens' judgments with sentiment analysis. *Business & Society* 57 (1): 60–97.

Etter, M., D. Ravasi, and E. Colleoni. 2019. Social media and the formation of organizational reputation. *Academy of Management Review* 44 (1): 28–52.

Falk, G. 2001. *Stigma: How we treat outsiders.* Amherst, NY: Prometheus Books.

Feather, N. T. 1989. Attitudes towards the high achiever: The fall of the tall poppy. *Australian Journal of Psychology* 41:239–267. doi:110.1080/0049538908260088.

Festinger, L. 1954. A theory of social comparison processes. *Human Relations* 7:117–140.

Festinger, L., H. W. Riecken, and S. Schachter. 2008. *When prophecy fails.* London: Pinter & Martin. Originally published 1965.)

Finney, A., and A. Hadida. 2019. *The king's speech: The road to production.* Cambridge Judge Business School, Case Study.

Fombrun, C., and M. Shanley. 1990. What's in a name? Reputation building and corporate strategy. *Academy of Management Journal* 33 (2): 233–258.

Foucault, M. 1977/2012. *Discipline and punish: The birth of the prison.* New York: Vintage.

Fraser, S. 2004. *Every man a speculator: A history of Wall Street in American life.* New York: HarperCollins.

Frooman, J. 1999. Stakeholder influence strategies. *Academy of Management Review* 24 (2): 191–205.

Galvin, T. L., M. J. Ventresca, and B. A. Hudson. 2005. Contested industry dynamics. *International Studies of Management & Organization* 34 (4): 56–82.

Gamson, J. 1994. *Claims to fame: Celebrity in contemporary America.* Berkeley: University of California Press.

Gamson, W. A., D. Croteau, W. Hoynes, and T. Sasson. 1992. Media images and the social construction of reality. *Annual Review of Sociology* 18 (1): 373–393.

García, C. 2011. Sex scandals: A cross-cultural analysis of image repair strategies in the cases of Bill Clinton and Silvio Berlusconi. *Public Relations Review* 37 (3): 292–296.

Garimella, K., G.D.F. Morales, A. Gionis, and M. Mathioudakis. 2018. Quantifying controversy on social media. *ACM Transactions on Social Computing* 1 (1): 3.

Gartrell, C. D. 1987. Network approaches to social evaluation. *Annual Review of Sociology* 13 (1): 49–66.

Gill, M., D. J. Gill, and T. Roulet. 2018. Constructing trustworthy historical narratives: Criteria, principles and techniques. *British Journal of Management* 29 (1): 191–205.

Gill, M. J., T. J. Roulet, and S. P. Kerridge. 2018. Mentoring for mental health: A mixed-method study of the benefits of formal mentoring programmes in the English police force. *Journal of Vocational Behavior* 108:201–213.

Gillmor, D. 2014. Is Silicon Valley the new Wall Street? *The Atlantic.* https://www.theatlantic.com/technology/archive/2014/07/is-silicon-valley-the-new-wall-street/375260.

Gioia, D. A., S. D. Patvardhan, A. L. Hamilton, and K. G. Corley. 2013. Organizational identity formation and change. *The Academy of Management Annals* 7 (1): 123–193.

Glynn, M. A., and C. Marquis. 2004. When good names go bad: Symbolic illegitimacy in organizations. *Research in the Sociology of Organizations* 22:147–170.

Goertzel, T. 1994. Belief in conspiracy theories. *Political Psychology*:731–742.

Goffman. 1961/2017. *Asylums: Essays on the social situation of mental patients and other inmates.* London: Routledge.

———. 1963. *Stigma: Notes on the management of spoiled identity.* Englewood Cliffs, NJ: Prentice-Hall.

———. 1978. *The presentation of self in everyday life.* London: Harmondsworth.

Goldenberg, J., B. Libai, S. Moldovan, and E. Muller. 2007. The NPV of bad news. *International Journal of Research in Marketing* 24 (3): 186–200.

Goldman, L., H. Giles, and M. A. Hogg. 2014. Going to extremes: Social identity and communication processes associated with gang membership. *Group Processes & Intergroup Relations* 17 (6): 813–832.

Goode, E. 1991. Positive deviance: A viable concept. *Deviant Behavior* 12 (3): 289–309.

Graham, C. and C. Grisard. 2019. Rich man, poor man, beggar man, thief: Accounting and the stigma of poverty. *Critical Perspectives on Accounting* 59:32–51.

Grandy, G., and S. Mavin. 2012. Occupational image, organizational image and identity in dirty work: Intersections of organizational efforts and media accounts. *Organization* 19 (6): 765–786.

Griffen, E. M. 2009. *A first look at communication theory.* New York: McGraw Hill.

Gutierrez, B., J. Howard-Grenville, and M. A. Scully. 2010. The faithful rise up: Split identification and an unlikely change effort. *Academy of Management Journal* 53 (4): 673–699.

Haack, P., M. D. Pfarrer, and A. G. Scherer. 2014. Legitimacy-as-feeling: How affect leads to vertical legitimacy spillovers in transnational governance. *Journal of Management Studies* 51 (4): 634–666.

Hall, P. M. 1972. A symbolic interactionist analysis of politics. *Sociological Inquiry* 42 (3–4), 35–75.

Hameiri, B., R. Porat, D. Bar-Tal, A. Bieler, and E. Halperin. 2014. Paradoxical thinking as a new avenue of intervention to promote peace. *Proceedings of the National Academy of Sciences* 111 (30): 10996–11001.

Hampel, C. E., and P. Tracey. 2017. How organizations move from stigma to legitimacy:

The case of Cook's travel agency in Victorian Britain. *Academy of Management Journal* 60 (6): 2175–2207.

———. 2019. Introducing a spectrum of moral evaluation: Integrating organizational stigmatization and moral legitimacy. *Journal of Management Inquiry* 28 (1): 11–15.

Hannigan, T., R.F.J. Haans, K. Vakili, H. Tchalian, V. Glaser, M. Wang, S. Kaplan, and P. D. Jennings. 2019. Topic modeling in management research: Rendering new theory from textual data. *Academy of Management Annals* 13 (2): 586–632.

Harmon, D. J., P. Haack, and T. J. Roulet. 2018. Microfoundations of institutions: A matter of structure vs. agency or level of analysis? *Academy of Management Review* 44 (2): 464–467.

Hearit, K. M. 1995. "Mistakes were made": Organizations, apologia, and crises of social legitimacy. *Communication Studies* 46 (1–2), 1–17.

———. 2006. *Crisis management by apology: Corporate response to allegations of wrongdoing.* London: Routledge.

Heider, F. 1958. *The psychology of interpersonal relations.* New York: Wiley.

Helms, W. S., and K. D. Patterson. 2014. Eliciting acceptance for "illicit" organizations: The positive implications of stigma for MMA organizations. *Academy of Management Journal* 57 (5): 1453–1484.

Helms, W. S., K. D. Patterson, and B. A. Hudson. 2019. Let's not "taint" stigma research with legitimacy, please. *Journal of Management Inquiry* 28 (1): 5–10.

Herek, G. M., J. B. Jobe, and R. M. Carney, eds. 1996. *Out in force: Sexual orientation and the military.* Chicago: University of Chicago Press.

Heugens, P. P., and M. W. Lander. 2009. Structure! Agency! (and other quarrels): A meta-analysis of institutional theories of organization. *Academy of Management Journal* 52 (1): 61–85.

Hewstone, M., M. Rubin, and H. Willis. 2002. Intergroup bias. *Annual Review of Psychology* 53 (1): 575–604.

Hilton, J. L., and W. Von Hippel. 1996. Stereotypes. *Annual Review of Psychology* 47 (1): 237–271.

Ho, K. 2009. *Liquidated: An ethnography of Wall Street.* Durham, NC: Duke University Press.

Hoelter, J. W. 1983. Factorial invariance and self-esteem: Reassessing race and sex differences. *Social Forces* 61 (3): 834–846.

Hudson, B. A. 2008. Against all odds: A consideration of core-stigmatized organizations. *Academy of Management Review* 33 (1): 252–266.

Hudson, B. A., and G. A. Okhuysen. 2009. Not with a ten-foot pole: Core stigma, stigma transfer, and improbable persistence of men's bathhouses. *Organization Science* 20 (1): 134–153.

Hughes, E. C. 1951. Work and the self. In *Social psychology at the crossroads,* ed. J. Rohrer and E. Sherif, 313–323. New York: Harper & Brothers.

Hughey, M. W. 2012. Stigma allure and white antiracist identity management. *Social Psychology Quarterly* 75 (3): 219–241.

Humphreys, L. 1970. *The tearoom trade: Impersonal sex in public places.* New York: Aldine.

Ingram, P., L. Q. Yue, and H. Rao. 2010. Trouble in store: Probes, protests, and store openings by Wal-Mart, 1998–2007. *American Journal of Sociology* 116 (1): 53–92.

Iyengar, S., and S. J. Westwood. 2015. Fear and loathing across party lines: New evidence on group polarization. *American Journal of Political Science* 59 (3): 690–707.

Jacobs, J. B. 1981. What prison guards think: A profile of the Illinois force. In *Prison guard/correctional officer: The use and abuse of the human resources of prisons*, ed. R. R. Ross, 41–53. Toronto: Butterworths.

Jaffe, G. 2018. How this veteran's company found profits in Trump-era patriotism and polarization. *Washington Post.* https://www.washingtonpost.com/politics/how-this-veterans-company-found-profits-in-trump-era-patriotism-and-polarization/2018/12/07/64b66ac4-f355–11e8-aeea-b85fd44449f5_story.html?utm_term=.14ead54fcc67&noredirect=on.

James, E. H., and L. P. Wooten. 2010. *Leading under pressure: From surviving to thriving before, during, and after a crisis.* New York: Routledge Academic.

Jepperson, R. L. 1991. Institutions, institutional effects, and institutionalism. In *The new institutionalism in organizational analysis*, ed. W. W. Powell and P. J. DiMaggio, 143–163. Chicago: University of Chicago Press.

Johnston, R., and Mehra, S. 2002. Best-practice complaint management. *The Academy of Management Executive* 16 (4): 145–154.

Jones, E. E., K. J. Brenner, and J. G. Knight. 1990. When failure elevates self-esteem. *Personality and Social Psychology Bulletin* 16:200—209.

Jones, K. P., and E. B. King. 2014. Managing concealable stigmas at work: A review and multilevel model. *Journal of Management* 40 (5): 1466–1494.

Karren, R., and K. Sherman. 2012. Layoffs and unemployment discrimination: A new stigma. *Journal of Managerial Psychology* 27 (8): 848–863.

Kavussanu, M. 2008. Moral behaviour in sport: A critical review of the literature. *International Review of Sport and Exercise Psychology* 1 (2): 124–138.

Keating, J. 2017. ISIS' end of the world problem. *Slate.* https://slate.com/technology/2017/09/isiss-apocalyptic-prophecies-arent-coming-true.html.

Kernis, M. H., and C. R. Sun. 1994. Narcissism and reactions to interpersonal feedback. *Journal of Research in Personality* 28 (1): 4–13.

Kraatz, M. S., and E. J. Zajac. 1996. Exploring the limits of the new institutionalism: The causes and consequences of illegitimate organizational change. *American Sociological Review* 61:812–836.

Kreiner, G. E., B. E. Ashforth, and D. M. Sluss. 2006. Identity dynamics in occupational dirty work: Integrating social identity and system justification perspectives. *Organization Science* 17 (5): 619–636.

Kreiner, G., E. Hollensbe, M. Sheep, B. Smith, and N. Kataria. 2015. Elasticity and the dialectic tensions of organizational identity: How can we hold together while we're pulling apart? *Academy of Management Journal* 58:981–1011.

Kuhn, T., and K. L. Ashcraft. 2003. Corporate scandal and the theory of the firm formulating the contributions of organizational communication studies. *Management Communication Quarterly* 17 (1): 20–57.

Kurzban, R., and M. R. Leary. 2001. Evolutionary origins of stigmatization: The functions of social exclusion. *Psychological Bulletin* 127 (2): 187.

Lander, M., T. J. Roulet, M. VanEssen, and P.M.A.R. Heugens. 2019. Tainting memories: The impact of stigmatization on the founding of Scotch whisky distilleries. EGOS Conference Proceedings 2019, Edinburgh.

Lashley, K., and T. G. Pollock. Forthcoming. Waiting to inhale: Removing stigma in the medical cannabis industry. *Administrative Science Quarterly.*

Lawrence, T. B., and S. L. Robinson. 2007. Ain't misbehavin': Workplace deviance as organizational resistance. *Journal of Management* 33 (3): 378–394.

Leach, C. W., R. Spears, N. R. Branscombe, and B. Doosje. 2003. Malicious pleasure: Schadenfreude at the suffering of another group. *Journal of Personality and Social Psychology* 84 (5): 932.

Leary, M. R. 2005. Sociometer theory and the pursuit of relational value: Getting to the root of self-esteem. *European Review of Social Psychology* 16 (1): 75–111.

Leary, M. R., and R. F. Baumeister. 2000. The nature and function of self-esteem: Sociometer theory. In *Advances in experimental social psychology*, ed. M. Zanna, Vol. 32, 1–62. San Diego: Academic Press.

Leary, M. R., and R. M. Kowalski. 1990. Impression management: A literature review and two-component model. *Psychological Bulletin* 107 (1): 34.

Leary, M., and L. Schreindorfer. 1998. The stigmatization of HIV and AIDS: Rubbing salt in the wound. In *HIV infection and social interaction, ed.* T. Derlega and A. Barbee, 12—29. Thousand Oaks, CA: Sage.

Lee, S. C., R. G. Muncaster, and D. A. Zinnes. 1994. "The friend of my enemy is my enemy": Modeling triadic international relationships. *Synthese* 100 (3): 333–358.

Lee, S. Y., E. R. Lim, and M. E. Drumwright. 2018. Hybrid happening: Organizational reputations in corporate crises. *Public Relations Review* 44 (4): 598–609.

Leskovec, J., D. Huttenlocher, and J. Kleinberg. 2010. Predicting positive and negative links in online social networks. In *Proceedings of the 19th international conference on world wide web*, 641–650. Raleigh, NC: Association for Computing Machinery.

Lewin, K. 1943. Psychology and the process of group living. *Journal of Social Psychology* 17:113–131. Reprinted in *The complete social scientist: A Kurt Lewin reader*, ed. Martin Gold, 333–345. Washington, DC: American Psychological Association.

Li, L., Z. Wu, S. Wu, M. Jia, E. Lieber, and Y. Lu. 2008. Impacts of HIV/AIDS stigma on family identity and interactions in China. *Families, Systems, & Health* 26 (4): 431.

Li, X., D. McAllister, R. Ilies, and J. L. Gloor. 2019. Schadenfreude: A counternormative observer response to workplace mistreatment. *Academy of Management Review* 44 (2): 360–379.

Link, B. G., and J. C. Phelan. 2001. Conceptualizing stigma. *Annual Review of Sociology* 27:363–395.

Lopes, P. 2006. Culture and stigma: Popular culture and the case of comic books. *Sociological Forum* 21 (3): 387–414.

Loury, G. C. 2003. Racial stigma: Toward a new paradigm for discrimination theory. *American Economic Review* 93 (2): 334–337.

Mackie, D. M. 1986. Social identification effects in group polarization. *Journal of Personality and Social Psychology* 50 (4): 720.

Madrick, J. 2012. *Age of greed: The triumph of finance and the decline of America, 1970 to the present.* New York: Vintage.

Malheiros, J., and B. Padilla. 2015. Can stigma become a resource? The mobilisation of aesthetic–corporal capital by female immigrant entrepreneurs from Brazil. *Identities* 22 (6): 687–705.

Maoz, Z., L. G. Terris, R. D. Kuperman, and I. Talmud. 2007. What is the enemy of my enemy? Causes and consequences of imbalanced international relations, 1816–2001. *Journal of Politics* 69 (1): 100–115.

Marsh, H. W., U. Trautwein, O. Lüdtke, J. Baumert, and O. Köller, O. 2007. The big-fish-little-pond effect: Persistent negative effects of selective high schools on self-concept after graduation. *American Educational Research Journal* 44 (3): 631–669.

Matthes, J., K. Rios Morrison, and C. Schemer. 2010. A spiral of silence for some: Attitude certainty and the expression of political minority opinions. *Communication Research* 37 (6): 774–800.

Mavin, S., and G. Grandy. 2013. Doing gender well and differently in dirty work: The case of exotic dancing. *Gender, Work & Organization* 20 (3): 232–251.

McCants, W. F. 2015. *The ISIS apocalypse: The history, strategy, and doomsday vision of the Islamic State.* New York: Macmillan.

McDonnell, M. H., and B. King. 2013. Keeping up appearances: Reputational threat and impression management after social movement boycotts. *Administrative Science Quarterly* 58 (3): 387–419.

McFarlin, D. B., R. F. Baumeister, and J. Blascovich. 1984. On knowing when to quit: Task failure, self-esteem, advice, and nonproductive persistence. *Journal of Personality* 52 (2): 138–155.

Meara, H. 1974. Honor in dirty work: The case of American meat cutters and Turkish butchers. *Sociology of Work and Occupations* 1 (3): 259–283.

Menon, T., and L. Thompson. 2007. Don't hate me because I'm beautiful: Self-enhancing biases in threat appraisal. *Organizational Behavior and Human Decision Processes* 104 (1): 45–60.

Merlan, A. 2019. Why we are addicted to conspiracy theories. *The Guardian*. https://www.theguardian.com/us-news/2019/may/02/why-we-are-addicted-to-conspiracy-theories.

Milgrom, P., and J. Roberts. 1986. Price and advertising signals of product quality. *Journal of Political Economy* 94 (4): 796–821.

Mill, J. S. 1863/2016. Utilitarianism. In *Seven masterpieces of philosophy*, 337–383. London: Routledge.

Mishina, Y., and C. E. Devers. 2012. On being bad: Why stigma is not the same as a bad reputation. *The Oxford handbook of corporate reputation*, 201–220. Oxford, UK: Oxford University Press.

Morrison, A. D., and W. J. Wilhelm. 2007. Investment banking: Past, present, and future. *Journal of Applied Corporate Finance* 19 (1): 42.

Muzio, D., J. Faulconbridge, C. Gabbioneta, and R. Greenwood. 2016. Bad apples, bad barrels and bad cellars: A "boundaries" perspective on professional misconduct. In *Organizational wrongdoing*, ed. D. Palmer, R. Greenwood, and K. Smith-Crowe, 141–175. Cambridge, UK: Cambridge University Press.

Nath, V. 2011. Aesthetic and emotional labour through stigma: National identity management and racial abuse in offshored Indian call centres. *Work, Employment and Society* 25 (4): 709–725.

Neuberg, S. L., D. M. Smith, J. C. Hoffman, and F. J. Russell. 1994. When we observe stigmatized and "normal" individuals interacting: Stigma by association. *Personality and Social Psychology Bulletin* 20 (2): 196–209.

Nietzsche, F. 1967. *On the genealogy of morals*, trans. W. Kaufmann and R. J. Hollingdale. New York: Random House. (Originally published 1887.)

Noelle-Neumann, E. 1974. The spiral of silence: A theory of public opinion. *Journal of Communication* 24 (2): 43–51.

Norton, M. I., E. W. Dunn, D. R. Carney, and D. Ariely. 2012. The persuasive "power" of stigma? *Organizational Behavior and Human Decision Processes* 117 (2): 261–268.

Nougayrede, N. 2019. Europe is in the grip of conspiracy theories—will they define its elections? *The Guardian*. https://www.theguardian.com/commentisfree/2019/feb/01/europe-conspiracy-theories-eu-elections.

Ohanian, R. 1991. The impact of celebrity spokespersons' perceived image on consumers' intention to purchase. *Journal of Advertising Research* 31 (1): 46–54.

Oliver, J. E., and T. J. Wood. 2014. Conspiracy theories and the paranoid style (s) of mass opinion. *American Journal of Political Science* 58 (4): 952–966.

O'Neill, M., A. Calder, and B. Allen. 2014. Tall poppies: Bullying behaviors faced by Australian high-performance school-age athletes. *Journal of School Violence* 13 (2): 210–227.

Ouvrein, G., H. Vandebosch, and C. J. De Backer. 2019. Celebrities' experience with cyberbullying: A framing analysis of celebrity stories in online news articles in teen magazines. In *Narratives in research and interventions on cyberbullying among young people*, ed. H. Vandebosch and L. Green, 181–198. Cham, Switzerland: Springer.

Palmer, D. 2012. *Normal organizational wrongdoing: A critical analysis of theories of misconduct in and by organizations*. Oxford, UK: Oxford University Press.

———. 2013. The new perspective on organizational wrongdoing. *California Management Review* 56 (1): 5–23.

Palmer, D., R. Greenwood, and K. Smith-Crowe, eds. 2016. *Organizational Wrongdoing*. Cambridge, UK: Cambridge University Press.

Palmer, D., and C. B. Yenkey. 2015. Drugs, sweat, and gears: An organizational analysis of performance-enhancing drug use in the 2010 Tour de France. *Social Forces* 94 (2): 891–922.

Paolella, L., and R. Durand. 2016. Category spanning, evaluation, and performance: Revised theory and test on the corporate law market. *Academy of Management Journal* 59 (1): 330–351.

Park, L. E., and J. K. Maner. 2009. Does self-threat promote social connection? The role of self-esteem and contingencies of self-worth. *Journal of Personality and Social Psychology* 96 (1): 203.

Parker, R., and Aggleton, P. 2003. HIV and AIDS-related stigma and discrimination: A conceptual framework and implications for action. *Social Science & Medicine* 57:13–24.

Paruchuri, S., T. Pollock, and N. Kumar. 2019. On the tip of the brain: Understanding when negative reputational events can have positive reputation spillovers, and for how long. *Strategic Management Journal* 40:1965–1983.

Pescosolido, B. A., and J. K. Martin. 2015. The stigma complex. *Annual Review of Sociology* 41:87–116.

Petriglieri, J. L. 2011. Under threat: Responses to and the consequences of threats to individuals' identities. *Academy of Management Review* 36 (4): 641–662.

———. 2015. Co-creating relationship repair: Pathways to reconstructing destabilized organizational identification. *Administrative Science Quarterly* 60 (3): 518–557.

Petrillo, G. 1990. The distant mourner: An examination of the American gravedigger. *OMEGA-Journal of Death and Dying* 20 (2): 139–148.

Pew Research Center. 2013. *The global divide on homosexuality*. https://www.pewresearch.org/global/2013/06/04/the-global-divide-on-homosexuality.

Pfarrer, M. D., T. G. Pollock, and V. P. Rindova. 2010. A tale of two assets: The effects of firm reputation and celebrity on earnings surprises and investors' reactions. *Academy of Management Journal* 53 (5): 1131–1152.

Pfeffer, J., and Salancik, G. R. 2003. *The external control of organizations: A resource dependence perspective*. Stanford, CA: Stanford University Press.

Phelan, J. C., B. G. Link, A. Stueve, and B. A. Pescosolido. 2000. Public conceptions of mental illness in 1950 and 1996: What is mental illness and is it to be feared? *Journal of Health and Social Behavior*:188–207.

Phillips, D., and E. Zuckerman. 2005. High-status deviance or conformity? Professional purity or impurity? Silicon Valley law firms' engagement in family and personal injury law. MIT working paper.

Phillips, M. 1994. Industry mindsets: Exploring the cultures of two macro-organizational settings. *Organization Science* 5 (3): 384–402.

Piazza, A., and F. Castellucci. 2014. Status in organization and management theory. *Journal of Management* 40 (1): 287–315.

Piazza, A., and J. Jourdan. 2018. When the dust settles: The consequences of scandals for organizational competition. *Academy of Management Journal* 61 (1): 165–190.

Piazza, A., and F. Perretti, F. 2015. Categorical stigma and firm disengagement: Nuclear power generation in the United States, 1970–2000. *Organization Science* 26 (3): 724–742.

Podolny, J. M. 1993. A status-based model of market competition. *American journal of sociology* 98 (4): 829–872.

———. 2010. *Status signals: A sociological study of market competition.* Princeton, NJ: Princeton University Press.

Pollock, T. G., K. Lashley, V. P. Rindova, and J. H. Han. Forthcoming. Which of these things are not like the others? Comparing the rational, emotional and moral aspects of reputation, status, celebrity and stigma. *Academy of Management Annals* 13 (2): 444–478.

Pontikes, E., G. Negro, and H. Rao. 2010. Stained red: A study of stigma by association to blacklisted artists during the "red scare" in Hollywood, 1945 to 1960. *American Sociological Review* 75 (3): 456–478.

Popper, K. 1971/2012. *The open society and its enemies.* London: Routledge.

Puglisi, R., and J. M. Snyder. 2011. Newspaper coverage of political scandals. *The Journal of Politics* 73 (3): 931–950.

Ragins, B. R. 2008. Disclosure disconnects: Antecedents and consequences of disclosing invisible stigmas across life domains. *Academy of Management Review* 33 (1): 194–215.

Ragins, B. R., and J. M. Cornwell. 2001. Pink triangles: Antecedents and consequences of perceived workplace discrimination against gay and lesbian employees. *Journal of Applied Psychology* 86 (6): 1244.

Ravasi, D., and M. Schultz. 2006. Responding to organizational identity threats: Exploring the role of organizational culture. *Academy of Management Journal* 49 (3): 433–458.

Reeve, E. 2018. This is what the life of an Incel looks like. *Vice News.* https://news.vice.com/en_us/article/7xqw3g/this-is-what-the-life-of-an-incel-looks-like.

Rege, M., and K. Telle. 2004. The impact of social approval and framing on cooperation in public good situations. *Journal of Public Economics* 88 (7–8): 1625–1644.

Reilly, P. 2019. No laughter among thieves: Authenticity and the enforcement of community norms in stand-up comedy. *American Sociological Review* 83 (5): 933–958.

Rhee, M., and T. Kim. 2012. After the collapse: A behavioral theory of reputation repair. *The Oxford handbook of corporate reputation,* 446–465. Oxford, UK: Oxford University Press.

Rindova, V. P., T. G. Pollock, and M. L. Hayward. 2006. Celebrity firms: The social construction of market popularity. *Academy of Management Review* 31 (1): 50–71.

Roberts, P. W., and G. R. Dowling. 2002. Corporate reputation and sustained superior financial performance. *Strategic Management Journal* 23 (12): 1077–1093.

Rodner, V., T. J. Roulet, F. Kerrigan, and D. Vom Lehn. Forthcoming. Making space for art: A spatial perspective of disruptive and defensive institutional work in Venezuela's art world. *Academy of Management Journal.*

Rosenberg, M., and R. G. Simmons. 1972. *Black and white self-esteem: The urban school child.* Washington, DC: American Sociological Association.

Roulet, T. 2013. Banking on illegitimacy: Logics, disapprobation and inter-organizational relationships in the post-crisis finance industry (2007–2011). PhD diss., HEC Paris.

Roulet, T. 2015a. "What good is Wall Street?" Institutional contradiction and the diffusion of the stigma over the finance industry. *Journal of Business Ethics*:1–14.

Roulet, T. 2015b. Qu'il est bon d'être méchant! *Revue française de gestion* (3): 41–55.

Roulet, T. 2017. Good to be disliked? Exploring the relationship between disapproval of organizations and job satisfaction in the French context. *Journal of General Management 42 (4): 68–79.*

Roulet, T. 2019a. Sins for some, virtues for others: Media coverage of investment banks' misconduct and adherence to professional norms during the financial crisis. *Human Relations 72 (9): 1436–1463.*

Roulet, T. 2019b. Les évaluations sociales en stratégie : Légitimité, réputation, statut, stigmate et cie. In *Les grands courants de management stratégique,* ed. S. Liarte. Paris: Editions EMS.

Roulet, T., and M. Clemente. 2018. Let's open media's black box: Media as a set of heterogeneous actors and not only as a homogenous ensemble. *Academy of Management Review 43 (2): 327–329.*

Roulet, T., M. Gill, S. Stenger, and D. J. Gill. 2017. Reconsidering the value of covert research: The role of ambiguous consent in participant observation. *Organizational Research Methods 20 (3): 487–517.*

Roulet, T. J., L. Paolella, C. Gabbioneta, and D. Muzio. 2020. Microfoundations of institutional change in the career structure of UK elite law firms. In *Research in the sociology of organizations,* Volume 65A, *Microfoundations of institutions,* 251–268. Bingley, UK: Emerald Publishing.

Roulet, T., and J. Salomons. 2018. An institutional perspective on return migration: The emotional baggage of "sending" or "returning home." EGOS Conference Proceedings 2018, Tallinn.

Roulet, T. J., and S. Touboul 2015. The intentions with which the road is paved: Attitudes to liberalism as determinants of greenwashing. *Journal of Business Ethics* 128 (2): 305–320.

Rousseau, D. M., and S. A. Tijoriwala. 1999. What's a good reason to change? Motivated reasoning and social accounts in promoting organizational change. *Journal of Applied Psychology* 84 (4): 514.

Roux-Dufort, C. 2016. Delving into the roots of crises: The genealogy of surprise. In *The handbook of international crisis communication research,* ed. A. Schwarz, M. W. Seeger, and C. Auer, 24–33. West Sussex, UK: Wiley.

Ruef, M., and W. R. Scott. 1998. A multidimensional model of organizational legitimacy: Hospital survival in changing institutional environments. *Administrative Science Quarterly:*877–904.

Scholten, W., and N. Ellemers. 2016. Bad apples or corrupting barrels? Preventing traders' misconduct. *Journal of Financial Regulation and Compliance* 24 (4): 366–382.

Schultz, F., S. Utz, and A. Göritz. 2011. Is the medium the message? Perceptions of and reactions to crisis communication via twitter, blogs and traditional media. *Public Relations Review* 37 (1): 20–27.

Scott, W. R. 1995. *Institutions and organizations,* Newbury Park, CA: Sage.

Shantz, A. S., E. Fischer, A. Liu, and M. Lévesque 2019. Spoils from the spoiled: Strategies for entering stigmatized markets. *Journal of Management Studies* 56 (7): 1260–1286.

Sherman, D. K., and G. L. Cohen. 2006. The psychology of self-defense: Self-affirmation theory. *Advances in Experimental Social Psychology* 38, 183–242.

Shymko, Y., and T. Roulet. 2017. When does Medici hurt DaVinci? Mitigating the negative signal of extraneous stakeholder relationships in the field of cultural production. *Academy of Management Journal* 60 (4): 1307–1338.

Simon, H. A. 1971. Designing organizations for an information rich world. In *Computers, communications and the public interest,* ed. M. Greenberger, 37–52. Baltimore: Johns Hopkins University Press.

Sirola, N., and M. Pitesa. 2018. The macroeconomic environment and the psychology of work evaluation. *Organizational Behavior and Human Decision Processes* 144:11–24.

Smith, R. A. 2012. Segmenting an audience into the own, the wise, and normals: A latent class analysis of stigma-related categories. *Communication Research Reports* 29 (4): 257–265.

Smith, R. H. 2013. *The joy of pain: Schadenfreude and the dark side of human nature.* New York: Oxford University Press.

Smith, R. H., U. Merlone, and M. K. Duffy. 2016. *Envy at work and in organizations.* New York: Oxford University Press.

Smith, R. H., C. A. Powell, D. J. Combs, and D. R. Schurtz. 2009. Exploring the when and why of schadenfreude. *Social and Personality Psychology Compass* 3 (4): 530–546.

Smith, S. 2019. Mitchell, J. Clyde, 1918–1995. *Biographical memoirs of fellows of the British Academy, XVIII.*

Soll, I. 1994. Nietzsche on cruelty, asceticism, and the failure of hedonism. In *Nietzsche, genealogy, morality: Essays on Nietzsche's On the Genealogy of Morals,* ed. R. Schact, Vol. 5, 168–192. Berkeley: University of California Press.

Solomon, D. 2012. Selective publicity and stock prices. *Journal of Finance* 67 (2): 599–638.

Spence, A. M. 1974. *Market signaling: Informational transfer in hiring and related processes.* Cambridge, MA: Harvard University Press.

Spreitzer, G. M., and S. Sonenshein. 2004. Toward the construct definition of positive deviance. *American Behavioral Scientist* 47 (6): 828–847.

Spring, V. L., C. D. Cameron, and M. Cikara. 2018. The upside of outrage. *Trends in Cognitive Sciences* 22 (12): 1067–1069.

Stacey, C. L. 2005. Finding dignity in dirty work: The constraints and rewards of low-wage home care labour. *Sociology of Health & Illness* 27 (6): 831–854.

Steele, C. M. 1988. The psychology of self-affirmation: Sustaining the integrity of the self. In *Advances in experimental social psychology,* Vol. 21, 261–302. Cambridge, MA: Academic Press.

Stenger, S. 2017. *Au coeur des cabinets d'audit et de conseil: De la distinction à la soumission.* Paris: Presses Universitaires de France.

Stenger, S., and Roulet, T. 2018. Pride against prejudice? The stakes of concealment and disclosure of a stigmatized identity for gay and lesbian auditors. *Work, Employment & Society* 32 (2): 257–273.

Suchman, M. C. 1995. Managing legitimacy: Strategic and institutional approaches. *Academy of Management Review* 20 (3): 571–610.

Suddaby, R., A. Bitektine, and P. Haack. 2017. Legitimacy. *Academy of Management Annals* 11 (1): 451–478.

Sutton, R. I. 1991. Maintaining norms about expressed emotions: The case of bill collectors. *Administrative Science Quarterly:* 245–268.

———. 2007. *The no asshole rule: Building a civilized workplace and surviving one that isn't.* London: Hachette UK.

Sutton, R. I., and Callahan, A. L. 1987. The stigma of bankruptcy: Spoiled organizational image and its management. *Academy of Management Journal* 30 (3): 405–436.

Tajfel, H. 1978. Social categorization, social identity, and social comparison. In *Differentiation between social groups: Studies in the social psychology of intergroup relations*, ed. H. Tajfel, 61–76. London: Academic Press.

Tajfel, H., M. G. Billig, R. P. Bundy, and C. Flament. (1971. Social categorization and intergroup behaviour. *European Journal of Social Psychology* 1 (2): 149–178.

Tajfel, H., and J. C. Turner. 1979. An integrative theory of intergroup conflict. In *Social psychology of intergroup relations*, ed. W. G. Austin and S. Worchel, 33–47. Monterey, CA: Brooks-Cole.

———. 1986. The social identity theory of intergroup behavior. In *Psychology of intergroup relations*, ed. S. Worchel and W. G. Austin, 2nd ed., 7–24. Chicago: Nelson-Hall.

Tarrant, S. 2016. *The pornography industry: What everyone needs to know*. New York: Oxford University Press.

Thomson, P. 2014. Field. In *Pierre Bourdieu: Key concepts*, ed. M. J. Grenfell, 65–82. Abingdon and Oxon, UK: Routledge.

Tiedens, L. Z. 2001. Anger and advancement versus sadness and subjugation: The effect of negative emotion expressions on social status conferral. *Journal of Personality and Social Psychology* 80 (1): 86.

Tilcsik, A., M. Anteby, and C. R. Knight. 2015. Concealable stigma and occupational segregation: Toward a theory of gay and lesbian occupations. *Administrative Science Quarterly*, 60 (3): 446–481.

Timming A. R. 2015. Visible tattoos in the service sector: A new challenge to recruitment and selection. *Work, Employment and Society* 29 (1): 60–78.

Tracey, P., and N. Phillips. 2016. Managing the consequences of organizational stigmatization: Identity work in a social enterprise. *Academy of Management Journal* 59 (3): 740–765.

Treadwell, D. F., and T. M. Harrison. 1994. Conceptualizing and assessing organizational image: Model images, commitment, and communication. *Communications Monographs* 61 (1): 63–85.

Turban, D., and Greening, D. 1997. Corporate social performance and organizational attractiveness to prospective employees. *Academy of Management Journal* 40 (3): 658–672.

Vadera, A. K., M. G. Pratt, and P. Mishra. 2013. Constructive deviance in organizations: Integrating and moving forward. *Journal of Management* 39 (5): 1221–1276.

Vandellen, M. R., W. K. Campbell, R. H. Hoyle, and E. K. Bradfield. 2011. Compensating, resisting, and breaking: A meta-analytic examination of reactions to self-esteem threat. *Personality and Social Psychology Review* 15 (1): 51–74.

Vartanian, L. R., and J. G. Shaprow. 2008. Effects of weight stigma on exercise motivation and behavior: A preliminary investigation among college-aged females. *Journal of Health Psychology* 13 (1): 131–138.

Vaughan, D. 1999. The dark side of organizations: Mistake, misconduct, and disaster. *Annual Review of Sociology* 25 (1): 271–305.

Venkataramani, V., and R. S. Dalal. 2007. Who helps and harms whom? Relational antecedents of interpersonal helping and harming in organizations. *Journal of Applied Psychology* 92 (4): 952.

Vergne, J. P. 2011. Toward a new measure of organizational legitimacy: Method, validation, and illustration. *Organizational Research Methods* 14 (3): 484–502.

———. 2012. Stigmatized categories and public disapproval of organizations: A mixed-methods study of the global arms industry, 1996–2007. *Academy of Management Journal* 55 (5): 1027–1052.

Vidaillet, B. 2016. Envy, schadenfreude & evaluation: Understanding the strange growing of performance appraisal. In *Envy at work and in organizations.*, ed. R. H. Smith, U. Merlone, and M. K. Duffy. New York: Oxford University Press.

Voss, G. 2015. *Stigma and the shaping of the pornography industry.* London: *Routledge.*

Waldo, C. R. 1999. Working in a majority context: A structural modelling of heterosexism as minority stress in the workplace. *Journal of Counseling Psychology* 46 (2): 218–232.

Waller, D., and R. Younger. 2017. *The reputation game: The art of changing how people see you.* London: Oneworld Publications.

Wang, T., F. C. Wezel, and B. Forgues. 2016. Protecting market identity: When and how do organizations respond to consumers' devaluations. *Academy of Management Journal* 59 (1): 135–162.

Wang, Y., B. F. Jones, and D. Wang. 2019. Early-career setback and future career impact. Cornell University, arXiv preprint, arXiv:1903.06958.

Ward, J., and B. Schneider, 2009. The reaches of heteronormativity: An introduction. *Gender and Society* 23:433–439.

Warren, D. E. 2007. Corporate scandals and spoiled identities: How organizations shift stigma to employees. *Business Ethics Quarterly* 17:477–496.

Weber, M. 1968. *Economy and society: An interpretive sociology.* Ed. Guenther Roth and Claus Wittich. New York: Bedminister Press. (Originally published 1922.)

Weick, K. E. 1993. The collapse of sensemaking in organizations: The Mann Gulch disaster. *Administrative Science Quarterly*:628–652.

Westphal, J. D., and D. L. Deephouse. 2011. Avoiding bad press: Interpersonal influence in relations between CEOs and journalists and the consequences for press reporting about firms and their leadership. *Organization Science* 22:1061–1086.

Whitaker, B. 2011. *Unspeakable love: Gay and lesbian life in the Middle East.* London: Saqi.

Willey, N. R., and B. R. McCandless. 1973. Social stereotypes for normal, educable mentally retarded, and orthopedically handicapped children. *The Journal of Special Education* 7 (3): 283–288.

Williams, T., D. Gruber, K. Sutcliffe, D. Shepherd, and E. Y. Zhao. 2017. Organizational response to adversity: Fusing crisis management and resilience research streams. *Academy of Management Annals* 11 (2): 733–769.

Williamson, E., and E. Steele. 2018. Conspiracy theories made Alex Jones very rich. They may bring him down. *New York Times.* https://www.nytimes.com/2018/09/07/us/politics/alex-jones-business-infowars-conspiracy.html.

Wolfe, A. W., and S. J. Blithe. 2015. Managing image in a core-stigmatized organization: Concealment and revelation in Nevada's legal brothels. *Management Communication Quarterly* 29 (4): 539–563.

Wood, G. 2015. What ISIS really wants. *The Atlantic.* https://www.theatlantic.com/magazine/archive/2015/03/what-isis-really-wants/384980.

Yammarino, F. J., and F. Dansereau. 2008. Multi-level nature of and multi-level approaches to leadership. *The Leadership Quarterly* 19 (2): 135–141.

Yardi, S., and D. Boyd. 2010. Dynamic debates: An analysis of group polarization over time on twitter. *Bulletin of Science, Technology & Society* 30 (5): 316–327.

Yudkin, D. 2018. The psychology of political polarization. *New York Times.* https://www.nytimes.com/2018/11/17/opinion/sunday/political-polarization-psychology.html.

Zavyalova, A., M. Pfarrer, and R. Reger. 2017. Celebrity and infamy? The consequences of media narratives about organizational identity. *Academy of Management Review* 42 (3): 461–480.

Zavyalova, A., M. D. Pfarrer, R. K. Reger, and T. D. Hubbard. 2016. Reputation as a benefit and a burden? How stakeholders' organizational identification affects the role of reputation following a negative event. *Academy of Management Journal* 59 (1): 253–276.

Zuckerman, E. W. 1999. The categorical imperative: Securities analysts and the illegitimacy discount. *American Journal of Sociology* 104: 1398–1438.

INDEX

Note: page numbers in italics refer to figures.